LOGICAL THINKING IN SECOND GRADE

Millie Almy

-with the collaboration of-

Lilly Dimitrovsky
Mildred Hardeman
Felice Gordis
Edward Chittenden
David L. Elliott

Teachers College Press
Teachers College, Columbia University

Library of Congress Catalog Card Number: 73-117980

The research reported herein was largely accomplished under
a grant from the Bureau of Research, Office of Education,
U.S. Department of Health, Education and Welfare. The docu-
ment containing the basic work is obtainable through the
ERIC system.

Manufactured in the United States of America

PREFACE

This study, extending over a three-year period, involved a grand total of 914 children, 26 kindergarten teachers, and 58 first grade teachers. Each child was interviewed at least once, some children twice, and a majority, three times. The teachers not only made the interviewing possible, but also responded to questionnaires, permitted observations and in some instances, tape-recording of their classrooms in action. We regret that we cannot give individual recognition, for we know that each teacher added participation in the study to a schedule that was already full. We are most grateful for the assistance they gave.

We are also appreciative of the contribution made by the children, who cheerfully answered questions, sharing some of their thoughts with us and giving us new insight into their complexity and also into the complexities involved in instructing them.

Our work was facilitated by the central administrative staffs of the school systems that were involved in the study and also by the principals in each of the 21 schools. We are particularly grateful to the individuals in the central staffs who helped us in the initiation of the study: Mr. Lloyd Peak in Pelham, New York; Dr. Mario Menesini in Orinda, and Mrs. Harriet Wood in Berkeley, California; Mr. George Clark in New Rochelle, and Dr. Edgar Farley in Garden City, New York; and Dr. Mark Shedd in Englewood, New Jersey. The principals gave gracious and helpful support throughout the entire three-year period.

Thanks also go to the staffs and the children in the schools where the interview schedules were tried out, and where the interviews were repeated for the purpose of establishing reliability: Riverside Nursery School, Agnes Russell School at Teachers College, Columbia University, Manhattanville Community Centers, and Yeshiva Chofetz-Chaim in New York City; and the Berkwood School in Berkeley, California.

The idea for the study began to take shape when the senior investigator participated in the 1963 writing conference for the Science Curriculum Improvement Study. Its evolution into a large-scale investigation came through the support provided in a Faculty Seminar in Learning in the Classroom that met at Teachers College during 1964-1965.

Encouragement in initiating the study and assistance in locating the school systems to participate in the study were given by Dr. Robert Karplus and Dr. Herbert Thier of the Science Curriculum Improvement Study, Dr. Henry Walbesser of the Commission on Science Education, American Association for the Advancement of Science, and Dr. Stanley Frank of Science Research Associates.

The study was associated with the Institute of Psychological Research at Teachers College. Its director, Professor Robert L. Thorndike, has been a source of support in matters both practical and theoretical. Professor Rosedith Sitgreaves gave consultation on the statistical analyses, Professor Arno Bellack on the study of classroom teachers. We are also grateful to other colleagues who in various ways furthered our work: Professor Elizabeth Hagen, Professor Arthur T. Jersild, Professor Jay Erickson, Professor Myron Rosskopf, Professor Mary Budd Rowe at Teachers College, and Professor Warren B. Searles of Queens College.

Dr. Lilly Dimitrovsky, as research associate in 1966-67 and in 1967-68, carried major responsibility for the final interviewing and initial data analysis. Dr. Paula Miller served as research associate during the first year of the study. Research assistants included Mildred Hardeman and Judith Garrettson in 1965-66, Nancy Helman and Felice Gordis in 1966-67, Ellen Goldstein and Fred Smith in 1967-68, and Paula Jean Martin in 1968-69. Dr. Hardeman and Mrs. Gordis gave invaluable assistance not only in preparing chapters for the final report but also in seeing it to its conclusion.

Several students, including Naomi Foner, Emma Redbird, Carole Steinboch (not directly involved in the study), conducted analyses of portions of the data. Not all of these analyses have been included in the present report. We are grateful for the insights provided by their work.

The collaboration of Dr. David Elliott and also Dr. Edward Chittenden needs special note. Dr. Elliott, who is an assistant professor of education at the University of California at Berkeley, served as coordinator for the gathering of the data in California. He also tape-recorded lessons in the California classes. Dr. Chittenden, currently at Educational Testing Service, who had collaborated in an earlier study, has maintained a continuing interest in the present one, giving special attention to the development of the tasks used in the final interviews.

The senior investigator acknowledges the support of her collaborators and colleagues with gratitude. Without them the study would never have been completed. However, the decisions as to what was to be done, what appears in this report, and the way the results are interpreted have all been hers. For these, she takes full responsibility.

Financial support for the study was largely provided under a grant from the Bureau of Research, U.S. Office of Education. Supplementary funds for certain aspects were provided by Teachers College through the Bailey K. Howard Fund and the Faculty Research Fund of the Horace Mann-Lincoln Institute. All these sources of support are gratefully acknowledged.

TABLE OF CONTENTS

LIST OF TABLES

LIST OF FIGURES

CHAPTER I

THE PROBLEM

The major question raised in this study is: Do children who receive systematic instruction in the basic concepts of mathematics and science when they are in the kindergarten think more logically when they reach second grade than do children who did not have such early instruction? The study is based on the theoretical formulations of Piaget, who for many years has maintained that a major shift in the nature of children's thinking occurs somewhere around the age of seven. At this point, the child becomes less prone to distractions than he was earlier, can hold on to and manipulate ideas more readily, is aware of contradictions, and can correct himself when he makes mistakes.

Piaget suggests that four important factors are involved in this transition. One of these is maturation. Another is social experience, including not only adult instruction but also the child's interaction with his peers. A third factor has to do with the child's encounters with his physical environment, that is, the opportunities he has for action on it. The fourth factor, equilibration or "self-regulation," involves the process whereby the child incorporates new learnings into his repertory and becomes able to employ them in new settings.

Piaget (1966) regards equilibration as the pedagogically fundamental factor. Maturation opens up possibilities but it is insufficient for their actualization. The influence of the physical and social environment depends on the child's active involvement in it. The structures of mental growth are built as the child acts on his environment, but they are continuously modified, corrected, reconstructed at new levels of complexity. This process of self-regulation in cognitive functions is seen by Piaget not only as analogous to but continuous with organic self-regulation.

Piaget's ideas have been invoked by those who have been concerned with curriculum revision for early childhood education, bringing the basic concepts of mathematics and science down into the first grade and kindergarten--and also by those who have opposed such revision. One basic issue has been whether or not appropriate ways could be found to teach such ideas to young children whose thinking still tends to be rather idiosyncratic and dominated by personal concerns.

Another issue has to do with whether the same concepts might not be more readily and easily grasped after the transition to more systematic and logical thinking is already clearly under way. Proponents of the new curricula have maintained that the instruction experiences provided the children are of such a nature as to facilitate, if not to accelerate, the transition.

In the present study, children whose mathematics and science instruction has been prescribed in teacher manuals and in workbooks

1

prepared by representatives of these disciplines are compared with children in classes where mathematics and science experiences were planned by each teacher on the basis of the children's interests.

The study began in the fall of 1965. At that time the recent spate of studies and curriculum innovations designed to facilitate logical thinking was just under way. Since then, Piaget-derived research has increased at a rapid rate, as has the study of curriculum innovation at the early childhood level.

The present study takes its place in a series of inquiries into children's thinking begun by the senior author in 1957. A major aim at the beginning was to investigate the effects of classroom experience, in certain areas of natural science, on the young child's thinking. Furtherance of that aim led to a three-year-longitudinal study dealing primarily with the early development of children's concepts of number (Almy, et al., 1966). The main intent of the latter study was to gather normative data to parallel those reported by Piaget. However, a question arose as to whether the somewhat better performance of one of the groups in the study could be attributed to their participation in an innovative mathematics curriculum. This renewed the earlier interest in the effects of classroom experience on thinking. The fact that several programs of an innovative nature were available in both mathematics and science made the present research feasible.

The present study addresses itself primarily to the question of the timing of certain aspects of the curriculum: What effect does early instruction have on the later development of logical thinking? It is also concerned with the issue of the content of the curriculum and with the issue of the instructional skills of the teacher.

Major Issues Concerning Curriculum

Curricular Timing and Transfer of Learning

Curriculum revision, beginning in the high school in the 1950's, gradually moved downward into the elementary school. By 1965 new programs in mathematics, designed to begin as early as kindergarten, were already in wide use. Experimental programs in science, also beginning in kindergarten, were being tried out in a number of schools. While major efforts in the areas of social studies and English were still going into revision of high school and upper elementary programs, there was widespread interest in what could be done to promote concept development at the earlier levels. Textbooks were already available for one program dealing with basic economic and social concepts.

These attempts to inject more intellectual content into the kindergarten and first grade curriculum reflected a recognition of the rapidity of intellectual development during the early years and a belief that this is the period when children acquire their basic orientation toward learning. The underlying assumption is that children who are introduced early to the most basic or elementary concepts in the various subject matter areas learn not only a vocabulary but also appropriate ways of organizing information that will facilitate their understanding of the more complex ideas they will encounter later on. It will be unnecessary for them to "unlearn" erroneous ideas derived from a more naturalistic, primitive and untutored experiencing of their physical and social environment. The ultimate test of the validity of this assumption rests in the progress the children make as they move into the later elementary grades and on into high school and college. But there are some questions that can be raised to test the shorter term effects of early instruction, and to investigate the practicality of offering such instruction in several different areas of subject matter.

Some of these questions have to do with the extent of "transfer" of learning from early instruction. Informal observation suggests, for example, that five-year-olds in a "new" mathematics program have no more difficulties in talking about "sets," and first graders about "equations" and "number lines," than their parents had in counting by rote or computing sums at the same ages. What is often not clear is how much of the new learning is limited to the particular classroom procedures and materials. Will a child who is confronted in another setting with a somewhat different problem, involving the same basic concept, reveal that he has grasped the underlying principle, or only that he has learned a specific set of associations? This is one aspect of the question of transfer of learning.

Curricular Content and Transfer of Learning

Another aspect of transfer has to do with the child's ability to apply a concept that he has learned in one area of the curriculum to a like problem in another area of the curriculum. Does the child who has learned to use the number line in the mathematics program readily bring this notion to bear, without further instruction, in making observations in the science program?

It may be, as the theory of Jean Piaget suggests, that the period of early childhood is one in which the child's learning from instruction is necessarily rather specific. Not until the child has had many encounters with the physical and social environment does he begin to develop the structures or conceptual systems that facilitate transfer. If this is the case then it may be inappropriate to look for "transfer" until a later point in development. Piaget's experimentation and various replications of his work indicate that the age of seven, on the average, represents the point at which truly conceptual thinking emerges. Accordingly, this may be the best time to test the initial effectiveness of early instruction.

In 1965, the content of the new programs of early instruction appeared to have been determined primarily by some consensus on the part of the representatives of a particular discipline regarding those concepts that are most elementary and can be regarded as fundamental. Although they were not unaware that the basic ideas of any two subject matter areas may overlap to some degree, they had made little attempt to

3

design a total curriculum that would take such common elements into direct consideration. Overlap is most obvious between science and mathematics. For example, the Commission on Science Education of the American Association for the Advancement of Science specified eight science processes to be taught in grades K-3. Among them are "Recognizing Number Relations" and "Measuring" (American Association for Advancement of Science, 1964). The Report of the Cambridge Conference on School Mathematics notes that work with real numbers can be closely related to work in science (Educational Services Incorporated, 1963). But there are other areas of overlap. For example, both science and mathematics programs call for experiences in grouping and ordering. Teachers are often struck by the similarity between these tasks and those more customarily given as part of early instruction for learning to read.

A program in economics education (Senesh, 1964), dealing with different kinds of concepts, demands similar logical processes. For example, the child classifies people according to their functions as producers or consumers. He must learn to deal with the fact that a person may have membership in more than one class, just as in science he learns to classify objects on the basis of different properties. Problems of order and of sequence are encountered as the children deal with the different costs of objects of different kinds and describe the steps in a production process.

Viewed from the standpoint of the intellectual tasks the children are expected to perform, as distinct from the information they are to learn, the new programs for early instruction appeared to have a great deal in common. To some extent programs later designed by linguists, anthropologists, historians and geographers also posed similar intellectual tasks. Accordingly, educators concerned with the total curriculum for kindergarten and first grade could raise the questions of how many different kinds of subject matter and how large are the amounts of information children can manage effectively, while still acquiring the basic ideas and concepts intended in the instruction. Is the goal for this educational level to provide the child with as much information as possible? Or is it to help him to develop ways of organizing and systematizing information of diverse kinds? To what extent are such goals compatible?

Although the ultimate answers to these questions lay outside the scope of the present study, it was designed to throw light on the underlying question of the extent to which learning acquired through early instruction in one area of subject matter affects the child's thinking in other areas and at a later period of development.

The Teacher and the Curriculum

Another major concern in the study had to do with the skills of the teacher. A program that has been specifically designed to promote concept formation seems unlikely to succeed if the teacher, rather than emphasizing the common elements in the children's experiences,

4

continually orients them toward learning specific information. The present investigation, although not primarily concerned with teaching, offered an opportunity to explore certain aspects of what teachers do when they teach young children.

Related Research

The study draws on three major areas of research as they appeared when the study was initiated. One is derived from the work of Piaget. The second has to do with the analysis of classroom teaching, and the third with curriculum content.

Piagetian Theory

The investigator concerned with the intellectual content of programs for children in kindergarten and first grade may turn to the work of Jean Piaget, not only for a theory of intellectual development, but also for a method of appraising that development. A tremendous variety of "experiments" may be found in his works that may be used to assess the child's thought and stimulate him to think further or more deeply.

Although the early work of Piaget has been well known in this country since the 1920's, the extent of his investigations has only recently come into prominence. Jerome Bruner in The Process of Education (1960) called attention to the relevance of Piaget's ideas for curriculum revision. At about the same time a group of psychologists concerned with cognitive processes in children devoted the first of their conferences entirely to the work of Piaget (Kessen and Kuhlman, 1962). Flavell's (1963) volume dealing with Piaget's theory and experimentation in both intelligence and perception summarized both his psychological and his epistemological views. In 1964 Piaget elaborated his views at conferences held at Cornell University and the University of California and supported jointly by the National Science Foundation and the United States Office of Education. Although these conferences were originally designed to inquire into the implications of current investigations of children's cognitive development for the science curriculum, it soon became apparent that such implications applied to the entire curriculum (Ripple and Rockcastle, 1964).

Widespread recognition of the importance of Piaget's views for curriculum had come somewhat earlier in England than in the United States. Typical of studies based on his ideas are Lovell's The Growth of Basic Mathematics and Scientific Concepts in Children (1961) and Churchill's Counting and Measuring (1961). The work of Nuffield Foundation (Matthews, 1968) is particularly noteworthy.

From the point of view of Piaget's theory, the period of early childhood marks the transition from thought that is perceptual and subjectively oriented to thought that is conceptual, objective, and systematic.

Piaget contrasts the perceptually bound, state-to-state, often illogical thinking of the younger child with the more conceptual, more mobile and systematic thought of the older child in many series of investigations on quantity (Piaget, 1941), number (Piaget, 1952), classification, and seriation (Inhelder and Piaget, 1964), space (Piaget and Inhelder, 1956), time (Piaget, 1946), elementary physics and chemistry (Inhelder and Piaget, 1958). Some of his earlier work dealt with children's ideas about naturally occurring events and ways of reasoning about problems in social relationships (Piaget, 1926, 1932).

The nature of the transition from one level of thinking to the other is highlighted in the classic "experiment" in which the child is given two balls of clay, identical in quantity. One of them is then elongated, or broken into smaller pieces. The child who is still perceptually oriented, or pre-operative, claims there is more clay in the ball, or in the pieces that are spread out. The child who has reached the level of "concrete operations" in thinking indicates that the amounts of clay remain the same, that is, he "conserves" quantity. The first child pays attention to the appearance or state of the clay, and deals with one state at a time. The second child pays attention to the aspects that remain the same even though the material is transformed in appearance. He moves back and forth mentally from one state to the other. The first child is untroubled by logical contradiction. The second child has developed the elements of a logical system.

According to Piaget, a true concept of number evolves only after the child has begun to "conserve" quantity. The number concept involves both cardination and ordination, which are aspects of classification and seriation respectively. When, for example, a child ignores differences in a set or collection of pencils, treats each simply as a unit of the total set, and notes how many pencils there are, he is dealing with the cardinal aspects of number (classification). When he systematically imposes differences upon the pencils in the set by specifying, "This one is first, that one is second, ..." he is dealing with the ordinal aspect of number (seriation). Piaget and Inhelder contend, in The Early Growth of Logic in the Child (1964), that the abilities involved in classifying and in making seriations are also basic to the development of logical thought. Accordingly, it would seem that the child who has arrived at an adequate number concept is likely to deal with problems in areas other than mathematics in a more logical fashion than the child who has not yet reached this level of thinking.

Many studies replicating Piaget's experiments (Beilin, 1962; Dodwell, 1960; Elkind, 1961; Smedslund, 1961; Wohlwill, 1960) confirmed this transition in thought, placed by Piaget at around seven years on the average. However, many questions having to do with the factors that are involved in the transition, and with the relative roles that maturation and experience play in it persist.

Piaget insists that the child must take an active part in making the transition, becoming, as it were, dissatisfied with his old view of the world, and accordingly impelled to construct his own new view.

6

Merely going through the motions of conforming to the view of the older child or adult (saying that the clay in the ball is the "same" when he sees it differently, for example) will not transform his thought. There is some experimental evidence (Smedslund, 1961; Wohlwill and Lowe, 1962) to support this contention. On the other hand, Piaget does not dispute the possibility that the early provision of appropriate experiences (involving actual manipulation of objects, as contrasted with mere observation or labeling) may hasten the transition from perceptually dominated thinking to that based on logic.

The differences in the rates of transition that may be associated with socio-economic status were strikingly underlined in cross-sectional and longitudinal studies completed under the direction of the senior investigator (Almy, Chittenden and Miller, 1966). The cross-sectional study involved 330 kindergarten, first-, and second-graders in two schools, one located in a middle-class area of New York City, the other in a lower-class area. The children's ability to conserve number and quantity was measured by their performance in three tasks derived from Piaget's Le Developpement des Quantités (1941), and The Child's Conception of Number (1952). Their thinking in an experiment dealing with the floating and sinking of objects was also appraised. The children's conservation abilities were studied in relation to their thinking in this experiment and in relation to other measures of verbal and mental ability and of academic achievement.

The patterns into which the children's performances fell corresponded closely to what would be anticipated from Piaget's theory and experimentation. The sequence of development he described, although holding for the children from both schools, showed that those from the school in the lower-class neighborhood made slower progress.

The sequence of development that had emerged in the cross-sectional study was confirmed in the longitudinal study when the progress of individual children was repeatedly assessed during a two and a half year period. However, in the middle-class school a substantially larger number of the children who had been re-interviewed four times conserved on all items at the final test than did their second grade counterparts who had been interviewed only once during the cross-sectional study. This finding did not hold for the lower-class school.

In the course of these studies the three tasks concerned with the conservation of number and quantity were presented to several additional groups of children in suburban schools. Accordingly, what may be regarded as normative data for these conservation tasks are available for approximately 500 children.

The investigators associated with these studies also inquired into other aspects of Piaget's theory. Their investigations dealt with children's concepts of substance and weight (Chittenden, 1964), their concepts of life and death (Steiner, 1965), the classification abilities of kindergarten and second grade children (Paula Miller, 1966) and with the "logical multiplication" abilities of elementary school children (Brodlie, 1966).

7

Involvement in all these studies led to an increased conviction that the theory and the methods of Piaget had considerable relevance for the education of young children. On the one hand, the theory, insofar as it suggested a sequence in which certain abilities develop, seemed applicable to the organization of curricula. On the other hand, and perhaps of more importance, the methods seemed promising for the assessment of the children's learning, during and following their participation in a particular curriculum.

The conference attended by Piaget and by representatives of several experimental curricula in mathematics and science (Ripple and Rockcastle, 1964) further explored the possibilities for the application of the theory to curriculum development. Piaget's studies had already guided the ordering of the presentation of certain concepts in some of the new curricula. However, many issues remained unresolved. One of these had to do with the relative usefulness of direct instruction, as opposed to self-discovery, in the formation of concepts. Another issue concerned whether language could serve as a sufficient as well as necessary condition in such formation. Resolution of these issues must rest on extensive research in cognitive development and learning, including not only "natural" experiments such as the present study, but studies in which more rigorous control of all variables is possible.

Research in Classroom Teaching

A crucial variable in the present study is the teacher. Whether or not a well-designed curriculum has any important cognitive effects is likely to depend in part on the ways the teachers attempt to structure the children's thinking.

The investigator who compares several different curricula needs some means of appraising the teachers' strategies. At least two possibilities are open to him. He may juxtapose the teaching as it occurs in each classroom against the teaching prescribed for each curriculum, or he may view the teaching in all the classrooms from a single framework or category system. In the latter case he assumes that the prescriptions of the various curricula will be reflected in varying amounts of certain kinds of teaching behaviors.

In the years prior to 1965 several different systems for the observation of classrooms, and more specifically of the teaching, had been devised (Medley and Mitzel, 1958). The majority of these systems focused more on the interpersonal and affective dimensions of the classroom interaction than on its cognitive dimensions, and more on upper-elementary and high school classrooms than on kindergarten and the lower grades.

Pioneer work on the development of category systems for analyzing the cognitive content of classroom interaction at the high school and upper elementary levels was done by B. O. Smith and Mary Jane Aschner.

8

Smith (1963) views teaching as "A system of action involving an agent, a situation, an end-in-view and two sets of factors in the situation, one over which the agent has no control (for example, size of classroom and physical characteristics of pupils) and one set which the agent can modify with respect to the end-in-view (for example, assignments and ways of asking questions)" (p. 4). The latter set of factors constitutes the means by which the end-in-view is reached.

Teachers proceed to the end-in-view by strategies, as, for example, minimizing the number of wrong responses when a pupil attempts to learn a concept. These strategies are subdivided into tactical episodes that may also be identified as logical operations. Examples are defining, describing, designating, stating, reporting, comparing, contrasting, and so on.

Aschner (1960) was specifically concerned with the kinds of verbal actions of the teacher that would be most effective in inducing various kinds of learning in pupils. In one of her studies (1963) she developed a category system based on Guilford's (1956) conception of intellectual structure. This system provides for categorization of the intellectual tasks set the child by the teacher and parallel categorization of the child's handling of the task. Aschner applied the system to junior high school classes.

Bellack (1966), also using a framework based on a logical analysis of the verbal interplay in the classroom, studied high school classes. He identified four basic "pedagogical moves." Structuring moves set the context for the ensuing behavior. Soliciting moves are further analyzed into components consisting of a task (substantive or instructional) and a set of activities dealing with the logical process and the information process. The logical process activities are again subdivided into analytic processes (defining and interpreting), empirical processes (fact stating and explaining), and evaluating processes (opining and justifying). The two additional basic moves are responding and reacting.

Whether or not schemes that are based mainly on verbal interaction could be adapted effectively for use in the earliest years of schooling, or for use in science programs where the manipulation of materials and equipment assumes importance on a par with verbalization, was not known. Indeed, relatively few attempts had been made to apply any kind of categorization scheme to the cognitive dimensions of classroom interaction at kindergarten, first, or second grade levels.

Hughes (1959) analyzed the verbal and non-verbal behavior of elementary school teachers, including some in kindergarten. Her system focuses on the functions the teachers perform in controlling the pupils' behavior and in developing content for them. Kohn (1963) studied the ways kindergarten teachers structured classroom activities to organize the children's learning. Taba (1964) included second grade children in a study that examined the effect of training on the development of thinking. Her multi-dimensional analysis relates teaching strategies to the children's cognitive behavior.

9

Despite the paucity of published reports of research concerned with the cognitive aspects of classroom interaction at the early childhood level, many investigators were interested in the problem. Much of the work appears to have coincided with the current emphasis on curriculum revisions extending downward into the kindergarten.

Research in Curriculum Content

If a single claim were to be made for the various new curricula that were being tried out in kindergarten and first grades during the early years of the 1960's, it would surely be that they were designed to further cognitive development. Zaccharias (1964), commenting on six years of major curriculum revisions, notes "a growing awareness that the capacity of children to learn has commonly been grievously underestimated. Mathematicians, particularly, have discovered that children by the age of ten years or even less can master extremely subtle concepts if those concepts are properly presented to them" (p. 69). On the other hand, as Woodring (1964) points out, "Academic scholars who work exclusively with selected college students are prone to overestimate the capacity of unselected school children while elementary and secondary school teachers, because they must work daily with students of all levels of ability and find their greatest frustrations with the slow learners, are prone to underestimate the ability of the kindergarten students" (p. 7).

The ideas of the academicians must ultimately be tested in the classroom, and one would judge, the younger the children, the more imperative the need for such testing. Assuming also a more limited range of abilities on the part of the younger children, identification of the level of concepts or cognitive operations typically available to them would seem important. By and large, however, curriculum workers, at least in 1965, appeared somewhat more concerned with the development and expansion of new programs than with an examination of their long-term cognitive outcomes.

Although the present study is an outgrowth of the senior investigator's studies based on Piaget's theories regarding the development of children's thinking, it should be noted that the idea that curriculum modification might produce an acceleration of the transition from pre-operational to operational thinking is not advocated by Piaget. Rather, in his view, schooling may affect the acquisition of information but is not likely to be crucial in changing basic ways of organizing and assimilating facts. The implications of Piaget's theories for curriculum development are so significant, however, that, at this juncture, a test of the effects of schooling in terms of Piaget's categories is not only timely but essential, both from a psychological and a pedagogical point of view.

Objectives of the Study

The primary objective of this study is to find out whether children who have received instruction in kindergarten and first grade in one or more of the "new" programs dealing with basic concepts in mathematics and science show a more advanced level of thinking when they reach second grade than do children of similar background who have not had such instruction.

The study has two subsidiary objectives. One is to examine the cognitive tasks posed by the programs of instruction in the different curriculum areas of mathematics and science and the extent of overlap among them. To what extent do the programs, as set forth in the workbooks and the teacher's manuals, call on the children to perform similar cognitive tasks, such as, for example, classifying and ordering? To what extent do they deal with similar phenomena, such as, for example, color, shape, texture, sound? A secondary subsidiary objective is to explore the ways the teachers instruct the children. To what extent are teachers able to adapt their instruction in ways appropriate to carrying out the intent of the "new" programs?

Some of the specific questions the study is designed to answer are:

1. Do children who have participated in any of the "new" programs reveal more advanced thinking at the second grade level than children who have not been involved in such instruction?

2. Do children who have participated in any of the new programs in kindergarten as well as in first grade reveal more advanced thinking at the second grade level than children who have participated in such programs only in first grade?

3. Do children who have participated in programs stressing the actual manipulation as well as the labeling of objects reveal more advanced thinking at the second grade level than children who were in classes where the experience was predominantly of a paper-and-pencil character?

4. Do children participating in any one program tend to be more advanced in their thinking at the second grade level than are children participating in any other program?

5. What evidence is there to suggest that variation in the level of thinking attained by the second grade may be associated with variation in the skills of the teachers of the "new" programs? Since the number of teachers involved in teaching any one program was small, and many other factors might also contribute to the variation in the children's performance, the intent here is to look for clues, rather than anticipating definite answers.

CHAPTER II

METHOD AND PROCEDURE

In the spring of 1965, when the plan for the study evolved, several programs designed to introduce first grade and, more especially, kindergarten children to the basic concepts of mathematics and science were available. The Third Report of the Information Clearinghouse on New Science and Mathematics Curricula listed eight projects that included materials for the kindergarten (Lockard, 1965).

Among the considerations guiding the selection of the programs to be included in this study were: the availability of manuals specifying in detail the lessons or experiences for the children; the opportunity for consultation with those who had designed the program; the cooperation of the school systems where the programs were being taught; and some comparability among the communities represented by those systems.

The Programs of Instruction

The Science Curriculum Improvement Study was chosen first. The senior investigator had been associated with the development of this program, as a consultant, beginning in the summer of 1963, when the first writing conference was held. Some acquaintance with the program of the American Association for the Advancement of Science, and the fact that a colleague on the Teachers College Faculty served as a consultant to it, led to consideration of that program. The schools using these science programs also used the Greater Cleveland Mathematics Program, so that it became the logical choice for a program of mathematics instruction.

The programs are described briefly below, and in more complete detail in Chapter III.

AAAS-Science--A Process Approach

The American Association for the Advancement of Science established the Commission on Science Education in 1962. To encourage the improvement of science education in the early grades, the Commission undertook the development of a science curriculum beginning in kindergarten. Using as its framework papers on "The Scientific Approach to Knowledge" prepared by Robert Gagné and a panel of scientists, an experimental curriculum was developed in writing conferences during the summers of 1963, 1964 and 1965.

Classroom teachers were involved in both the writing conferences and in trying out successive versions of the curriculum. Fourteen school systems served as experimental centers. AAAS provided materials, books, and some compensation for the cooperating teachers. The teachers attended meetings at the experimental centers, and regional meetings. In addition, at the end of the year, each teacher prepared reports on the testing of three children who had participated in the program.

12

In the fall of 1965, when the present study began, the materials for the kindergarten and first grade had just undergone their third revision. With this revision the major impetus in the program had moved to the upper grades of the elementary school.

Science Curriculum Improvement Study (SCIS)

This project was established in 1962 by Robert Karplus, a professor of theoretical physics at the University of California. Karplus was concerned with the development of scientific literacy through the provision of experiences of a scientific kind beginning in the early elementary school.

The first writing conference was held in 1963 when work on the kindergarten and first grade materials was initiated. Revision of these materials continued through 1964 and 1965, when the present study began. As Karplus notes in a recent publication,

> Because of the integrated nature of the SCIS program, the trial and revision procedures are quite time-consuming. The first-grade program, for instance, may have to be reviewed in the light of work done by the first graders when they come to second or third grade or even later. There is also a reason for conducting classroom trials for more than one year between revisions. During the first year, the ideas and procedures of a unit are so novel to many teachers that their reactions are not indicative of actual difficulties in pedagogical design. Only on repetition are the teachers able to plan instruction satisfactorily because then they know what range of behaviors to expect from the pupils. (1967, pp. 17-18)

The kindergarten program used in the present study was undergoing classroom trial in 1965. It was preliminary in nature and a year later was regarded as quite outmoded.

The first grade program used in the present study in 1966 had reached the stage of preliminary commercial publication. Members of the SCIS staff were frequent observers in the classrooms, particularly in the case of those located in California.

The program developed by the Science Curriculum Improvement Study and that developed by the American Association for the Advancement of Science, at the kindergarten and first grade level, are similar in many respects. Both are parts of a complete and integrated elementary science program formulated by men who are themselves scientists. The SCIS program emphasizes concepts and the child's involvement with phenomena in the world around him. It assumes that the child will learn the processes of science as he experiments, discusses, and analyzes. In contrast, AAAS puts the practice of the processes in the foreground, using the phenomena as a means for learning the processes, and the concepts as tools for understanding them (Karplus and Thier, 1967, p. 8).

13

Greater Cleveland Mathematics Program (GCMP)

Unlike the science programs, the Greater Cleveland Mathematics Program had progressed beyond the experimental period when the present investigation was begun. The program developed under the aegis of the Educational Research Council of Greater Cleveland. Beginning in 1959, participating teachers from 25 school districts participated in foundations courses in mathematics and received supplementary materials to use in their classrooms. By the second year, teacher guides and exercise sheets for the children had been prepared by teams of teachers and project staff members. These materials were revised during the spring and summer of the third year and were commercially published in 1961 (Deans, 1963).

No Prescribed Lessons

To provide a contrast to the programs where the lesson plans were specified in considerable detail by academicians, a program allowing the teachers more freedom was selected. The curriculum guides for this program had been prepared by committees of teachers and supervisors in a single school system for science in 1958, and for mathematics in 1961. The guides, intended to meet local needs, recommended the general topics to be covered in kindergarten and first grades, but did not include any detailed prescriptions for teaching such topics. The teachers using these curriculum guides could not refer to them for detailed instructions as they taught each day as could the teachers in the other three programs.

Other Instructional Programs Used in the Classes in the Study

Except for reading readiness materials and first grade readers, which varied considerably from one school system to another, there were no other specified programs of instruction in any of the kindergarten classes included in the main study. At the first grade level, as will be noted in the next section, the mathematics programs that were used varied somewhat.

The Classes That Were Studied

Selection

Table 1 shows the number of children in each of the programs at the beginning of the study, 1965, and remaining in it in subsequent years.

Each kindergarten teacher taught two classes--one in the morning, one in the afternoon. While a random selection of children from both morning and afternoon classes would have been desirable in certain ways, the plan for observation of the classes necessitated the selection of a single class for each teacher--with two exceptions. In the latter cases both classes were included.

The first group of classes to be selected were those representing the SCIS program. Located in Berkeley and Orinda, California, these classes were generally taught by teachers who had been associated with the SCIS program for a year, and who were visited frequently by members of the SCIS staff. The teachers also attended regular sessions with the staff. The class size in the six classes ranged from 24 to 29.

Table 1

Experimental Programs, Number of Schools, Classes and Children, 1965-1967

Program	Schools	1965-1966		1966-1967		Fall, 1968	
		Classes	Children	Classes[b]	Children	Classes[c]	Children
		Program Initiated in Kindergarten					
AAAS (GCMP)	5	7	189	8	105	11	94
SCIS (GCMP)	3	6	159	10	118	13	79
GCMP only	4	7	168	17	143	16	122
No Pre-scribed Lessons	4	16	181[a]	11	152	14	136
		Program Initiated in First Grade					
SCIS (Math)	3	–	–	8	139	15	115
Math only	2	–	–	8	113	14	87

[a] Does not include children in these classes enrolled in public kindergarten, but scheduled for first grade in parochial school.

[b] Classes include children who had not participated in program in kindergarten.

[c] Classes include children who had not participated in program in kindergarten and/or first grade.

The AAAS classes were chosen next. They represented all of the kindergarten teachers who were involved in the AAAS program in Pelham, New York. These teachers were attending regular meetings with the AAAS consultant, but the focus in these meetings was on the teaching of the program in third grade and up. In the five Pelham classes class size ranged from 18 to 27.

One of the Berkeley, California, schools had served as an AAAS try-out center. Two kindergarten classes taught by one teacher using the AAAS program were included in the study to round out the numbers of children and classes representing AAAS.

The classes representing the Greater Cleveland Mathematics program with no pre-planned science program were found in New Rochelle, New York. The number of children in six classes ranged from 19 to 24, but a seventh class of 35 had a head teacher and an assistant teacher.

The kindergarten teachers in New Rochelle had participated in a number of in-service sessions with the system's mathematics coordinator prior to the introduction of the Greater Cleveland Mathematics Program, but there were no special training sessions going on at the time the study began.

The classes chosen as a contrast group, having no prescribed lessons, were located in Garden City, New York. Class size ranged from 16 to 23. In this community a number of children customarily attended public school kindergarten, then shifted to parochial school for first grade. Only those kindergarten children whose parents indicated that they would continue in first grade were included in the study.

The classes representing science instruction in the first grade but not in kindergarten used the SCIS program. (The AAAS program was designed to be initiated in kindergarten and no beginning first grade classes were available.) In the fall of 1966 SCIS programs beginning in first grade were initiated in three different school systems in the New York metropolitan area. One of these, Englewood, New Jersey, cooperated in the present study. The teachers participated in an in-service training program that was centered at Teachers College, Columbia University. To some extent these circumstances paralleled those that prevailed in California for the training of the kindergarten and first grade teachers whose SCIS classes were included in the study. An important difference, however, is that by 1966 most of the California first grade teachers were experienced in teaching SCIS. On the other hand, the in-service program in the New York Center could benefit from earlier experience in California and was organized to prepare the teachers in advance for some of the problems they were likely to encounter.

The choice of the Englewood classes was based on two considerations. First, the population appeared to be sufficiently varied to provide an appropriate comparison with the other schools in the study. Second, the schools were involved in an evaluation study with consultation from a member of the Teachers College faculty who also served as a consultant to the present study. Accordingly some collaboration in gathering data could easily be arranged.

An additional advantage in selecting the Englewood schools lay in the fact that their mathematics program was regarded as comparable to the Greater Cleveland program by the mathematics consultants to the present study. Further, since half of the first grade classes were not involved in the SCIS science program, they could be included in the study to represent instruction beginning in first grade, in mathematics, but not in science. Accordingly, all of the first grades in the Englewood schools were involved in the study. Eight of them in three schools had SCIS science, and a mathematics program based on GCMP (1962) or Addison-Wesley (1963) beginning in first grade, and eight classes, in two other schools, had only the mathematics. The kindergarten programs from which these classes had come did not involve any special instruction in either science or mathematics. At this time in New Jersey the use of any text book program in the kindergarten was prohibited. The class size ranged from 17 to 25. In some instances in the Englewood schools, teachers worked in clusters so that the children could receive instruction from a specialist in a particular subject.

Comparability of the Groups Representing Different Programs

Although lacking specific information regarding the communities and school systems from which the classes were drawn, the reader will none-theless have taken note of many sources of variation unrelated to the programs of instruction that may contribute to the final results. Included are such factors as geographic differences, the size of the classes, the mixtures of children of varying background within each class, the different backgrounds and experience of the teachers apart from the effectiveness of whatever in-service training they received, the level of morale within the school, and so on. While the researcher who deals with large numbers of classes can impose some degree of statistical control on such variation, its effects cannot be ignored.

In the present study, the initial intent was to achieve maximum comparability by selecting schools in middle-class communities, with Orinda, California, serving as a prototype. Census-tract data for it and for suburban communities in the New York area were studied, as was information furnished by the New York Metropolitan School Study Council. Information was also secured from publishers regarding school systems that were using either innovative or more traditional programs of instruction and from colleagues who served as consultants in those systems. School systems in over 20 communities were approached in the process of selection.

Eventually it became clear that the attempt to limit the selection to relatively homogeneous middle-class communities was not feasible. To obtain an adequate sample of teachers as well as children, SCIS classes

17

in Berkeley, California, had to be included. Since these classes were in schools located near the University so that children of students and, more rarely, a child of a professor accounted for a portion of each class, a wide variety of ethnic and socioeconomic backgrounds was represented.

As far as AAAS centers were concerned, Pelham, New York, a Westchester County community with a predominately upper middle-class population, appeared to be roughly comparable in income level to Orinda. It is, however, an older community, and has a few areas where the income level is considerably lower, although probably not as low as the lowest in Berkeley. Classes in AAAS centers in Philadelphia, and in Ithaca, New York, were given some consideration, but their distance from New York, and the fact that they were already involved in other research projects made their inclusion impractical.

New Rochelle, New York, representing GCMP, is, like Berkeley, a city with a mixed population. However, it borders on Pelham and has large areas that closely resemble Pelham. Certain classes were clearly comparable to others in Pelham. Others presented a mixture resembling those in Berkeley.

The selection of a school system where there was no detailed prescriptive manual for instruction in mathematics or science in the kindergarten presented a number of problems, in addition to that of comparability to the systems where such special programs were offered. For purposes of strict control, classes where there was no professed concern with the children's intellectual development might have been sought. Indeed, it was suggested that "it should not be difficult to locate some mediocre kindergartens." While this is unfortunately true, it is also true that school systems and teachers identified in this way would cooperate in a study of the present kind only if its purpose were concealed. Instead, an effort was made to secure the cooperation of a school system that had earned a reputation for having good kindergartens, but was committed to waiting for the children to demonstrate "readiness" before confronting them with systematic instruction. Garden City, New York, had such a system, and several kindergarten teachers had expressed an interest in participating in the study. Spontaneous cooperation of this sort seemed desirable since it might well balance out whatever enthusiasm the teachers in the more experimental programs might have. In considering the results, however, it must be noted that Garden City is, with the possible exception of Orinda, the most homogeneous of any of the communities in the study. It is a well-to-do community that appears to have been relatively untouched by population changes typical in the suburban areas surrounding it.

Englewood, New Jersey, where the study did not begin until the children were in the first grade, is a community with a heterogeneity in population similar to New Rochelle and to Berkeley. There are living areas comparable to those in Pelham and Garden City, and there are low-income pockets. Within all its schools there is a considerable mixture of backgrounds.

Table 2 presents comparable census data for the six communities involved in the study.

Table 2

Census Information for Communities in Which Schools Were Located

Community	Program	Population 1960	Median Income of Families	Median Years of Schooling Completed by Persons 25 Years and Over
Pelham, N.Y. (total)	AAAS (GCMP)	13,404	Not Available	Not Available
North Pelham		5,326	7,494	11.7
Pelham Manor		6,114	10,000 +	13.3
Pelham Village		1,964	Not Available	Not Available
Berkeley, Calif.	SCIS (GCMP)	111,268	6,576	12.9
Orinda, Calif.	SCIS (GCMP)	4,712	10,000 +	14.2
New Rochelle, N.Y.	GCMP only	76,812	8,131	12.2
Garden City, N.Y.	No Prescribed Lessons	23,948	13,875	12.9
Englewood, N. J.	1st grade SCIS (Math)	26,057	7,827	12.1
	Math only			

The Subjects

Table 3 shows the sex, chronological age, and Peabody Picture Vocabulary Test I.Q. for all the children at the initiation of the programs. Programs that were studied from the kindergarten through the first grade were initiated in the fall of 1965. Programs not initiated until the first grade began in the fall of 1966. Table 4 shows the comparable figures for the children who remained in the study to its completion.

19

Table 3

Sex, Chronological Age and I.Q.[a] of Children in
Six Instructional Programs at the Outset of the Study

Program	No. of Children	Sex		Chronological Age in Months		PPVT	I.Q.
		Boys	Girls	Mean	S.D.	Mean	S.D.
Program Initiated in Kindergarten							
AAAS (GCMP)	189	97	92	63.81	3.47	103.25	18.31
SCIS (GCMP)	159	84	75	64.97	3.56	101.09	16.97
GCMP only	168	99	69	64.82	3.34	106.55	13.84
No prescribed lessons	181	89	92	65.13	3.42	109.28	14.77
Total	697	369	328	64.66	3.48	105.12	16.37
Program Initiated in First Grade							
SCIS (Math)	139	74	65	75.73	3.02	108.22	14.73
Math only	113	57	56	74.83	3.45	104.87	16.01
Total	252	131	121	75.33	3.25	106.72	15.37
Grand Total	949						

[a] I.Q. is based upon Peabody Picture Vocabulary Test, Form A.

20

Table 4

Sex, Chronological Age and I.Q.[a] at Initiation of Study
of Children Remaining to Completion

Program	No. of Children	Sex		Chronological Age in Months		PPVT	I.Q.
		Boys	Girls	Mean	S.D.	Mean	S.D.
Program Initiated in Kindergarten							
AAAS (GCMP)	94	50	44	64.28	3.61	105.41	17.62
SCIS (GCMP)	79	43	36	64.42	3.67	100.66	18.24
GCMP only	122	67	55	64.80	3.37	106.76	12.55
No prescribed lessons	137	63	74	64.92	3.31	109.20	14.73
Total	432	223	209	64.66	3.46	106.13	15.76
Program Initiated in First Grade							
SCIS (Math)	115	61	54	75.63	3.06	107.87	13.93
GCMP only	87	45	42	75.24	3.23	104.31	14.96
Total	202	106	96	75.46	3.13	106.34	14.45
Grand Total	634	329	305			106.19	15.34

[a] I.Q. is based upon Peabody Picture Vocabulary Test, Form A.

21

Mean PPVT I.Q.'s for children who dropped from the study did not differ significantly from those for the children who remained in the study.

Parent Occupational Level

When children enter kindergarten the abilities they have already developed and their readiness for instruction reflect to some degree the educational experiences they have had in their families. These in turn are correlated with socioeconomic status. Recent work with disadvantaged young children has highlighted the extent of educational handicap in homes of lower socioeconomic status. However, as Wolf (1964) has pointed out, status per se is an imprecise indicator of the effects of a given environment. Correlations of family environment with general intelligence, usually running between .20 and .40, and with academic achievement, around .50, can be raised 20 to 30 points when specific aspects of the environment are appraised. Among such aspects are "the climate created for academic achievement," "the level of intellectuality," and "the opportunities provided for and emphasis on verbal development." Wolf measured these and other aspects of the family environment through the use of an interview averaging one and a half hours in length.

In the present study it seemed clear that the family environments could either enhance the children's learning, or inhibit it, not only as the children began school, but also as they continued through the various programs. Accordingly, some measure of the home situation was needed. Although a detailed appraisal such as that made by Wolf was not feasible, information regarding the number of years of education of the parents and their occupations seemed essential.

The initial arrangements with the various school systems indicated that their records consistently included information on parental occupation but not on years of schooling. The possibilities for securing information regarding schooling varied from system to system.

The summer of 1965, in many communities, including some whose schools participated in the present study, was a period of turmoil related to school integration. In such a climate, questions having to do with socioeconomic status and with educational background were increasingly regarded as potentially inflammatory. In some schools research that included I.Q. measures also became suspect. None of the schools that had agreed to participate in the present study asked to withdraw, but it was apparent that inquiries going beyond the school records, and the interviews with the children as they had been projected would not be regarded with favor. Tentative plans for securing somewhat detailed information about parental occupation and years of schooling were abandoned. At the time, it seemed that such information might be gleaned at the end of the study. Unfortunately when the study was completed, pressures on the schools had increased rather than lessened, and it was not feasible to attempt to gather any more data.

Information regarding the occupation of the father, or in his absence, of the mother, was either copied from the school records, or in some instances, supplied by the kindergarten teachers. In some cases the information supplied was very precise, and with some knowledge of the surrounding community, could readily be categorized. In other instances it was more vague, and could be categorized with difficulty, if at all.

Occupations were coded according to the index developed by the U.S. Bureau of the Census (1963). This index was based on the average of the three scores assigned to occupation, years of education, and income, using a one in a thousand sample from the 1960 U.S. Census. A scale was then constructed ranging from 01 to 99 and occupations assigned scale values on it. Table 5 shows some occupations that are typical of the various levels. It should be noted that the points on the scale are not necessarily equidistant, and that a large portion of the socioeconomic range is represented at the two upper levels.

Although most of the occupations were clearly enough described to be coded immediately, a number were classified only after consultation with an individual who was familiar with the scale and with the communities. In some instances ambiguous descriptions could be coded on this basis, in others they had to be eliminated. Cases where no information was available or the occupation as reported could not be classified were coded 0.

Table 5

Examples from U.S. Occupational Index

Level	Occupation
01-09	household worker, laundress
10-19	kitchen worker, janitor, sanitary services
20-29	garage laborer, recreation attendant
30-39	hospital attendant, cleaning operator, barber
40-49	truck driver, bartender, auto mechanic
50-59	delivery man, glazier, metal worker
60-69	bus driver, plumber, machinist
70-79	policeman, clerk, electrician
80-89	salesman, draftsman, manager, teacher
90-99	doctor, lawyer, engineer, psychologist

Table 6 shows the socioeconomic status of the parents of the children who remained in the study to its completion.

Table 6

Socioeconomic Status of Children[a] Remaining to Completion

| Program | No. in Program | No Information Available | Occupational Scale | | | | | |
| | | | 0-39 | | 40-70 | | 80-99 | |
			N	%	N	%	N	%
	Program Initiated in Kindergarten							
AAAS (GCMP)	94	9	9	10	11	13	65	77
SCIS (GCMP)	79	11	9	13	20	29	39	57
GCMP only	122	10	7	7	20	18	85	76
No prescribed lessons	137	13	1	1	16	12	105	86
	Program Initiated in First Grade							
SCIS (Math)	115	20	29	31	28	30	38	40
Math only	87	7	18	23	31	39	30	38

Note.--Socioeconomic status based on U.S. Bureau of the Census, Methodology and scores of socioeconomic status. Working Paper No. 15, Washington, D. C., 1963, transforming occupations to socioeconomic status.

[a] Per cents based on children for whom information was available.

24

The Teachers and Their Teaching

Whatever effects differences in the communities and related differences in the interests and abilities of the children may have on the outcomes of early instruction, an equally crucial variable is represented by the teachers. Table 7 shows the educational background and experience of the teachers in the study. A more detailed analysis of the teachers' responses to questionnaires given them at the beginning and the end of the school year is presented in Chapter IV. Chapter IV also includes information related to teacher attitudes regarding early instruction and the specific programs they were teaching.

While it seems reasonable to believe that a teacher who is enthusiastic about a particular instructional program is likely to use it more effectively than one who is opposed to or even neutral toward it, only direct observation can furnish evidence that the program is being taught as it was intended.

In the present study, such evidence is particularly important. For example, if a particular program were to require that the children answer questions based on actual manipulation of materials, and the teacher failed to provide for such manipulation, the effectiveness of the program would be inadequately tested. Again, the intent of the program would be violated if the program were designed to have the children reflect on their answers and the teacher posed the questions in such a fashion as to provide cues to the answer.

To obtain evidence on these matters, arrangements were made to observe in the classrooms. In the classes where SCIS and AAAS programs were being taught, the teachers were not unaccustomed to having observers in their classrooms. Nevertheless, the presence of an observer, particularly for a short period, can distract both the teacher and the children, thereby providing an inadequate picture of the typical activity of any classroom. While the teachers in the present study appeared to understand that the investigators needed to know the variety of ways concepts were presented to the children, and also the kinds of responses the children made, they clearly had reservations about having their classes observed. It was not feasible to ask for repeated observations. Nearly all classrooms were, however, observed twice, and most of the kindergartens three times. In addition, nine of the SCIS first grade classes were tape-recorded once and four others were tape-recorded during four consecutive lessons.

The initial plans for the classroom observations called for the development of a check list whereby the kinds of cognitive tasks the teacher posed the children could be recorded as they occurred. While work on the construction of such a check list was under way, the senior investigator and an associate spent a full morning or afternoon session in each of the kindergarten classrooms. In general, one observer recorded the verbal and other activity of the teacher, while the other observer kept a record related to the children's activities.

Table 7

Educational Background and Experience of Teachers

| | Kindergarten, 1965-1966 | | | | | | | | First Grade, 1966-1967 | | | | | | | |
| | | | Highest Degree | | | Experience | | | | | Highest Degree | | | Experience | | |
Program	No.of Tchrs.	No. Rspdg.	B.A.	M.A.	No. Rspdg.	0-3 Yrs.	4-12 Yrs.	13+ Yrs.	No. of Tchrs.	No. Rspdg.	B.A.	M.A.	No. Rspdg.	0-3 Yrs.	4-12 Yrs.	13+ Yrs.
	Program Initiated in Kindergarten															
AAAS (GCMP)	5	5	3	2	4	0	3	1	8	7	3	4	8	2	6	0
SCIS (GCMP)	5	4	4	0	4	0	3	1	10	9	9	0	9	3	3	3
GCMP only	7	7	2	5	7	1	5	1	17	14	10	4	13	5	6	2
No Pre-scribed Lessons	9	9	1	8	9	0	4	5	11	10	1	10	10	5	3	2
	Program Initiated in First Grade															
SCIS (Math)									6	6	1	5	5	0	3	2
Math only									6	6	1	5	6	2	1	3

Note.--Data are derived from questionnaires at the initiation of the study.

26

As these observations progressed it became increasingly clear that none of the check lists or category systems then available could be put to effective use soon enough to secure data from all the classes involved. Further, it could be argued that for the present study the question of whether the programs were being taught as their authors had intended was at least as crucial as the question of the kinds of cognitive tasks actually required.

Accordingly, the observations of the classroom were turned over to representatives of the various programs who were asked to make judgments on the extent to which teaching of the programs conformed to the intent of the authors. The qualifications of these observers, the observation schedule used, as well as their findings are described in Chapter IV. The tape-recorded observations of the SCIS lessons are treated separately in Chapter V.

The Measures of Logical Thinking

Tasks derived from the work of Piaget were used to appraise the logical abilities of the children as they began kindergarten, again as they entered first grade, and finally, as they entered second grade. The "pre-test" interviews, in kindergarten and first grade, included only two kinds of tasks. In the "post-test" interviews these same tasks were repeated and also supplemented by four other kinds of tasks. Complete interview schedules are found in Appendix A.

Construction of Pre-Test Interview Schedules

The tasks used in the pre-tests were taken directly from two previous studies. One set dealt with the conservation of number and quantity (Almy, Chittendon and Miller, 1966). The other set was composed of class inclusion tasks used in a study by Miller (1966).

Conservation of Number. The first two tasks involved the conservation of number, patterned after Piaget (1952). (See Figure 1.) *

During orientation in Task A the child compares eight yellow cubes with eleven red ones, and adds yellow cubes to make the rows the same, then compares the rows with one red removed, one red added, two yellows removed, two added, and so on. For the experiment, the red blocks are bunched and the child is asked "What about now?" If no response is forthcoming, "Are there more red blocks, or more yellow blocks, or are they the same?"

---

* Full details of the interview schedule will be found in the Appendix. In the schematizations that follow (Figures 1 - 7), questions involving no manipulation of materials and calling for purely verbal responses have been omitted. Tasks in which essentially similar procedures are repeated have been shown only once.

Figure 1

CONSERVATION OF NUMBER

Task A: Orientation

ARE THERE JUST AS MANY YELLOW BLOCKS AS RED BLOCKS? YOU TAKE SOME MORE
AND MAKE IT SO THERE ARE JUST AS MANY. After child does so (or is
assisted in doing so), E removes 1 red, asks WHAT ABOUT NOW? and, if
necessary, ARE THERE JUST AS MANY RED ONES AS YELLOW ONES? ARE THERE
MORE YELLOW ONES? Continues removing 2 yellows, returning 2 yellows,
etc. ending with child's statement of equality.

WHAT ABOUT NOW?

WHAT ABOUT NOW?

WHY DO YOU THINK SO?

28

Task B: Counting

□ □ □ □ □ □ □ □ □ □ □

CAN YOU COUNT? CAN YOU FIND OUT HOW MANY BLOCKS THERE ARE? YOU COUNT
THEM. Assist as necessary. SO HOW MANY BLOCKS ARE THERE?

□ □ □ □ □ □ □ □ □ □ □

HOW MANY NOW? (CAN YOU TELL WITHOUT COUNTING?)

HOW MANY NOW?

The yellow blocks are then spread apart, and the above question or questions are repeated. Finally the child is asked, "Why do you think so?"

Conceivably, a child might respond differently to the bunching of the blocks than to the spreading of the blocks, so that the order in which these were presented might affect the results. However, in a small study testing this possibility, no differences were found between the protocols of children under the "bunched" or "spread" conditions.

In the second part of this experiment, Task B, only the yellow cubes are used. The child is asked to count them. Then they are spread and he is asked to indicate how many (without counting). Again they are bunched and the question "How many?" is repeated.

Conservation of a Quantity of Liquid. (See Figure 2.) During orientation in Task C, the child compares the water in two identical glass tumblers, indicating when one has more water than the other, and filling them to indicate when the water is "the same."

The experimenter then empties the water from one tumbler into a shallow glass bowl, asking "What about now?" In the event of no response the question is put, "Is there more here, or more here (pointing), or are they the same?" The final question is "Why do you think so?"

Class Inclusion. (See Figure 3.) These tasks, used in Miller's study (1966), are based on experiments designed by Piaget (1964) to ascertain children's understanding of logical classes. In a hierarchy of classes formed on attribute similarity, the class inclusion relationship is understood when the child is able to recognize the attributes defining a particular subclass or superordinate class and also the quantitative superiority of the superordinate class to any subclass. The classic example of this type of problem is one in which the child is confronted with a box of wooden beads, most of them brown, but two of them white. He is then posed the problem of whether there are more wooden beads or more brown beads. The pre-operational child is unable to think simultaneously of the whole class (wooden beads) and the two subclasses (brown beads and white beads), but he is "well aware that the brown beads are made of wood and that they therefore form part of the same whole as the white ones. . . . But when it is a question of envisaging simultaneously the class of wooden beads and the class of brown beads, i.e., of taking the point of view of the inclusion, in their extension, of two classes" (Piaget, 1952, p. 171) difficulties arise. The problem, as Lunzer (Piaget, 1964) puts it, is that in this kind of task the child must not only abstract from the objects experienced, but he must also abstract the criteria of a classification. This involves a "turning round" on his actions of grouping and regrouping (p. xv).

Varying the materials used in the experiments, the criteria used for forming the classes and subclasses, and the number of elements in the classes and subclasses, Inhelder and Piaget (1964) studied exten-

Figure 2

CONSERVATION OF A QUANTITY OF LIQUID

Task C: Orientation

WHICH HAS MORE?   CAN YOU MAKE THEM SO THEY ARE THE SAME?   When child has
established equality, E returns some of the water from one glass to
pitcher.

WHAT ABOUT NOW?

WHAT ABOUT NOW?

WHAT ABOUT NOW?   WHY DO YOU THINK SO?

Figure 3

CLASS INCLUSION TASKS

Task A: Fruit (4 plastic bananas, 6 plastic grapes)

Orientation: HOW ARE ALL THESE OBJECTS ALIKE? WHAT DO YOU CALL THEM?
CAN YOU FIND SOME WAY TO PUT THESE OBJECTS INTO TWO GROUPS
WHICH BELONG TOGETHER? PUT ALL THE FRUIT INTO ONE GROUP.

SUPPOSE I WANTED ALL THE GRAPES AND YOU WANTED ALL THE FRUIT.
WHO WOULD HAVE MORE PIECES OF FRUIT?

HOW CAN YOU TELL?

Task B: Wooden Blocks (6 blue and 3 orange)

Orientation: CAN YOU FIND SOME WAY TO PUT THESE OBJECTS INTO TWO GROUPS
WHICH BELONG TOGETHER? PUT ALL OF THE WOODEN BLOCKS INTO
ONE GROUP.

WOULD A TOWER MADE OUT OF ALL THE WOODEN BLOCKS BE TALLER
OR SHORTER THAN A TOWER MADE OUT OF ALL THE BLUE BLOCKS?

HOW CAN YOU TELL?

Task C: Metal Cars (8 blue and 4 red)

Orientation: HOW ARE ALL OF THESE ALIKE? WHAT DO YOU CALL THEM? CAN YOU FIND SOME WAY TO PUT THESE OBJECTS INTO GROUPS WHICH BELONG TOGETHER?

PUT ALL THE <u>METAL</u> CARS INTO ONE GROUP.

ARE THERE MORE RED CARS, MORE BLUE CARS OR ARE THEY THE SAME? HOW CAN YOU TELL?

ARE THERE MORE <u>BLUE</u> CARS, MORE <u>METAL</u> CARS OR ARE THEY THE SAME?

HOW CAN YOU TELL?

Task D: Metal Cars (4 red cars added)

ARE THERE MORE RED CARS, MORE METAL CARS OR ARE THEY THE SAME?

HOW CAN YOU TELL?

33

sively the ways children of different ages handle class inclusion problems (pp. 100-149; 196-216). On the basis of their clinical procedures they find that for the majority of the children, truly operational solutions appear only after the age of seven.

Both of the science programs in the present study placed considerable emphasis on the rudiments of classification, although not on the logic of hierarchical classification. If, as Miller's (1966) work suggests, practice in classification facilitates an understanding of class inclusion, one might expect children, particularly in the science programs, to excel in class inclusion.

The procedures for each of the four class inclusion tasks are similar. Each begins with orientation procedures in which the interviewer ascertains the child's understanding that the objects in the collection are all alike in some way (that is, the superordinate class is represented by fruit in Task A, wooden blocks in Task B, metal cars in Tasks C and D), and also that each of the collections can be grouped in two separate collections (that is, the subclasses represented by grapes and bananas in Task A, blue blocks and orange blocks in Task B, blue cars and red cars in Tasks C and D).

The test questions are of two kinds. In Tasks A and B the questions pose the child two options--that is, to indicate whether the superordinate class or a single subclass is larger. In Tasks C and D three options are posed: the superordinate class is larger, or the subclass is larger, or they are the same. It should be further noted that in Tasks A, B and C, the number of objects in the subclasses are unequal, while in Task D the numbers in the subclasses are equal. In each task the child is asked for an explanation--"How can you tell?"

Some concern as to the extent to which the ways of posing the questions may affect the child's understanding of the problem is inevitable. At the time Miller designed her study (1966), she tested several versions of questions for each task. Tape recordings of children's responses to these suggested that when a child appreciated that the issue confronting him had to do with the relationships between the collection viewed simultaneously as a totality and as two separate parts, he responded correctly. For a child lacking such insight the rephrasing of the question made little if any difference in his response.

Construction of Post-Test Interview Schedules

Both theoretical and practical considerations guided the selection of the tasks that were included in the post-test interviews.

Review of a considerable portion of the experimental work done by Piaget and his colleagues and of related replication studies resulted in the consideration of many tasks and variations. Some of these were discarded without trial while others were tested with a few children and then discarded. Finally, four kinds of tasks were added to the conservation and class inclusion tasks of the pre-test. The new tasks involved the conservation of weight, seriation, transitivity of length, and multiple classification (matrices).

Theoretical Considerations. Since the study raised questions regarding the age at which a transition from pre-operational to operational thinking could occur, the post-test tasks needed to provide an adequate measure of operational thinking. Or, to put the matter another way, the tasks selected had to be ones that have been used by Piaget to demonstrate a shift from egocentric, perceptually dominated, inflexible thought, to thought that is operational, that is, logical and systematic. Such thought is "no longer tied to particular states of the object, but is obliged to follow successive changes with all their possible detours and reversals; and it no longer issues from a particular viewpoint of the subject, but coordinates all the different viewpoints in a system of objective reciprocities" (Piaget, 1959, p. 142).

The central position of conservation in Piaget's theory is well known. He maintains that "conservation is a necessary condition of all rational activity" (Piaget, 1952, p. 1) and has devised many tasks to demonstrate the child's ability to conserve substance, quantity, number, weight, and volume. Since the pre-test had included conservation tasks dealing with number and quantity, the addition to the post-test of another and presumably more difficult one seemed appropriate. Accordingly, a conservation of weight task was included.

The centrality of the other tasks to Piaget's theory is suggested by his comment on:

> . . . the operational groupings,which are constituted at about seven or eight years of age (sometimes a little earlier) . . . lead to the logical operations of fitting classes together [class inclusion] . . . and of seriali- zing asymmetrical relations. Hence the discovery of transitivity which permits the deductions: $A = B$; $B = C$, therefore $A = C$; or $A < B$, $B < C$, therefore $A < C$ . . . when a child aged seven has arranged a series of mannikins in order of size, he will be able to make a series of sticks or bags correspond to them and he will be able to identify which element in one series corresponds to which in another, even when they are all jumbled (since the multiplicative character of this grouping adds no difficulty to the additive serial- izing operations which have just been discovered). (Piaget, 1959, p. 143)

In addition to testing cognitive processes that are central to Piaget's theory, the additional tasks selected represented a sufficient number of operations to provide multiple indices to the level of the children's thinking. A child who reveals operational thinking in several different kinds of tasks is obviously more advanced toward the attainment of concrete operational thinking than one who can success- fully handle only one or two such tasks.

Piaget's studies are replete with varied tasks designed to reveal different operations. Piaget's clinical approach allows the interviewer to probe any suspect answers and so to guard against false conclusions of either positive or negative kinds. In a large-scale study such as the present one, where standard rather than clinical procedures are necessary, the tasks themselves must be so designed as to guard against misunderstanding on the part of either the child or the interviewer.

To a considerable extent, the selection of tasks for the present study was guided by Smedslund's (1964) specifications for tests of concrete reasoning. According to Smedslund:

> . . . all situations permitting a diagnosis of the
> presence vs. the absence of concrete reasoning have
> the following characteristics: the initial events
> are perceived by the subject . . . and are then
> removed. . . . The initial events have one necessary
> conclusion. If the subject arrives at this conclusion,
> he is, in this situation, capable of concrete reasoning.
> If he does not arrive at this conclusion, he is, in
> this situation, not capable of concrete reasoning.
> (Smedslund, 1964)

Smedslund further specified methodological rules to ensure that the tasks are not contaminated by irrelevant factors. These together with certain other practical considerations further directed the selection of the tasks used in this study.

Practical Considerations. Smedlund's caveats can be subsumed under the major consideration "evidence that a task works." Accordingly, with the exception of the matrices, no tasks were chosen that had not been used, in relatively comparable form, by researchers other than Piaget.

The work of these researchers provided evidence not only regarding the probable ease of administration of tasks, and of their scoring, but also of the age at which they were discriminating. Assuming that the children to be interviewed would be seven-year-olds, all of the tasks included had to show a spread in performance at that age. This criterion was particularly important in view of the possibility that the experimental groups might be advanced for their age.

Information from other research also provided some indication of the extent to which the tasks might provide reliable evidence regarding the children's operational abilities. In addition, all the tasks to be included were repeated within a two-week period with enough children so as to provide further information on the question of reliability.

A final practical consideration was that the tasks chosen should have some relevance to the experimental curricula, although the tasks themselves should not be ones in which the children had been instructed.

Ease of administration became an extremely important criterion in view of the fact that approximately 700 children were to be interviewed, sometimes in rather cramped quarters, by interviewers who varied somewhat in the amount of prior interviewing experience they had had. Some tasks had to be modified from their original forms, and recording procedures simplified in order not to place an undue burden on the interviewers.

All of the tasks were presented in a standard order, beginning with the pre-test conservation and class inclusion items, and continuing with seriation, transitivity of length, matrices and conservation of weight. This order permitted something of an alternation between tasks in which the child was given relatively little opportunity to handle materials, and those in which he had more freedom. Occasional opportunities for the child to gather up used materials gave the interviewer time to arrange the next task. The transitivity of length task provided a break in the interview time and an opportunity for the child to walk to the opposite side of the table.

Serial Ordering. The procedures for these tasks were derived fairly directly from Piaget's investigation of "seriation, qualitative similarity and ordinal correspondence" (Piaget, 1952, pp. 96-121).

Dodwell included somewhat similar tasks in an early study (1960, pp. 191-205). He presented dolls and canes of graded sizes to the child. After eight dolls had been arranged in order from the smallest to the largest, and the appropriate canes given to the two smallest dolls, the child was asked to arrange the remaining canes so that each doll would have the cane which belonged to him. Then the dolls were spread apart and the child was asked to indicate the dolls to which certain specified canes belonged. He was then asked to explain his selection. Dodwell found no consistent age trends.

Hood (1962, pp. 273-286), using drawings of ten boys differing in size and a complementary set of ten hoops, required the child to put each set into serial order and then to make the two sets correspond. She found this to be one of the most difficult of the tasks related to the concept of number. At age seven only 6 per cent of her normal subjects had reached the level of operational thought that enabled them to solve this problem of seriation. Of the eight-year-olds, 34 per cent, and of the nine-year-olds, 75 per cent, were at this level.

In the present study, as in the Hood study, pictures rather than objects were used. The initial tasks corresponded to those used by Hood. However, these tasks were posed with two different sets of pictures, and in addition, questions relating to the child's understanding of ordination, and his ability to maintain relationships after the visual correspondence was destroyed by scrambling, were included.

The tasks closely resembled those described by Piaget (1952a,

37

pp. 97-98). A standardized rather than a clinical procedure was
followed, and pictures rather than objects were used. The pictures
were drafted on transparent material and reproduced on cards by means
of a diazo process.

The materials for the task consisted of two sets of ten cards,
5" x 2 1/2" in size, with pictures of monkeys and balloons, and two sets
of 7" x 2" cards with pictures of knives and forks. The first picture
of the largest monkey was four inches in height. Each of the remaining
nine pictures was successively scaled down in size so that the smallest
monkey was one inch in height. The pictures of balloons were similarly
scaled from four inches to one inch. The knives were scaled from 6 1/2"
to 2" and the forks from 5 1/2" to 1 3/4".

Three kinds of problems were posed with these materials: arranging
the cards in corresponding series from smallest to biggest; identifying
ordinal positions; and reordering a series after the order had been
broken. All of the cards were coded so that the interviewer could readily record the children's responses and reassemble the cards correctly.

In the first of the seriation tasks (see Figure 4) with cards showing
monkeys and balloons, the interviewer placed the two smallest and two largest
monkeys about 20 inches apart, asking the child to arrange the remaining
six cards in order from the smaller to the bigger. If the child did this
correctly, he proceeded directly to the second seriation task. If the
order was incorrect, the interviewer made the necessary rearrangement,
commenting on the sizes of the monkeys (this one is just a little bigger,
etc.) as he did so. In the second task the interviewer placed the biggest and smallest balloons above the biggest and smallest monkeys, and
asked the child to arrange the rest (eight cards) so that each monkey
would have the right sized balloon. Incorrect orders were rearranged
by the interviewer.

For the ordination task, the interviewer pushed the row of monkeys
closer together and spread the row of balloons, moving them to the left,
then asked the child to identify the correct balloon for each of three
pre-specified monkeys. Finally, in the reordering task, leaving the
series of monkeys intact, the interviewer scrambled the balloons and
asked the child to identify a fourth monkey's balloon.

The procedures with the knives and forks were similar except that
the interviewer ordered two series and put them into correspondence himself. He then displaced the correspondence, moving the top series to
the left to pose the ordination problem. The child was asked to locate
the correct fork for three different knives, and was also asked to
explain his procedure. Finally, for the reordering tasks, the knives
were scrambled and the child asked to locate the correct knife for a
specific fork.

The interviewer recorded the cards chosen, the method used in
reordering, and the explanation given.

Transitivity Tasks. The ability to understand transitivity (A > B;
B > C; A > C), that is, to grasp the relationship between A and C without the necessity for directly comparing them may, of course, be revealed in tasks involving a wide variety of materials and different
attributes. Such understanding is an essential element in measurement.
In The Child's Conception of Geometry (Piaget, Inhelder, and Szeminska,
1960, pp. 123-128), Piaget poses the problem of transitivity of length
by asking children to build on a low table a tower of blocks equal in
height to one built on a higher table by the experimenter. Sticks of
various lengths are available for the child's use, but according to
Piaget's findings, are not used adequately before the age of seven or
eight years. Braine (1959) using non-verbal methods challenged Piaget's
age norms since, in his sample, 50 per cent of the children between four
years, two months and five years, five months appeared to grasp transitivity. Smedslund (1963) in turn questions Braine's methods, pointing
out the possibility that the children were giving "correct" responses on
the basis of non-transitive responses. Smedslund designed a new test of
transitivity, as applied to length, administered it to 107 children
between the ages of four and ten years and concluded that the average
age of acquisition of transitivity of length probably lies near eight
years.

        Smedslund's procedures were incorporated in Tuddenham's (1968)
attempt to develop a scale of intelligence based on Piaget's theory of
cognitive development. He found that about 20 per cent of second-graders,
40 per cent of third grade boys and 20 per cent of third grade girls had
the concept.

        In the present study, Tuddenham's procedures were used with very
few modifications. (See Figure 5.)

        In all of these studies, transitivity is investigated in situations
in which the child who follows the perceptual cues cannot maintain the
concept of transitivity. The child is asked to compare three sticks.
The longest stick, A, has lines subtending at each end to make it look
shorter, as in the Müller-Lyer illusion. Similarly, the shortest stick,
C, has lines extending at each end to make it look longer. The third
stick, B, used as a measuring stick, is longer than C and shorter than A.
The operational child deduces from this relationship that A is longer
than C, but the child who is dependent on perceptual cues maintains that
A is shorter than C.

        The sticks and their V-shaped figures were glued to white oilcloth
sheets to aid the interviewer in presenting identical stimuli to each
child. A practice session was designed to familiarize the child with
the illusion. (One child designated the phenomenon as an "obstacle
illusion.") The sticks used were as follows:

39

Figure 4

SERIATION

I. Monkeys and Balloons

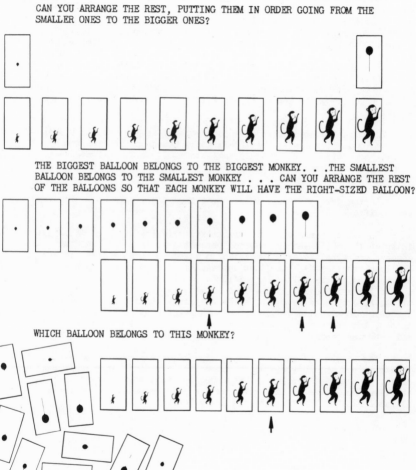

CAN YOU ARRANGE THE REST, PUTTING THEM IN ORDER GOING FROM THE
SMALLER ONES TO THE BIGGER ONES?

THE BIGGEST BALLOON BELONGS TO THE BIGGEST MONKEY. . .THE SMALLEST
BALLOON BELONGS TO THE SMALLEST MONKEY . . . CAN YOU ARRANGE THE REST
OF THE BALLOONS SO THAT EACH MONKEY WILL HAVE THE RIGHT-SIZED BALLOON?

WHICH BALLOON BELONGS TO THIS MONKEY?

CAN YOU FIND THIS MONKEY'S BALLOON NOW?

II. Knives and Forks

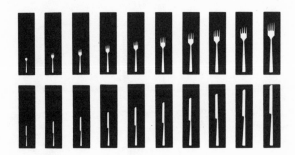

HERE ARE SOME KNIVES . . .IN ORDER, FROM LARGEST TO SMALLEST . . . HERE ARE SOME FORKS . . . I'LL PUT EACH FORK ABOVE THE KNIFE IT GOES WITH.

WHICH FORK GOES WITH THIS KNIFE?

CAN YOU FIND THE KNIFE THAT GOES WITH THIS FORK?

Figure 5

TRANSITIVITY

Practice I

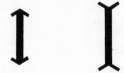

WHICH ONE OF THESE TWO STICKS IS LONGER? DON'T COUNT THE ARROWS.
JUST LOOK AT THE STICKS.

Practice II

WHICH ONE OF THESE TWO STICKS IS LONGER? REMEMBER NOT TO COUNT
THE ARROWS, JUST THE STICKS.

Test A.

BEFORE YOU TELL ME WHICH IS LONGER I WILL PLACE THE BLUE STICK
LIKE THIS.

WHICH IS LONGER, THE BLUE OR THE BLACK?

WHICH IS LONGER, THE BLUE OR THE BLACK?

WHICH OF THE BLACK STICKS IS LONGER?

	Stick A	V-Figures	Stick C	V-Figures	Stick B
Practice 1	14"	Extending	10"	Subtending	
Practice 2	12"	Subtending	9 7/8"	Extending	
Test 1	10 1/8"	Subtending	9 7/8"	Extending	10"
Test 2	9 7/8"	Extending	10 1/8"	Subtending	10"
Test 3	12 1/8"	Subtending	11 7/8"	Extending	12"
Test 4	11 7/8"	Extending	12 1/8"	Subtending	12"

All A and C sticks and corresponding V-figures were black, while the
B measuring sticks were light blue. Two cloths were used for the presentation of practice 1 and practice 2, and two additional cloths for
the four test items. After test 1, the first of these was reversed for
test 2, and after test 3 the second was reversed for test 4.

In the practice session the interviewer assisted any child who did
not correctly respond to the question "Which of these two sticks is
longer?" by measuring the shorter stick with his fingers showing him
that "it only comes up to here" on the other stick.

In the test sessions the interviewer placed the measuring stick B
against stick A, pointing out that the ends of the stick nearest him
coincided but that there was a difference in the ends nearest the child.
He then asked the child to indicate which stick was longer, the blue or
the black. The measuring stick was then moved against stick C and the
question repeated. Finally, the interviewer asked "Which of the black
sticks is longer?" and, "How can you tell?" This procedure was repeated
for each of the three remaining tests.

Matrix Tasks. The matrix tasks deal with what Piaget terms multiplicative classification. For example, a collection of circles and
squares, some red, some blue, some small, and some large, can be classified on the basis of color or form. Multiplicative classification involves the simultaneous classification of each element in the collection
according to both criteria, and may be symbolized by a matrix. In this
example, the collection is arranged so that the rows are classified
according to color, and the columns according to form. A red square is
at once located in the row of red elements and the column of square
elements.

The correct placement of a particular element in a matrix can, in
such an example, be arrived at in either of two ways. The perceptual
solution is to "extend the graphic properties by following the vertical
and horizontal symmetries in the matrix arrangement" (Inhelder and
Piaget, 1964, p. 153). The conceptual solution involves reasoning in
terms of classes.

43

In their initial studies Inhelder and Piaget (1964) used 14 matrices, each containing four or six pictured objects. These were grouped according to shape, color, size, number or orientation (in the case of animals whose heads were turned to the right or left). All but two of these tests were answered correctly by 75 per cent of the eight- to nine-year-olds (pp.154-155). However, for those items involving three attributes, four- to five-year-olds did about as well as the eight- to nine-year-olds, while the six- to seven-year-olds were far worse. Clinical inquiry suggested that the younger children were using perceptual or graphic solutions, while the older ones were struggling to handle the problems more conceptually. To check these results Inhelder and Piaget devised a more standardized series of tests. These are the ones used in the present study. It should be noted that while Inhelder and Piaget's results with this series indicated that "Operational solutions increase steadily with age while graphic solutions decrease after the age of six" (p. 164), there is no fully satisfactory way to determine which solution the child may be using. Despite this known limitation in the use of the matrices, two considerations supported their use in the present study. First, the inclusion of a classification measure less difficult than the class inclusion tasks seemed essential in view of the emphasis on sorting and grouping in the various curricula. Second, the matrices are interesting to second-graders, are relatively easily administered, and at this age level provide a good spread in scores.

The pictures for the matrices were copied from those presented by Inhelder and Piaget (1964, pp. 160-161). (See Figure 6.) There were eight test matrices and one practice matrix. For the present study an additional practice matrix was constructed. Four of the matrices had four cells, one of which was empty. Four of the matrices had six cells, with one empty. Each matrix was presented on a 5" by 5" card. Each of the pictured objects, from which the one to fill the empty cell was to be chosen, was presented on a 2 1/2" by 2 1/2" card. The number of these choice cards for each matrix varied from four (for the initial practice tasks) to eight. The matrices were presented to each child in the same order, as were the choice cards. (The position of the correct choice, and of the various distractors had been predetermined by randomization.)

In the procedure used by Piaget and Inhelder (1964, p. 159) the multiple choices were presented one by one and the child allowed to try each of them in the empty cell. In the present study, this procedure was followed for the initial practice matrix, but modified in the succeeding practice matrix and the test matrices. The modification consisted in showing the child each of the choice cards, one by one, asking him to look at them carefully and <u>think</u> about "Which one is the correct one." Then the choice cards were re-shown, one by one, and the child asked to indicate by "yes" or "no," whether each, in turn, was the one that "goes best with the others." This procedure was intended to guard against an impulsive choice, and was also an attempt to elicit a conceptual rather than a perceptual approach. After the child had indicated "yes" or "no" for each one, the interviewer returned to the child's selection for "yes," and asked "How can you tell that is the best one?"--recording the attributes mentioned. In instances where children selected one card, and in the process of justifying their choice, changed their selection, the change as well as the original selection was recorded.

        Conservation of Weight. The conservation of weight task represented an extension of the other kinds of conservation items. In Le Developpement des quantités chez l'enfant (1941), Inhelder and Piaget report that the conservation of weight is achieved subsequent to the conservation of substance, and typically not before the age of ten.

A replication study by Elkind (1961) confirmed both the sequence and the ages of acquisition. Studies by Smedslund (1961) and Chittenden (1964) confirmed the general trends but suggested that the difference in difficulty of the two tasks is not very great. In any case, the conservation of weight seemed an appropriate addition.

Consideration was given to the possibility of including a conservation of substance task, to contrast with the task involving conservation of a quantity of liquid; but this idea was excluded when the length of the interview became apparent.

The procedures used in the conservation of weight task were based on those of Chittenden (1964), except that the use of a balance scale was eliminated. (See Figure 7.) In view of the number of children to be interviewed in diverse settings, it did not seem feasible to add a piece of equipment that in the previous more leisurely study had sometimes been the source of various kinds of difficulty. The equivalence of weights of two balls of Play-Doh was established in a series of "hefting" procedures. The child lifted in his hand in turn a standard ball and four comparison balls, one of which was equivalent in both size and weight to the standard. The other comparison balls had been weighted with lead curtain weights so that the smallest in quantity and diameter was the heaviest, and the largest, the lightest. This procedure was intended to focus the child's attention on weight as contrasted with quantity. The standard ball of Play-Doh (blue) and its equivalent (red) weighed three ounces and was 2" in diameter. The weight and diameters of the other red comparison balls were 2 1/2 ounces plus two weights, 1 3/4"; 1 1/2 ounces plus four weights, 1 1/2"; and 3/4 ounces plus six weights, 1 1/4" respectively.

The interviewer began this section of the interview by placing the blue ball in front of the child, and the four red balls in front of himself. He then asked the child to find the red ball that weighed the same as the blue, taking the blue ball in one hand, and then trying each of the others. The response of the child who immediately chose the right ball was confirmed as correct but he was also asked to try each of the others to "make sure." However, if his choice was incorrect, the interviewer indicated to the child that his choice was "pretty good" but that it was heavier (or lighter) than the correct choice. The interviewer then indicated the correct choice, making sure the child agreed.

Figure 6[*]

MATRICES

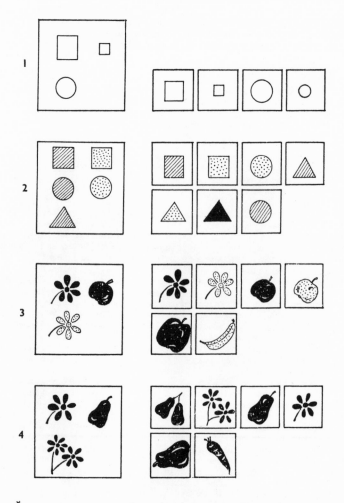

46

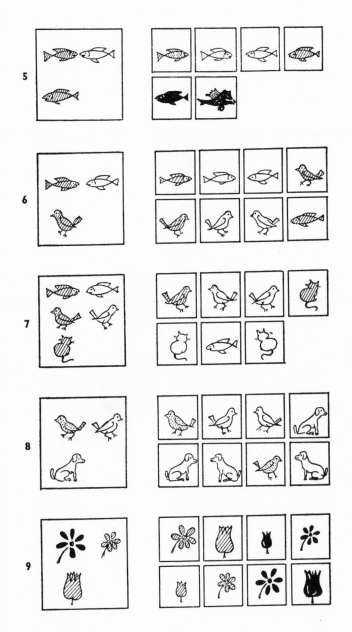

5

6

7

8

9

47

Figure 7

CONSERVATION OF WEIGHT

Orientation

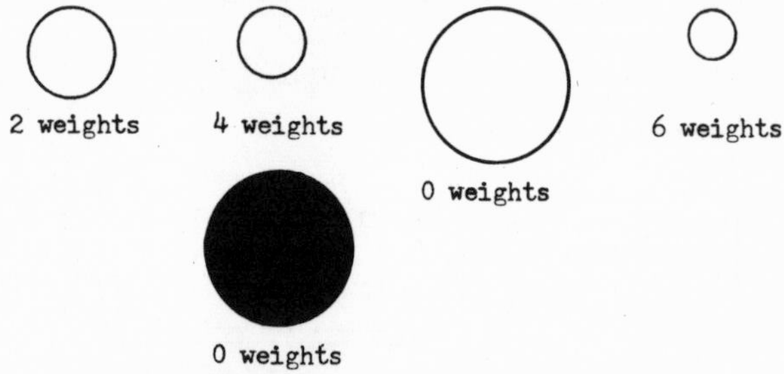

2 weights   4 weights   6 weights

0 weights

0 weights

CAN YOU FIND OUT WHICH RED BALL WEIGHS THE SAME AMOUNT AS YOUR BLUE BALL?

Test Section

A.

DOES MINE WEIGH AS MUCH AS YOURS OR DOES ONE OF THEM WEIGH MORE?

B.

DO THESE PIECES ALTOGETHER WEIGH MORE, LESS OR THE SAME AS THAT PIECE?

DOES MINE WEIGH AS MUCH AS YOURS OR DOES ONE OF THEM WEIGH MORE?

C.

48

After the child had accepted the equality of the two unweighted balls, the weighted balls were put out of sight and the inquiry proceeded with the two equivalent balls. In the test items that followed, the red Play-Doh was elongated on the first two test items while the comparison blue Play-Doh remained unchanged until the final test item, when it was broken into three pieces. The standard question for the elongations was "Does mine weigh as much as yours, or does one of them weigh more?", and for the broken pieces, "Do these pieces all together weigh more, less, the same as that piece?" In each instance an additional question was allowed if the child did not answer or appeared not to understand, "Is the blue Play-Doh heavier, the red Play-Doh heavier, or do they weigh the same?" In each instance a justification question, "How can you tell?" was also asked.

Reliability

The usual problems surrounding the testing of young children whose responses are extremely erratic are compounded when the investigator attempts to combine Piagetian tasks and standardized procedures. Since standardization prohibits probing of suspect answers, there is always the possibility of the "false positive" where the child is credited with thinking on an operational level when, in fact, his answer misleadingly reflects that level of understanding. Perhaps less probable, but still not unlikely, is the "false negative" where the child responds as though he did not understand because he does not grasp the intent of the interviewer soon enough and is not given further opportunity to demonstrate his understanding.

Increasing the number of tasks should increase the probability of getting a more adequate demonstration of the child's abilities, but may also lead to fatigue, and in the case of many children, a wariness or even withdrawal. The "how can you tell" and more especially, "why do you think so" questions that are intended to elicit further thought, may be interpreted by the child as evidence of his error and tempt him to change his original response.

Assuming that the number of tasks given the child is adequate to sample his typical ways of thinking about a certain kind of problem, what is the likelihood that he will respond in the same way if the interview is repeated? If his responses the first time can, without any equivocation, clearly be classed as operational, this level should be sustained over repeated interviews. If he is clearly pre-operational and the next interview occurs within a short time, his responses should remain at the same level. However, allowance must be made for the possibility that his initial responses represent impetuous behavior and that learning and maturation may intervene to change them. The case of the child whom Piaget would term "transitional" is even less predictable, for he may vacillate in his responses until the new level is firmly established.

49

The relative stability over short periods of children's performances in the conservation and class inclusion tasks was established in earlier studies. No significant differences in conservation performance were found when first-graders were re-interviewed after a two-week period (Almy, Chittenden and Miller, 1966, p. 57). Miller (1966) found no improvement in class inclusion performance among either kindergarten or second grade children who were re-interviewed after a six to eight week interval.

For the present study, assessment of the reliability of the post-test measures was combined with the training of the interviewers. Before the interviewers were permitted to interview any of the children serving as subjects in the study, they had to demonstrate their competence with a child who was not included. For all of the tasks, except transitivity, 21 children were interviewed twice, within a two-week interval. Twenty-three children repeated the transitivity tasks. The interviewer for the first presentation was not the same as for the second. Considering this shift, and the fact that the interviewers were not as skillful as they were to become, stability of performance from one interview to the next, when it occurred, can probably be regarded as genuine.

Because the number of children is small, and the tasks vary in complexity, the comparisons of performance from one testing to another are, in most instances, based on the extent to which the responses are in agreement at the two testings rather than on the correlation between scores.

Serial Ordering Tasks. Since these tasks were scored according to a formula that took into account the extent of the error the child made, a comparison of scores was necessary. The extent of the differences in the seriation and ordination tasks is apparent in the following summary:

Differences in Test-Retest Scores	Number of Children	Number of Children
Seriation	First Task	Second Task
0	15	11
1	6	7
2	0	2
Ordination		
0	14	17
1	4	3
2	2	1
3	1	0

In response to the question, "How did you do these [ordinations] ?" 21 children gave the same response in both testings.

Reordering after Scrambling. These are the most difficult of the serial ordering tasks. Twelve of 21 children gave the same response in both testings for the first of these tasks. Fourteen children gave the same response on the second task.

Transitivity Tasks. In these tasks the children's answers and explanations were categorized on the basis of their quality. The extent of agreement from the first to the second testing is indicated below:

Task	No. of Children	No. of Agreements
A	23	20
B	23	18
C	23	18
D	23	19

On the basis of the overall category to which their responses on the four tasks were assigned, 22 out of 23 children were in exact agreement.

Conservation of Weight. As in the transitivity tasks, answers and explanations on the conservation of weight tasks were categorized separately, and then placed in an overall category. The agreement on individual tasks is shown below:

Task		No. of Children	No. of Agreements
A	Answer	21	18
	Explanation	21	15
B	Answer	21	19
	Explanation	21	18
C	Answer	21	18
	Explanation	21	12

On the basis of the overall category, 19 of 21 children were in exact agreement.

Matrix Tasks. Since these tasks produced a range of scores (6 to 20), a Pearson Product moment correlation coefficient between test and re-test scores of 21 children was calculated. It was .76.

Measure of Verbal Ability

Since previous studies (Almy, Chittenden and Miller, 1966) have shown an association between performance in Piaget-derived tasks and mental maturity, and since the ability to understand verbal directions is clearly a requisite for coping with such tasks, some measure of verbal ability seemed essential. The Peabody Picture Vocabulary Test

(1965) was chosen for its ease of administration and interest for kindergarten children. It appraises the child's auditory comprehension vocabulary, rather than his expressive vocabulary.

The reported alternate form reliability coefficient for age five is .73, age six .67 and age seven .74.

It should be noted that although the manual reports substantial correlations with other measures of intelligence, such as the Stanford Binet and the Wechsler Intelligence Scale for Children, the populations rarely included a wide range of five, six, and seven year olds. Studies correlating PPVT scores with school achievement have not been extensive, nor have they included many children, other than those with mental handicaps, in the five to seven year range. However, the author of the test (Dunn, 1965) suggests that "apparently one can do about, but not quite as well estimating school achievement from PPVT scores as from Binet and Wechsler scores" (p. 41).

In the present study, the PPVT was used as one means of differentiating the level of ability of the children in the various programs at the beginning of the study. It was administered in kindergarten to those children whose instructional programs began in kindergarten, and in first grade to those children whose instructional programs began in first grade.

The Interviewing

All of the interviewing was done in the fall of the year. The intent was to complete it before the children began the special programs of instruction. The number of children to be interviewed, and the fact that few schools had space for working with more than two children at a time, made realization of this intent difficult. However, with the exception of the classes having no prescribed lessons where in the first year of the study interviewing did not get under way until November, the interviewing was nearly completed in the first two months of the school year.

The Interviews

Most of the interviewers were graduate students in psychology, with some, but not extensive experience in either interviewing or working with young children. Each worked two or three days a week. Four of the interviewers were not students but had had previous graduate work. The first year there were 17 interviewers, the other two years, 18 interviewers. Seven individuals served as interviewers for two years, two for three years.

Training of the Interviewers

Piaget (1961, p. 8) in describing his own clinical method of interviewing states that "a year of daily practice is necessary before pass-

ing beyond the inevitable fumbling state of the beginner." With standardized procedures, the fumbling stage is not so extended but is none-
theless inevitable. Just as in the individual intelligence testing of
young children, rapport must be established; materials,of which there
are many, must be presented in a prescribed fashion; the interviewer
must be prepared for the unexpected answer and alert to those instances
where the procedure allows or does not allow for a probing question;
finally, the child's responses must be recorded systematically.

To facilitate the training of the interviewers in the present study,
eight millimeter cartridge films showing the correct administration of
each section of the interview were produced. A detailed descriptive
guide keyed to the film enabled the viewer to pace the interviewer's
manipulations of the materials with the proper verbal instructions and
questions to the child. Interviewers-in-training first reviewed the
interview schedule and discussed the purpose for each of the tasks with
the senior investigator, or with her research associate. Then, after
viewing the films, the interviewers rehearsed the procedures with a
partner until they felt ready to attempt them with children. Following
one or more trial interviews with children not involved in the study,
some interviewers returned for further rehearsal, others moved directly
to an interview which was observed by a senior staff member. No interviewer was permitted to interview a child in the study until he had
satisfactorily completed at least one, and in many instances, two training interviews with children who were not involved in the study.

Administration of the Interviews

After the classes to be included in the study had been selected and
the teachers and the parents informed about it, lists of names and birth
dates were prepared. Arrangements were made so that not more than half
the boys and half the girls in each class were tested by a single interviewer. The children were interviewed in whatever space was available
outside their classroom, such as a nearby hall, a vacant office, a large
supply closet or nurse's room.

At the first interview, usually lasting for 20 to 30 minutes, the
Peabody Picture Vocabulary Test was administered first, and followed by
the other tasks. At the kindergarten level, when some children seemed
fatigued, the interviews were sometimes given in two sittings. To provide a break between the conservation and class inclusion tasks, all the
kindergarten children were asked to stand up and show how they could pat
their heads and rub their stomachs. The interviews concluded with tasks
that were varied from one child to another, such as reciting a nursery
rhyme, or repeating digits, in order to avoid possible classroom discussion of the Piaget tasks.

The post-test interviews at the beginning of the second grade took
about 45 minutes. The conservation and class inclusion tasks, which the
children had done before, were presented first, and succeeded by the
seriation, transitivity, matrices, and conservation of weight tasks, in
that order. Relatively few of the second-graders seemed to find the
interview unduly fatiguing.

Scoring and Categorization of the Data

Experience in a previous study (Almy, Chittenden and Miller, 1966) dictated many of the precautions taken in the present study to insure adequate recording and correct categorization of the children's responses.

While not all of the tasks included in the post-test interview presented exactly the same problems as did the conservation tasks of the previous study (Almy, et al., 1966), the general approach to categorizing and scoring was quite similar. Each set of tasks (except seriation) included orientation or practice that enabled the interviewer to ascertain whether the child's attention was appropriately focused and whether he appeared to understand the questions. Wherever possible his responses were categorized on a check list as they occurred, but, in many instances, they had to be recorded verbatim. If the procedure provided for a probe question, it was also recorded.

Because the questions were standardized, and relatively little probing was included, responses had to be taken at face value. The general procedure for each task consisted of categorizing each of the responses in a particular task and then recategorizing the performance for the total task on the basis of the patterns formed by the separate responses. The categorization scheme that evolved for each set of tasks was first applied to the protocols obtained in the test-retest reliability study. It represented the collaboration of staff members who were familiar with Piaget's theory, who had considerable experience in interviewing. Only minor modifications were made in applying the scheme to the protocols in the main study.

Each categorization scheme attempted to differentiate responses that provided clear evidence of operational thinking from those that were clearly non-operational or ambiguous. It also attempted to distinguish responses that were spontaneous from those that were given in response to a probe question. On this basis the evidence for a set of tasks could then be categorized as clearly indicative of operational thought; clearly indicative of thought that is not operational; and insufficient. As can be seen in the detailed description of the categories, finer distinctions can be drawn for some tasks. However, in the present study most of the analyses dealt only with the children whose responses are clearly operational as contrasted with all others.

Conservation of Number and Liquid

Each of the three conservation tasks was categorized independently but the procedure for each was basically similar. It consisted of weighing the evidence for or against conservation in the child's response to each opportunity presented in a particular task. (The initial task presented three such opportunities; the second, two, and the final task, two.) This evidence was accordingly classified in one of four

categories: clearly indicative of conservation; uncertain, that is
apparently indicating conservation but based on responses that could be
inspired by clues in the questioning; clearly indicative of non-
conservation; or evidence lacking. After the evidence for each of the
opportunities to conserve had been so classified, the evidence for the
total task was weighed and the total performance on that task classified
in one of five categories. These categories were: clear evidence of
conservation; probable evidence of conservation; uncertain evidence of
conservation (a category to include the performance of a child for whom
there is evidence of both conserving and not conserving, a child whose
performance on this task might go either way if more evidence were
available); clear evidence of non-conservation; insufficient evidence
regarding conservation (a category for the child who says he does not
know, gives no response, or uses gestures).

For the analyses of the present study, the five-fold categorization
for each task was collapsed and each task scored 0 if the evidence for
conservation was classified as uncertain, or clearly in favor of non-
conservation, or insufficient. If the evidence for the task had been
categorized as clear or probable, the task was scored 1. The possible
range of scores for the three tasks was 0 to 3.

Class Inclusion

Each of these four tasks required an answer and an explanation.
These two parts were examined as a unit. In a correct answer, the child
indicated that there were more objects in the superordinate class than
in either sub-class. A correct explanation focused upon the defining
attributes of the superordinate class or indicated the total number of
objects in it. A correct solution of the task required both a correct
answer and a correct explanation. The incorrect solutions were also
categorized to indicate whether the child recognized the defining attributes of the superordinate class, although he did not verbalize its
quantitative superiority, focused his attention on the quantitative relationship between the sub-classes, or gave ambiguous responses. In the
analyses of the present study, each class inclusion task received a
score of 1 for a completely correct solution. All other solutions were
scored 0. The range of scores for the four tasks was 0 to 4.

Serial Ordering Tasks

Since the cards the child used in these tasks had been coded with
letters, the interviewer had only to record on the protocol the identifying letters for the child's ordering or selection in each task. These
were then scored right or wrong. The interviewer also categorized the
child's explanation as ordination, one-to-one correspondence, or other.
The categorization of the explanations was not used in the major
analyses of the data.

Seriation. For each of the two seriation tasks, the child's order-

ing of the items was recorded and then compared with the correct ordering. The sum of squares of the differences between his ranking and the
correct ones was obtained and then converted into a corrected score on
the basis of the formula, Score = (Number of things ranked) S r_R^2
(Stanley, 1964, p. 380). For task A, the possible range of scores was
0-12. The range for task B was 0-18.

Ordination. Each of the three ordination items in the two series
was scored 0 or 1. The possible range of scores was 0-6.

Reordering. The child's rearrangement of each series of cards
after they had been scrambled by the interviewer was scored 1 if correct,
0 if there were errors. The possible range of scores was 0-2.

Transitivity Tasks

Each of the four tasks required an answer and an explanation. Each
answer was scored 0 if incorrect, 1 if correct. The explanations were
scored correct if the child included both sides of the statement,
$A > B > C : A > C$. After the answers and explanations for each task
were separately scored, they were categorized 3 for a correct answer and
explanation; 2 for a correct answer and partially correct or incorrect
or missing explanation; 1 for a correct explanation and incorrect answer;
and 0 for incorrect answer and incorrect explanation.

It should be noted that in these tasks the child was asked to
justify each answer, that is to make the same explanation four times.
As the interviewing proceeded, it became clear that children who responded correctly and fully in one task often evaded further explanation.
Accordingly, after the distribution of responses had been examined, it
was decided to assign the four transitivity tasks an overall score of 1
if none of the four tasks was categorized less than 2 and if there was
at least one at the category 3 level. All other combinations were
scored 0. The possible range of scores was 0-1.

Matrix Tasks

For each of the eight test items, the card chosen by the child was
scored according to the number of attributes (shape, color, direction)
correct on any one item. The first four items involved two attributes,
the last four involved three. On the first four a choice might earn the
child a score of 0, 1, 2 or 3. The possible range of scores was 0-20.

Since the procedure permitted the child to change his mind, he was
given a separate score indicating the total score after such changes.
Thus the changed scores could range from 0 to 20.

The highest number of attributes on any one item was also scored.
The possible range of scores was 0-3.

Conservation of Weight

This task had three separate items, each consisting of an answer categorized for evidence of conservation, and an explanation similarly categorized. The system used corresponded to that in the earlier conservation tasks. The combinations of answers and explanations in all three tasks were then categorized, taking into account the fact that the explanations were demanded three times. In the overall score the child received a 1 if all of his answers were correct, and if at least one of his explanations provided clear evidence of conservation, and none was uncertain, clearly non-conserving or lacking in evidence. The possible range of scores was 0-1.

Reliability of Scoring and Categorization

The data for each of the three years of the study were scored and categorized in the same year they were gathered. For successive samples of 30 protocols the agreement between pairs of coders ranged from 95 per cent to 96 per cent on conservation, and from 91 per cent to 95 per cent on class inclusion. For conservation of weight in the post-test, two coders were in agreement on 96 per cent of the items. The coding and scoring for the remainder of the post-test items was so explicit that two coders could agree on 100 per cent of the items.

CHAPTER III

THE PROGRAMS[1]

One of the subsidiary objectives of this study was the examination of the content of the programs of instruction. Since this analysis provides the reader a framework against which he can view the major results of the study, it precedes the chapters dealing with such findings. In the present chapter, the programs of instruction are described, and their content is analyzed.

Bases of Content Analysis

The content of the special programs considered in the present study, namely AAAS, SCIS, and GCMP, was examined in three ways. The teacher's manuals provided for each program were analyzed in terms of (1) the information taught in each program, (2) the cognitive processes presumably required of the children in the various prescribed activities, and (3) the extent to which each program required direct manipulation of objects by the children. The fourth program, devised by educators in Garden City as a general guide in the local schools, provided very few specific directives to the teachers. Therefore, a comparable content analysis could not be made for the Garden City program except in the area of general information. No analysis was made for the mathematics program in Englewood since it was derived from several sources, including the Greater Cleveland Mathematics Program, and varied from class to class.

Information

The content of the special programs was analyzed in terms of the subject matter, or information, that was prescribed in each of the manuals. The subject matter was categorized according to whether it was concerned with physical objects and their properties or with concepts dealing with number. The kinds of measurement taught were also itemized. In addition, the programs were analyzed in terms of the number of special words recommended for teaching to the children.

Cognitive Processes

In order to examine the cognitive processes required of the children by the special programs, categories were established, based upon Piaget's theory of the development of logical thinking. The ages of the children in the present study placed them roughly in a transitional period between the earlier preoperational stage and the stage of concrete operations, toward which they were growing.

According to Piaget, such a transitional child is moving out of the stage in which he is overwhelmed by the way things appear to his senses

---

[1]This chapter was prepared by Mildred Hardeman.

and into the stage in which logical necessity becomes a reality for him and is more convincing to him than his wavering sense perceptions. "Logical necessity" entails the development of concrete operations, which are applied to classes, relations, and numbers. In other words, the child becomes "able to structure relationships between classes, relations, and numbers objectively" (Inhelder and Piaget, 1958, p. 343).

Such objectivity in regard to objects in the external world is a necessary prelude to objectivity in relation to one's own thoughts, the latter, according to Piaget, coming to existence only at about the time of puberty. According to Piaget, the concrete operational child deals very directly with facts as he goes about classifying and ordering objects and dealing with numbers, ignorant of both the methods he is using and his own thought processes. The child "never thinks about his own thoughts. . . . In other words, the child has no powers of reflection, i.e., no second-order thoughts which deal critically with his own thinking" (Inhelder and Piaget, 1958, p. 339-340).

The mathematics and science programs considered in the present study may be viewed as efforts to help the children move more completely into operational thinking. There is some emphasis, too, in the manuals on helping children to become aware of their thought processes, and hence more critical of their own logic.

In view of the foregoing aspects of Piaget's developmental theory, categories were established in terms that permitted the cognitive processes of the mathematics and science program to be analyzed. Each activity recommended in the manuals was first categorized as to whether it required cognitive activity in relation to concrete reality or in relation to the child's own process of thinking. If the former, it was then classified as to whether the activity pertained to classification (e.g., recognizing, naming, describing, defining, grouping), relations (e.g., ordering), or number (e.g., counting, joining sets, separating sets, adding, subtracting, etc.). Activities that required that the child think about his own thinking included explaining, predicting, checking of predictions, judging adequacy of criteria, viewing objects, events, or relations in more than one way.

No attempt was made to count the number of times a specific activity might have been repeated, for the manuals often recommend that an activity be repeated as long as the children are interested. In GCMP (Kindergarten, p. 56), for example, the teacher is asked to put ten paper fish on a flannel board, each being labelled "1" through "10." "Tell the children that the fish were swimming along in order when a big wave scattered them. Ask a child to line the fish up again, in order. Have many different 'waves' come along to scatter the fish and each time let a child rearrange them on the board."

When there was no reasonable basis for making a judgment concerning what cognitive processes might be required of the child, the activity was not categorized. For example, the general instruction that the teacher should discuss a given topic with the children did not lend itself to the present content analysis.

Several limitations in the present content analysis need to be considered. First, there is no way of knowing whether any given teacher actually carried out the activities in the precise way prescribed by the manual.

A second limitation is related to Piaget's warning against trying to analyze isolated statements in terms of their logical components, pointing to his own failure in such an attempt. "The question is psychologically meaningful only when the subject's entire reasoning or a sufficiently systematic series of inferences is taken as a context" (1958, p. 278). In the present context, the child's responses are not being analyzed, nor the teacher's presentation of activities and questions, but only the presumed cognitive processes required of the child as stated in the printed manual.

A third difficulty results from the fact that the mathematics and science programs cover a time span of two years, proceeding from very simple demands on the child to considerably more complex requirements. Yet some of these processes may be classified in the same way. A kindergarten child, for example, may be asked to describe a ball, and may reply that the ball is red, or that the ball is round. A first grade child may be asked to "Tell the story of this equation." The responses of both, in the present scheme, were categorized as one form of classifying, namely, describing. No distinction was made between the more and less sophisticated forms of description.

This difficulty is related to another, namely, the fact that the children in the present study were in a transitional stage, and when they were asked, for example, to "name" an object or an attribute, there is no way of knowing whether the pronouncing of the appropriate label is a pre-classificatory experience of the kind that Piaget calls "recognitive assimilation," or whether this pronouncing of the name genuinely implies awareness of a classification scheme, however rudimentary such a scheme might be.

Finally, the classification system itself only very roughly approximates the logical requirements of an exhaustive, mutually exclusive set of categories. For example, the process of "grouping" (noting similarities) was distinguished from the process of "distinguishing" (noting differences). Piaget's theory requires such a distinction, and although one process or the other is usually clearly called for in various activities prescribed in the manuals, yet in actuality, it would seem that the child who is asked to "put the blue blocks together" (grouping, or noting similarities) is implicitly also noting differences, i.e., the distinction between the blue blocks and those of another color.

In spite of the foregoing limitations involved in the examination of presumed cognitive processes required by the special programs, it seems reasonable to suppose that an indication of similarities and differences in the programs might be helpful in understanding the findings of the present study.

Direct Manipulation of Objects

According to Piaget, four factors contribute to the development of the child's logical abilities: maturation, experience with the physical world, social transmission, and equilibration (Piaget, 1964, pp. 176-186). Concerning experience with the physical world, Piaget has further stated that ". . . a child learns very little indeed when experiments are performed for him. . . . [instead] he must do them himself rather than sit and watch them done" (1966, p. v). Through direct manipulation of concrete objects, the child can not only discover properties of objects, but he can also discover ways of giving logical structure to the objects of the concrete world.

> For example, a child may be surprised to learn that when he counts three groups of two objects he gets the same total as when he counts two groups of three objects. When he learns that the sum is independent of the order of counting he is discovering the properties of the actions of ordering and uniting. He is learning something from these actions themselves, rather than from the objects independent of these actions. (Piaget, 1966, p. vi.)

In view of this emphasis on actual experience with physical reality, the science and mathematics programs were analyzed in terms of the extent to which, according to the teacher's manuals, the children were given the opportunity to manipulate objects physically. Examples of such activity included sorting buttons, planting seeds, measuring the floor, matching children and chairs, etc.

Description and Analysis of Programs

American Association for the Advancement of Science

For the early elementary years, AAAS has provided four manuals entitled Science--A Process Approach. The first two manuals, Part IA and Part IB, have been used frequently in kindergarten, and Part IIA and Part IIB in the first grade. Each of the four manuals begins with the same one-page foreword, in which the chief task of science education for young children is stated to be that of awakening "a sense of . . . joy and excitement" in searching for knowledge, and an awareness of the intellectual power of science.

In the foreword, the hope is expressed that in the primary grades, skills will be developed in "Observing, Recognizing and Using Number Relations, Measuring, Recognizing and Using Space-time Relations, Classifying, Communicating, Inferring, and Predicting." The stress is placed on developing these skills rather than upon a systematic presentation of information. Content is thus intended to be placed in a secondary role.

Our hope is that by the end of the third grade, the child who has been instructed by means of these exercises has acquired some important fundamental process skills, a good many basic scientific concepts, and some organized knowledge about the natural world. . . .

These instructional materials consist of descriptions for the teacher of exercises drawn from a variety of science fields. They are arranged as an orderly progression of learning experiences. The objectives, the student performance expected by the time each exercise is completed, are clearly specified. To ensure that these objectives have been attained, an associated appraisal exercise is provided. (Science--A Process Approach, 1965)

The activities themselves occupy 120 pages for kindergarten and 179 for first grade, totalling 24 lessons for kindergarten and 26 for first grade. Some of the objects studied are animals, plants, shells, magnets; and stress is placed on such properties as shape, size, color, and texture. Several concepts pertaining to number are emphasized, such as sets, numerals, addition, and measurement (linear, time, volume, weight).

In the AAAS manuals, each lesson is presented in the following form: objectives, rationale, vocabulary, materials, suggestions for originating the program with the children, instructional procedure (usually several different activities), one or more generalizing experiences, and ways of appraising what the children have learned. Instructions to the teachers are detailed and specific.

The specificity of directions may be illustrated by the lesson taught in the kindergarten on recognizing time intervals (IB, pp. 89-94). After stating three immediate objectives of the lesson, a rationale, a vocabulary of 38 words (year, month, week, etc.), and itemizing the materials needed, 21 questions are then given that the teacher may ask the children ("Originating the Problem"). As "Instructional Procedure," three activities are presented, each with details of activity and questions to be asked of the children. Frequently the answers that are required by the questions are given in parentheses after the question, e.g., concerning clocks: "Are the hands alike? How are they different? (One is longer than the other--or one moves faster than the other.)"

As a "generalizing experience," the manual asks the teacher whether the children select appropriate time intervals in describing the age of various people and objects, and whether they can order various time units in terms of length of interval. In order to appraise what the children have learned, three additional activities are provided.

Although the stated objective of the AAAS manuals is to develop processes, the present content analysis indicates considerable emphasis on specific information. For example, the first four AAAS manuals together recommend a total of 430 words to be taught.

When cognitive responses were examined, it was found that nearly half of those responses presumably required in the kindergarten and first grade pertain to the logic of classes, approximately 15 per cent to the logic of relations, and approximately 20 per cent to number. The logic of relations receives more emphasis than any one of the processes involved in the logic of classes (recognizing, naming, describing, grouping, distinguishing). Further, if the responses concerned with the logic of relations are added to those that require numerical ordering (ordination and cardination), then almost one-third of the AAAS responses are concerned with ordering.

Approximately 17 per cent of the responses to AAAS activities seem to require that the children think about their thought processes. Special emphasis is placed on predicting, explaining, and checking of the predictions and observations.

Approximately one-fourth of the required responses gave children the opportunity to manipulate physical objects directly.

Science Curriculum Improvement Study

Karplus presented the underlying philosophy of the SCIS program as he saw it in 1964 in the following way:

> In order to reach the objective of scientific literacy, . . . the science curriculum has to provide the pupils with experiences that are different from their usual ones. . . .
>
> A most interesting pedagogical question concerns the manner in which these experiences should be incorporated into the teaching program. . . . it is clear that the experiences should be direct ones for the children, not told by the teacher or read in a book. . . . There is, however, the question of how much guidance the teacher or the book should provide for the children as they manipulate and observe, and how much discussion and review should follow the experience. How much verbalization should take place?
>
> It is my belief that there should be substantial guidance and discussion. There should be an effort to relate the unusual experience to the more usual experience of which it represents an extreme case. In this way, the abstract concepts that are at the basis of the scientific point of view are built up. As the children make further observations, they will look at them more scientifically. The abstractions will form a link between their earlier experiences and later experiences, so that the children can bring their knowledge to bear in a systematic way. Perhaps the gulf between scientific thinking and common-sense thinking can be reduced!

Each lesson in the science program may fulfill one or
both of these functions: to provide a new experience
and to establish or reinforce an abstract concept.
Connections between different lessons are created by
use of the same phenomenon to illustrate different concepts and the use of the same concept to interpret different phenomena. The conceptual structure creates a
context for the new experience that enables it to be
assimilated rationally in relation to other experiences.
One might say that the conceptual structure provides
discipline for mental organization. (Karplus and Thier,
1967, pp. 5-6)

The teacher's manual used for the SCIS kindergarten program in 1965
contains 33 pages, of which nine provide a rationale of the program and
give suggestions for the development of an appropriate standpoint on the
part of the teacher for introducing young children to science.

In general, the teacher is asked to experiment with the presentation of various activities in the manner of a scientist, not evaluating
the results in terms of the children's excitement or what may appear to
be their immediate understanding, but looking rather for evidence of
"the children's growing ability and interest in dealing with objects and
events in more analytical ways." The teacher is further asked not to
make introductory or concluding generalizations for the children, but
rather to let them arrive at various conclusions themselves.

Concerning the content of the kindergarten program, the authors
state that they are concerned with "some simple ideas underlying the
basic concepts" (p. 7) to be encountered later in the study of complex
scientific theories. The particular concepts basic to the sciences
presented in the kindergarten manual are physical "objects" and their
"properties." According to the instructions to the teacher, emphasis
is to be placed on helping children to make accurate observations and
verbal descriptions of what is observed. Observation is to include
tactile observation, actual manipulation, and playing with objects.

Twenty-four pages of the manual are devoted to 15 different activities designed to carry out the objectives stated above. The objects
observed included those in the classroom, on a neighborhood walk, at a
zoo, and such items as leaves, buttons, blocks, beans, nuts and washers,
and plants. Properties emphasized included shape, color, size, and
texture. The manual does not offer special recommendations concerning
vocabulary to be taught, with the exception of the words "object,"
"property," "shape," "color," and "texture."

For the first grade, in 1966 SCIS provided an instructional manual
entitled Teacher's Guide: Material Objects, an equipment kit, and 60
"Student Activity Pages."

As in the teacher's manual for kindergarten, here, too, a lengthy
rationale is provided along with recommendations concerning the

teacher's general attitude toward both the teaching of science and the use of specific activities. Two long-range goals of the teaching of science are affirmed: intellectual development in which reliance is placed on one's own ability to reason, and "scientific literacy," or understanding of basic scientific concepts.

The immediate goals "of the program are to acquaint a child with specific examples of objects and organisms, to let him investigate examples of natural phenomena, and to help him develop skills of manipulating equipment and recording data" (SCIS, First Grade, p. vii).

The emphasis in the first grade again is on material objects and their properties. The authors express the hope that children will develop "habits of careful observation, a vocabulary that is useful in describing objects, methods of recording observations and experiences, and the ability to discriminate fine differences and to recognize broad similarities" (SCIS, First Grade, pp. x-xi).

In order to assist the teacher in carrying out these objectives, stress is again placed on the development of an appropriate attitude on the part of the teacher. Just as she is to help the child to trust his own observations and reasoning, so she, too, is to rely on her own observations and judgment: "If you feel hampered by the directions, modify the procedure to suit your own situation" (SCIS, First Grade, p. xi). She is instructed to ask questions without expecting answers, to refrain from drawing conclusions from experiments, and to refrain from urging the child to give verbal conclusions. The general emphasis in teaching is to be on open-endedness as exemplified in the question, "What have you observed today?" in contrast to the more traditional question, "What have we learned today?"

The chief recommendation for the use of the 60 activity pages is flexibility and judgment on the part of the teacher. "In general, your decision to use a student page, as well as all your other decisions in regard to the handling of this unit, should be based on the children's abilities, the objectives of the activity, and the teaching opportunities present in the classroom at the time" (SCIS, First Grade, p. xiv).

It is recommended that teachers make use of the distinction between "invention" lessons and "discovery" lessons. "Invention" lessons are those in which the teacher presents a "new" concept (i.e., new to the children) by giving it a label and a definition. A "discovery" lesson is one in which children are encouraged to pursue their own explorations in relation to an "invented" concept (Karplus, Thier, 1967).

In summary, the SCIS program has relied more on teaching the teachers than on providing a teacher-proof program for the children. For example, the AAAS program places emphasis on the how of specific activities. The SCIS program seems to place more emphasis on enabling the teacher to develop a scientific spirit through encouraging intellectual modesty, open-mindedness, non-manipulative observation, and objective inquiry.

Concerning the content of the first-grade SCIS program, the specific activities recommended to the teachers, a total of 30 units, are grouped into four categories: (1) introducing objects and their properties, (2) introducing the concept of material, (3) comparison and serial ordering of objects, and (4) experimenting with material objects. Specific objects studied include animals, plants, metal, wood, rocks, liquids, gases, shells, etc.

According to the present tabulation of cognitive processes in the SCIS program for kindergarten and first grade, there was a preponderance (approximately 70 per cent) of responses concerned with the logic of classes, with the heaviest emphasis on grouping and describing. There was some emphasis on the logic of relations (approximately 10 per cent), and none on number. Approximately 20 per cent of the responses seemed to push the child in the direction of becoming aware of his thought processes, requiring him to explain, predict, check his predictions, and after grouping objects according to one criterion, to group them according to some other criterion.

Approximately one-third of the responses required of children in kindergarten and first grade were found to give them an opportunity for direct manipulation of physical objects.

Greater Cleveland Mathematics Program

A teacher's guide, Key Topics in Mathematics for the Primary Teacher, is provided as part of the Greater Cleveland Mathematics Program. It contains the suggestion that the teacher who has an overview of all the mathematical concepts that are developed in the first four grades will understand better those that are specific to his grade level. It continues:

> The Greater Cleveland Mathematics Program is a new approach to the teaching of mathematics. It shifts the emphasis from teaching mathematics as a way of doing something, to teaching it as a way of thinking. The GCMP places major emphasis on the understanding of basic mathematical ideas which are sometimes hidden within computational techniques. Computation is an important part of mathematics and it must be taught, but it should be taught after the child understands the underlying mathematical ideas.

> The child makes use of inductive and deductive reasoning as he progresses from intuitive learning to basic information, and then to an understanding of more abstract concepts. The discovery approach to learning is employed; the child is given the opportunity to discover mathematical ideas for himself.

> New topics and vocabulary are included in GCMP to make mathematical concepts more meaningful, more precise, and more exciting to the child. The GCMP is taught as

> a continuous structure and not as a basis for the
> development of other concepts; each idea is presented
> in such a way that it will not have to be unlearned
> at a later date. (1962, p. 7)

Manuals giving detailed instructions for teaching mathematics are provided. A one-page introduction precedes 78 pages of 45 lessons for use in the kindergarten. Similarly, a one-page introduction precedes 250 pages of 129 lessons for first grade. For kindergarten 80 work pages are provided, and for first grade, 332 work pages.

In the introduction to the kindergarten manual, the teacher's responsibility is considered to be that of keeping the child's natural curiosity alive, encouraging him "to examine his environment critically in search of new patterns and new ideas," and helping him to "find relationships among these ideas." The author holds the general view that the area of arithmetic provides the teacher with "her greatest chance to help the child begin to develop his powers of reason."

According to the manual, the GCMP works toward this goal. "The importance of patterns and relationships is stressed as the child moves from concrete experiences to abstract ideas and as he applies these ideas to new situations. Basic mathematical concepts are developed, then tested and extended again and again. Continuity and creativity are stressed throughout the program."

Each lesson includes a statement of specific objectives, such as "To help children to develop a technique for demonstrating the fact that two sets are equivalent;" a section entitled "Fundamentals," offering suggestions to help the teacher conceptualize her activity in teaching mathematics to children; a section entitled "Readiness for Understanding," stating what is needed on the part of the children, such as "Ability to listen and follow directions."

"Development experiences" include a list of the materials needed for the lesson, a list of words to be learned, and specific activities to be carried out with the children. In addition, instructions are given for the use of the work pages. A final section entitled "Supplemental experiences" provides additional activities.

GCMP is as detailed and specific in the material it provides for teachers as AAAS. This may be seen, for example, in a GCMP kindergarten lesson entitled "Numbers and Numerals, Five - 5," in which one of the objectives is "To provide practice in recognizing sets containing five objects."

> Tell the children to listen as you clap your hands.
> Say that they must be ready to tell how many claps
> they hear. Start with three claps. Go on to five
> claps, four claps, and two claps. Have the children
> take turns clapping and choosing another child to
> give the number. (p. 34)

Six other activities are provided, including directions for the use of
the appropriate work pages. As "Supplemental experiences," five additional activities are described.

Concerning the subject matter taught by GCMP, the first few lessons
for kindergarten are concerned with shape, size, and pattern, without
introducing concepts pertaining directly to number. With the exception
of these lessons, all the others in both kindergarten and first grade
are concerned directly with concepts of number. Chief topics include
sets and their relations, counting, addition, subtraction, place value,
fractions, and measurement (linear, time, liquid, money value). The
special vocabulary for kindergarten and first grade included 195 words.

Of the cognitive processes required by GCMP in kindergarten and
first grade together, the count in the present analysis shows that
approximately 70 per cent are concerned with number, 20 per cent with
the logic of classes, and 3 per cent with the logic of relations (non-
numerical ordering). Only 7 per cent seem to push the child in the
direction of thinking about his thought processes.

Approximately one-third of the required responses give children the
opportunity for direct manipulation of physical objects.

No Prescribed Lessons

The teachers at Garden City were provided with two mimeographed
curriculum guides, one for science, the other for mathematics in the
elementary grades. Both had been compiled by local educators. While
these guides may in a sense be regarded as prescriptions for the overall content of the curriculum, they differ from the manuals provided
for the special programs in two important ways. The choice of activities
to teach or illustrate particular concepts or facts is left to the
teacher. The sequence in which concepts are presented is also a matter
of teacher choice, although the guides, particularly in mathematics, do
include reference to their relative difficulty.

In the science manual, charts are provided organizing nine different areas of the sciences into aspects that would be appropriate at different grade levels, kindergarten through sixth grade. The nine areas
include: living things; keeping healthy;using electricity; lifting and
moving things; using heat, light and sound; common chemical and physical
changes; the atmosphere; the earth; and earth and space. A brief preliminary statement indicates that these areas are aspects of the larger
concepts of space, time, change, interrelatedness, variety, and
adaptation.

Thirty-four pages of the manual are devoted to kindergarten and
first grade combined.

For each of the nine areas, an outline first presents simple concepts or facts to be taught, followed by suggested general activities.
The outline includes a variety of questions, and activities for school,

68

home, and field trips. In the first lesson, for example, on "living things," one of the facts to be taught is that "Animals live in many places." Thirteen different activities are suggested as relevant to this fact: e.g., "Collect pictures of pets at home, pets on farm, jungle animals, pond animals. Are they wild or tame? Briefly show map of country to indicate where certain animals are found." Another recommendation is, "Visit a farm. Discuss types of animals and what they give us. Supplement with many stories, films" (Garden City, Science ... p. 2).

In the teacher's manual for mathematics, two pages are provided for a teaching outline for kindergarten, five pages for first grade. These are a small part of the total manual, "Teaching Elementary School Mathematics: Tentative Guide. Kindergarten through Sixth Grade."

The manual includes a preface in which the general purpose is stated, namely, that of meeting the needs of the children of the community. It is pointed out that the guide attempts to combine the content taught by the various local teachers with recommendations by mathematics experts concerning the order of presentation. Stress is placed on the positive value of each teacher's unique way of presenting content.

An additional preliminary statement encourages teachers to allow children to find their own solutions to problems and to accept any valid method of solution before encouraging shorter or more accurate solutions. Warning is given of the importance of timing in encouraging children to move from manipulating material objects to functioning on a more abstract level.

The manual includes 38 pages of outlines for the various grade levels, 104 pages devoted to a presentation of basic concepts which form the mathematical background for the teacher, a bibliography, an appendix explaining the septimal system of notation, an appendix presenting a list of professional books and films, and a final appendix presenting a glossary of mathematical terms.

The outline for kindergarten gives a list of nine concepts to be taught, with one or two examples of each: e.g., "The need to count on a one to one correspondence. Example: We need ten chairs, twelve napkins." According to the manual, "Unhurried opportunities for children to explore, discover, select, and use their curiosity and ideas are important elements in building mathematical understanding in the kindergarten" (Garden City, Math . . . , p. 1).

Seven concepts are recommended for first grade: number; addition and subtraction; multiplication and division; measurement (temperature, time, linear, liquid and bulk, weight, speed, money value); graphs and tables; form and position (shape, directions); formulas and equations; ratio and proportion. Recommendations are made concerning the level at which each of the concepts is to be taught, but very little is given in the form of specific teaching activities.

69

Summary and Predictions

The purpose of the present content analysis was to explore the similarities and differences among the various special programs in science
and mathematics in three areas: the kinds of information taught, the
cognitive processes presumably required of the children, and the extent
to which the children were permitted to manipulate the physical world
directly. Because the recommendations to teachers in the Garden City
manuals do not prescribe detailed, specific activities and experiences,
no attempt was made to analyze cognitive processes that might have been
required or the extent to which opportunity might have been provided for
direct manipulation of objects.

As far as general information is concerned, whereas SCIS is exclusively concerned with science, and GCMP to a very large extent with
mathematics, AAAS includes both, without presenting as many mathematical
activities as GCMP. Whereas the SCIS and AAAS science programs stress
the study of objects and properties that can be directly manipulated by
the children in the classroom, the Garden City program includes a wider
range, stressing also areas that are not directly manipulated in the
classroom, such as the night sky, the day sky, and keeping healthy.
GCMP and the mathematics program of Garden City are similar in the concepts that are emphasized.

AAAS, GCMP, and Garden City all stress the teaching of various
kinds of measurement. SCIS is the exception to this major emphasis.

Concerning vocabulary, AAAS recommends the largest number of specific words to be taught, and GCMP ranks next. Both SCIS and Garden
City apparently leave this matter to the individual teachers.

As far as cognitive processes are concerned, examination shows that
SCIS has the highest proportion of responses requiring the child to
think about his thought processes, with AAAS having a slightly lower
proportion, and GCMP having the lowest. Responses concerned with the
logic of classes are stressed most by SCIS, somewhat less by AAAS, and
least by GCMP. Those responses concerned with the logic of relations
are emphasized to the greatest extent by AAAS, less by SCIS, and least
by GCMP.

GCMP contains the highest proportion of responses involving numbe
concepts, AAAS ranks next, and SCIS lowest.

Concerning the extent to which children are encouraged to manipulate directly the objects of the physical world, SCIS and GCMP are similar, both requiring such manipulation in approximately one-third of
their responses. The proportion of such responses in the AAAS program
is slightly lower.

In the present study of logical thinking in the second grade, the
post-tests are similar in that none seems to require information that
the children did not have an opportunity to learn. The tasks are sim-

70

ilar, too, in that they all require direct manipulation of material objects. However, there are differences among the tasks in the cognitive processes required.

The logic of classes is required for the class inclusion problems and the problems involving matrices. Logic of relations, as well as numerical ordering, are required in the tasks involving conservation of number and liquid, those involving conservation of weight, and those concerned with seriation and transitivity.

Coordination of relations, which is required in the tasks dealing with the conservation of liquid and the conservation of weight, was not emphasized in any of the manuals, nor was the multiplication of classes, which is required in the matrix tasks and in the class inclusion problems. Also, the class inclusion operation required by the class inclusion problems received no emphasis in any of the programs.

If the cognitive processes were actually emphasized in the classroom in approximately the same proportions as indicated in the teachers' manuals in the various programs, and if relative emphasis on a given cognitive process during the transitional period is an important factor in enabling the child to make use of that process in such tasks as those in the present study, then one might make certain predictions regarding the outcomes of the present study. However, the reader will recall that all of the children in all the kindergarten groups that had prescribed lessons in science (either SCIS or AAAS) also had the GCMP. It is difficult to weigh the effect of these combinations.

Assuming that the children having the SCIS program actually had the greatest exposure to the logic of classes, one might predict that they would make the highest scores on the matrix and class inclusion tasks, the AAAS children the next highest, and those who were exposed only to GCMP would make the lowest scores.

Similarly, those children whose teachers had presumably placed a relatively greater emphasis on the logic of relations (AAAS) would obtain the highest scores on the conservation, the transitivity and seriation tasks. It would be difficult to predict whether SCIS or GCMP children would rank second, for SCIS has a higher proportion of responses involving the logic of relations (non-numerical), whereas GCMP requires a higher proportion of responses involving numerical ordering.

The general trends indicated in the printed teacher's manuals may or may not have been reflected in the actual teaching of the programs. In Chapter IV some of the factors that may have affected the teaching are examined, while Chapter V deals with the actual teaching of some of the lessons of the SCIS program.

71

CHAPTER IV

SOME ASPECTS OF THE TEACHING

This chapter considers some of the variations among the teachers and their teaching of the programs that might have affected the outcomes of the study either directly or indirectly.

Just as the most rigorous test of the effectiveness of a given program comes when the children participating in it can be matched on certain crucial variables with children who do not participate, so also the teachers involved in the experimental programs should be matched with those in the non-experimental programs. Unfortunately, not enough is known about teaching to enable the researcher to specify all the crucial variables for such matching. But there are some variables too obvious to be ignored. These include the teachers' educational background and experience, their expressed attitudes and convictions regarding the programs, and their understanding of them. Samples of their teaching are obviously also germane. In the present study, a variety of circumstances precluded the matching of the teachers in the various programs, but they can be compared retrospectively. In such comparison, the nature and limitations of the available data need to be considered. Perhaps these can be viewed most effectively from the perspective of the teachers.

The Study as the Teachers Saw It

Although none of the teachers was asked to describe the study as it progressed, the questions they raised initially, the comments they wrote on the questionnaires they received, and their remarks to interviewers and observers provide some notion of their reactions.

In the first year of the study, the kindergarten teachers in the AAAS and SCIS programs knew that in agreeing to teach the experimental programs, they had also agreed to being observed occasionally. They had not bargained for the additional responsibilities placed before them when their participation in the present study was requested by the curriculum director or the principal. The teachers in the program involving only GCMP had no commitment to being observed by any one outside the school system although they were increasingly involved in research projects of various kinds. Arrangements for the involvement of the teachers who taught programs with no prescribed lessons were made at a meeting of the principals. They felt that the teachers would be enthusiastic about research that might justify the stance their school system had taken with regard to prescribed programs planned without regard to the particular characteristics and readiness of a kindergarten group.

The senior investigator met with all of the teachers in all of the programs to describe the study. In the case of AAAS and the kindergartens with no prescribed lessons, group conferences included all of the kindergarten teachers who would be involved. In the other programs, meetings were held either individually or with two or three teachers at a time.

At these meetings, and also in a statement of information sent to each teacher, the study was described as "designed to test the effects of early instruction in the basic concepts of mathematics, science, and social studies on the child's later ability to think in a logical fashion." The statement continued:

> As every kindergarten and first grade teacher knows, the intellectual content of the curriculum for these early years has been much emphasized of late. In some programs the concepts the children are expected to grasp are outlined in advance and presented to them in a specified, systematic fashion. In others, the concepts are expected to evolve according to the interests and apparent readiness of the children. Whatever the approach, teachers find that some children learn new concepts easily, other children have difficulty in comprehending many concepts, and certain concepts are hard for most young children to grasp. Most of the research related to the ways young children learn concepts has not been conducted in classrooms, nor has it dealt very extensively with those instances, so familiar to teachers, where a child initially appears to understand a concept but cannot apply it in a new situation, or after a lapse of time.

The teachers were also informed that each of the children in their class would be individually interviewed. Statements about the interviews were prepared for them to send to the parents. These indicated that the "study is concerned with the ways children's ideas about various aspects of mathematics and science change as they move from kindergarten into the first and second grades. The children will be asked questions individually concerning the concepts in these areas." The teachers were also told that in order to avoid the possibility of special coaching, the questions in the interviews would not be shared with them until after the study had been completed.

The classroom observations to be made were described as "very much dependent on your willingness to cooperate with us. . . . We wish to investigate the variety of ways science (or mathematics) concepts can be conveyed to young children, and the responses the children make, by observing two specified lessons during the year." It was noted that the observations would be coded and edited in such fashion that the identity of the teacher would be revealed only to the original observer.

Finally, responses to two brief questionnaires, one for the beginning of the study, and one for the end of the year, were requested.

In general, the responses of the teachers to the proposed plan were cooperative, and in some instances most enthusiastic. Several teachers in both the SCIS-GCMP and the GCMP programs expressed concern about the number of structured programs that were taking an increasing amount of the children's time, leaving them too little opportunity to engage in creative play. Several of the teachers in the schools having no prescribed lessons indicated their conviction that the children in their classes would do better than those in the experimental group because they were free to move along at their own pace, rather than being pushed through a particular schedule of activities. In retrospect, it seems likely that some of these teachers may have felt themselves to be in competition with the classes having prescribed lessons.

In all the programs the teachers expressed two kinds of reservations. One had to do with the interviews with the children and the difficulties of establishing sufficient rapport with each child to insure getting the best responses from him. The teachers were concerned that the interviewers be people who were experienced with young children, and expressed a strong preference for interviewers who had been teachers, as opposed to those who were psychologists, with little knowledge of classrooms.

A second reservation concerned the observations. Although the teachers did not then indicate that they themselves would object to being observed, they pointed to the difficulties involved in getting an adequate picture of the class in a short time, the possibility that some really important learnings might occur quite apart from the lessons, and the distractibility of the children when they had a visitor.

The questionnaires were sent out and the interviewing of the children began at approximately the same time. The questionnaires were returned fairly promptly by all but one teacher who mislaid the original and never completed the duplicates that were sent her.

Meanwhile the interviewing of the kindergarten children went considerably more slowly than had been anticipated. Although it was carried on outside the classroom, there is little question that it occasionally disrupted classroom routine. Furthermore, communications with parents about the study, provision of information from the records, and the location of space for the interviews all took considerable time.

After the interviews were completed, information from the Peabody Picture Vocabulary Tests was sent to each school. In most instances the principals passed this information along to the teachers. Suggestions for and cautions regarding interpretation of the results were included.

Classroom observations began shortly after the middle of the year when the senior investigator, usually accompanied by an associate, spent a full morning or afternoon in each classroom. Such observations had been suggested by some of the teachers who thought it would be difficult to plan a lesson for a pre-specified time. These observations provided a wealth of descriptive detail about the classes.

It should be noted that the investigators had not asked for such extensive observations from the beginning. Most teachers appeared to be unflustered by their visitors but surface appearances may have been misleading. Some of the most competent individuals later commented that they had been quite shaken by the experience. The two observations made later by experts in the particular programs were also unsettling to a few of the teachers. Under such circumstances the appraisal of the effectiveness of a program is open to question.

The second questionnaires together with a brief statement regarding the progress of the study were sent out well in advance of the end of the year with the suggestion that teachers estimate the class progress for the remainder of the term. Despite this attempt to avoid the inevitable piling up of reports, the questionnaires were returned slowly, and two were never returned (See Table 8). It should be noted that these omissions were not from the classes having no prescribed lessons even though those teachers in that group were asked to describe in considerable detail both the mathematics and science experiences the children had.

Much the same procedures were followed with the first grade teachers the following year. In most instances the senior investigator met with the teachers to explain the study to them. In several cases, however, the principals judged that no meeting was necessary since the teachers were acquainted with the study from their contacts with the kindergarten teachers of the previous year. These teachers received only the explanatory letter sent with the beginning-of-the-year questionnaire.

From the meetings that were held, and from comments made on the questionnaires, it appears that the first grade teachers viewed the study with less enthusiasm and less commitment than their colleagues in the kindergarten. Another indication of this comes from the fact that the teachers in only one program, AAAS, returned all the beginning-of-the-year questionnaires. For the end of the year the number of returns was even smaller.

Insufficient communication about the nature of the study (although the first grade teachers received mimeographed material almost identical to that given their kindergarten colleagues), unexpressed resentment about the observations, greater pressures from the community and from within the school system on matters not concerned with the present study are all factors that may have contributed to the apparent decline in interest in the study.

One teacher wrote on an earlier questionnaire, "We always begin our participation in a research project in high anticipation but we never reach the plateau of realization." With this criticism in mind, the second questionnaires for the first grade teachers were accompanied by a nine-page progress report outlining the study, showing the numbers of children and teachers involved, discussing the bearing of certain variables on the outcome, and reporting on the number of children who had given correct solutions to all the tasks posed in the kindergarten and first grade interviews. The nature of the tasks was not discussed. Also included were brief summaries of some of the opinions of the kindergarten and first grade teachers as expressed in the beginning-of-the-year questionnaires.

Table 8

Number of Questionnaires Completed by Teachers

Program	No. of Tchrs.	Fall 1965 Question-naires Completed	Spring 1966 Question-naires Completed	No. of Tchrs.	Fall 1966 Question-naires Completed	Spring 1967 Question-naires Completed
	Program Initiated in Kindergarten					
AAAS (GCMP)	5	5	5	8	8	6
SCIS (GCMP)	5	4	2	10	9	6
GCMP only	7	7	7	17	14	9
No Pre-scribed Lessons	9	9	9	11	9	9
	Program Initiated in First Grade					
SCIS (Math)				6	6	5
Math only				6	6	5

From the viewpoint of the investigators, the items on the question-naires were relatively unambiguous. Whether more extensive pretesting of some of the items could have eliminated the ambiguities the teachers perceived is not clear. In some instances they wrote at length in order to clarify their own points-of-view, in other instances they simply omitted occasional items. In either event it seems likely that many, if not most, of the teachers found responding to the questionnaires more time-consuming and possibly more frustrating than had been anticipated.

Despite the various difficulties over the two-year period, fewer than 20 per cent of the 74 teachers who were involved failed to respond to the questionnaires. In considering the possible differences in the teaching from program to program, the reader must bear in mind the extent of missing information and also the fact that within any program

the children could have any one of several possible combinations
of kindergarten and first grade teacher. He should also remember that
within all of the programs that were studied in both kindergarten and
first grade, several pairs of kindergarten and first grade teachers
were involved. A few kindergarten classes moved as groups into first
grade and shared the same first grade teacher. More often some of the
children from a particular kindergarten class had one first grade
teacher, others another, and still others may have had a third. The
number of combinations increased the difficulties of studying the
effects of the teaching.

Educational Background and Experiences of the Teachers

As Table 7 in Chapter II indicates, a majority of the kindergarten
teachers had Master's degrees, while a majority of the first grade
teachers had only Bachelor's degrees. The kindergarten teachers also
had more years of teaching experience than the first grade teachers.
The greatest differences among the programs are found in the classes
with no prescribed lessons where most of the kindergarten and first
grade teachers had Master's degrees and in the GCMP classes with a somewhat higher proportion of teachers who had only Bachelor's degrees.

Attempts to determine the amount of college or graduate work each
teacher had had in mathematics and science were not very successful,
since many teachers omitted the question. Among those responding there
were no apparent differences from program to program.

All of the teachers were asked to indicate whether and for how long
they had participated in teaching the experimental program(s) in use in
their school, and also whether they had participated in any other experimental programs. In general, the responses coincided with what was
known about the introduction of the experimental programs in the various
school systems. Some teachers indicated that they had had an earlier
introduction to GCMP. Teachers in the classes having no prescribed
lessons indicated participation in experimental reading or language arts
programs, but, with one exception, did not mention mathematics or
science.

Teachers' Attitudes and Convictions

Several items on the questionnaires were designed to elicit the
teachers' positive or negative feelings about involvement in a program
of early instruction, or in the research project, and their convictions
regarding the effects of early instruction.

Both kindergarten and first grade teachers in the fall questionnaire were asked to respond to the following statement:

> When teachers are faced with the necessity of teaching
> new material their reactions vary. When they like the
> material, feel it is appropriate for the children they
> are to teach, and know they will have sufficient time
> and help in preparing it, they are likely to be

enthusiastic. On the other hand, when they are dubious
about the material, uncertain that it is within the interest or the grasp of their particular group of children, or are teaching too large classes with too little
time for preparation, they are likely to feel opposed
to the innovations. We would like to know how you felt
when you first learned you were to teach the _____
program this year.

For the group having no prescribed lessons this statement was modified to "participating in a research project," and enthusiasm made contingent on interest "in the issues inherent in the research" and the
anticipation "that it will not be unduly disruptive of classroom learning or take an undue amount of time." Opposition was contingent on
being "dubious about the importance of the research," "uncertain of what
will be required," or "subject to too many other pressures."

Similar alternatives were offered in the end-of-year questionnaire
when the teachers were asked to indicate how they felt as the year came
to an end. The alternatives offered ranged from "very enthusiastic . . .
something I really wanted to do"; through "enthusiastic . . . positive
reactions outweighed misgivings"; and "not enthusiastic . . . misgivings
outweighed positive reactions"; to "opposed . . . something I really did
not want to do."

On the basis of the alternatives they selected, one can only judge
that the teachers were, by and large, enthusiastic about the experimental programs, or in the case of the group with no prescribed lessons,
about the research. Only once was the alternative "opposed" selected,
and the alternative "not enthusiastic" was selected a little more than
one time out of ten. However, about as frequently as this, the given
alternatives were ignored and a comment not readily classifiable as
either positive or negative was written in. At least some of these
comments can probably be taken as reservations. At the other extreme,
about one time out of three, the alternative chosen is the most positive,
"very enthusiastic."

It is difficult to discern any differences among the programs in
the degree of enthusiasm reported by the teachers. Only one program,
AAAS, never received a negative or ambiguous response. The proportion of
negative attitudes among the first grade teachers was not appreciably
greater than among those teaching kindergarten.

The questionnaires provide a pallid reflection of the actual attitudes and views of the teachers. As their comments indicated, some of
them appreciated the necessity for the multiple-choice approach of the
questionnaire but felt that it over-simplified matters that were in fact
complex.

Two of the questions were designed to get at some of the underlying
beliefs and attitudes that might contribute to the teacher's enthusiasm

or lack of it. One of these presented the frequently quoted statement by Bruner (1960), "Any subject can be taught effectively in some intellectually honest way to any child if the basic ideas can be translated into the child's way of seeing things." The statement was identified as one that had been widely quoted but the author was not cited. The teachers were asked to indicate whether they believed the statement to be true for any child, almost all, most, or very few children, or none. They were also asked to indicate whether they thought the statement applied in first grade and above, or in kindergarten, or in nursery school. The kindergarten teachers who had no prescribed lessons were more divided in their views than their colleagues in the other groups. This difference did not hold for the first grade teachers.

Perhaps indicative of a difference between the kindergarten and the first grade teachers, although the numbers are so small as to preclude much comment, is the number of first grade teachers who apparently believe the statement does not apply before the first grade.

An additional question had to do with the applicability of the statement to various areas of the curriculum. About half of those responding checked mathematics, but there were no apparent differences from one program to another. Perhaps the belief that mathematics can be made comprehensible at an early age reflected the general emphasis on that subject in current curriculum revision.

The notion that prescribed instruction in the basic concepts of mathematics or science might prove disruptive to a typical kindergarten program was explored in the fall questionnaire given to the kindergarten teachers. The question intended to give those teachers who were apprehensive about fitting a series of prescribed lessons into a loosely structured, child-centered kindergarten program an opportunity to express their views. It began with an unidentified textbook description of a kindergarten program:

> The kindergarten program is not subject matter oriented,
> nor is its curriculum prescribed. The teacher cuts
> across any and all bodies of subject matter, not by way
> of "lessons" and paper-and-pencil techniques but by
> drawing knowledge of all kinds from the ordinary expe-
> riences of the children. Through these she helps the
> children build for themselves a broad base of under-
> standing.

When asked to indicate whether they agreed strongly, or agreed with most of the statement, disagreed with most of the statement or disagreed strongly, every kindergarten teacher indicated agreement, half of them "strongly." The next question asked them to indicate to what extent the kindergarten described in the statement would be modified if the experimental program they were teaching (AAAS, SCIS, or GCMP) were incorporated in it. For the teachers having no prescribed lessons the statement referred to "a program of instruction in the basic concepts of mathematics or science." Most of the teachers in all the programs responded that such incorporation would be easy, or would change the program very little. Four teachers thought such incorporation would be difficult and one chose the alternative of indicating that the described kindergarten program would be changed "completely." It is interesting that only two of the five teachers whose responses suggested doubt that the typical kindergarten program could readily accommodate to instruction in the basic concepts were among those having no prescribed lessons in their kindergartens.

To ascertain the view of the first grade teachers regarding early instruction,the fall questionnaire contained the following hypothetical situation:

> A first-grade teacher is in an elementary school that has adopted a structured program for teaching mathematics and science in the first grade. She finds that her first-grade class is made up of children who have similar mental ability and come from similar home backgrounds. Also, they have all attended kindergarten classes that were well taught and well equipped. However, the kinds of kindergarten program they had differed.

> One group of children had only the usual kindergarten activities. The program for a second group included these usual kindergarten activities but some of their time was taken up by special lessons in both mathematics and science. In these lessons, the teacher took the children through activities and exercises that had been designed and prescribed by mathematicians and scientists. The program for a third group included the special mathematics lessons, but did not include any special science lessons.

> The first-grade teacher who has these three groups of children is expected to teach all of them the first-grade lessons for the science and mathematics programs described above.

The teachers were asked to choose alternatives to indicate their opinions as to the responsiveness of the three groups at the beginning of the year, both in general and specifically in relation to the first grade science lessons, and their expected progress in the science lessons, at mid-first grade and at the end of the first grade.

This question posed many alternatives, some of which were ignored. It also elicited many spontaneous comments from teachers who were clearly aware of the complex issues underlying it. On the whole, however, the responses were more striking in their similarities than in their differences. Most of the teachers thought that the children who had had both mathematics and science in kindergarten would be more responsive to the first grade mathematics and science lessons. Over half of the teachers responded that the children who had had mathematics would be more interested in the science lessons in first grade than those who had not had mathematics. However, of the remaining half all but six indicated that there would be no difference between the children who had had mathematics and those who had had no prescribed lessons in kindergarten.

In expressing views concerning the children's progress through first grade, about two-thirds of the teachers predicted greater progress on the part of the group that had had both mathematics and science in kindergarten. The remainder indicated a belief that there would be no difference when that group was compared with those having only mathematics and those having no prescribed lessons. Since the proportions of the responses differ little among the various programs it seems reasonable to assume that the expectations for the outcomes of early instruction were similar among all of the groups of teachers.

While a majority of the first grade teachers evidently believed in the efficacy of early instruction in mathematics and science, many of them, like their colleagues in kindergarten, did not feel markedly confident about undertaking innovative programs in those subjects. Such a conclusion is derived from the responses they made to a question regarding their participation in innovative programs.

In this question they were asked to assume that they were teaching in a school making major changes in its kindergarten or first-grade curriculum and that they could choose between one of two new programs. What choice would be made in each of the six possibilities: reading or mathematics, reading or science, reading or social studies, mathematics or science, mathematics or social studies, social studies or science? Reading is the subject in which most of the teachers would prefer to be innovative. The next popular choice is mathematics, then science, and social studies, with each receiving about the same number of choices. Apparently in all of the instructional programs there were a number of teachers who were less confident in teaching science or mathematics than in teaching reading. However, those who consistently preferred science or mathematics were not found more often in one program than another.

The Teachers' Views of the Programs They Taught

When a teacher undertakes to teach an innovative program for the first time, it is natural for her to wish to have help from someone who is knowledgeable about it. Before teaching begins she needs to be familiar with the program's requirements, and as the teaching proceeds she is likely to need assistance in both planning for and evaluating her teaching.

Since the circumstances under which each of the programs in the study were operating varied, it appeared that the best way to get a picture of the adequacy of the help given the teachers would be to ask how much they had and whether it was as much as they had anticipated. Accordingly, they were asked to indicate on the fall questionnaires the amount (number of hours) and kind of help (group meeting, individual

81

consultation) they had had preparatory to beginning the program, and that they expected during the year.

Ambiguities in estimating time are perhaps inevitable. Confusions arise in deciding whether a fifteen minute session at which experimental materials are handed out counts as a group meeting, or whether the five minutes the science consultant spends with a group of children really provides an opportunity for individual consultation. With allowance for such ambiguities, all that is clear from the questionnaires is that the amount of time given to preparatory help and consultation did not differ substantially as far as AAAS and SCIS were concerned in the kindergarten year. In the first grade, the time for SCIS was somewhat greater, largely because the teachers in the classes beginning the program in first grade had so many inservice training sessions. Both the GCMP group and the group having no special program reported that they received some help in preparation for teaching. In the first grade, however, almost no such help was reported for GCMP.

In the questionnaires given them at the end of the year the teachers were asked to indicate whether they thought they had had as much help as they needed in the concepts of science and mathematics, and also in the methods of teaching such concepts. They were also invited to specify the kinds of additional help they would have liked.

In nearly a third of the questionnaire returns there was no response to these questions. Among those who did respond, less than 20 per cent indicated that they had had less help than they needed. Help with the concepts of science was regarded as necessary by four of the first grade teachers in the SCIS program that had begun in kindergarten. The remainder of the teachers who indicated a wish for more help were scattered among the programs.

Several questions at the end of the year were designed to get the teachers' appraisal of the teacher's manuals and the lessons as they taught them to their particular group.

Since the AAAS manual for the kindergarten was considerably longer and more detailed than the SCIS, some negative comment regarding lack of specificity from the teachers of SCIS was anticipated but did not occur. Both AAAS and SCIS teachers noted that the manuals encouraged modification, although one teacher believed that AAAS discouraged it. Comments on the lessons suggested that SCIS teachers were less well satisfied than the AAAS teachers. This difference was not apparent at the first grade level where the proportion of negative comments and no responses was roughly equivalent for the two groups.

Teachers in the AAAS and SCIS programs, as well as those in the GCMP program, commented on the GCMP manual and lessons. At the kindergarten level there was little indication that these were seen as any less satisfactory than those for science. At the first grade level, particularly in the classes having only the GCMP program, there were many instances where the teachers made no responses.

For the experimental groups in the study, the objectives of the particular science program and of GCMP were set forth in the questionnaires at the end of the year. The teachers were asked to indicate the extent to which they thought the program had been successful in developing the specific attitudes, abilities, and skills described in these objectives. In addition to checking the degree of success they were asked to give reasons for their rating. The results indicated that all the programs were regarded at least as "somewhat successful" in achieving their stated objectives.

It may be that the most accurate measure of differences among programs, and perhaps also of their success, is the amount of time per week devoted to them. The fact that most classes, even at the kindergarten level, operate on a somewhat regular schedule probably means that the teacher has a fairly firm basis for making an estimate in this area.

Although there was some variation in the time estimates made by the teachers, the mode for each group emerges rather clearly. In the kindergarten most classes appeared to spend from one to two hours per week in both science and mathematics. There are two exceptions to this. SCIS teachers typically appeared to spend only one hour, and teachers in GCMP, lacking any special program of instruction in science, did not report any time spent in science activities.

In the classes where there were no prescribed lessons in either science or mathematics at the kindergarten level, science activities were reported to take up to three hours in two classes, but the more typical time spent was one hour. For activities that were designated mathematical, the time spent was typically one hour but ranged to as much as three hours per week. While the typical teacher in these classes reported spending no more time on science or mathematics than was typical in the classes with prescribed lessons, two teachers reported spending more time.

Some kindergarten teachers had indicated that the new programs, together with an increased emphasis on reading readiness, were consuming time that had previously been devoted to play. Accordingly, it seemed appropriate to find out how much time was devoted to these activities and whether or not there were differences among the groups.

As far as play is concerned, the AAAS teachers reported times ranging from three to five hours per week. The information from SCIS is not complete but one teacher indicated as little as two hours. It is not known whether or not she included the ten minutes of every hour that is required as "recess" in the California schools. For GCMP the amount of play ranged from two or three hours typically, to as much as six hours. The classes with no prescribed lessons presented the greatest variation, with none reporting less than two hours and one as much as six.

In the kindergartens in all the programs, one to two hours typically was spent in reading activities. Again, the widest variation was reported in the group having no prescribed lessons.

The amount of time spent in a particular program may be less important than the depth of the children's involvement in the lessons. Such involvement may come more readily when the class is organized as a total group, so the children are not distracted by other activities, or they may participate more fully when the organization of the class is such that they may have the full attention of the teacher in smaller groups. Small group organization may also provide more opportunities for children to learn from one another. This possibility has been emphasized in some of the SCIS activities where it is assumed that children develop greater flexibility and become less bound to their own egocentric ideas if they must confront the ideas of their peers.

In the end-of-the-year questionnaire the teachers were asked to indicate how they usually organized their classes for instruction in the programs. Not all the teachers responded to this question. However, most of the kindergarten teachers who did respond indicated that they worked with the total group. In all programs the first grade teachers who responded were fairly evenly divided between those who reported that they worked with only the total group and those who also worked with smaller groups. All but one of the SCIS first grade teachers whose children did not begin the program until first grade reported working with small groups, perhaps reflecting the inservice program in which they were involved.

A question dealing with the progress the children had made in the programs as measured by "the lesson or page completed by all the children" and by those "who went furthest if some went ahead of the others" brought forth specific responses and a number of spontaneous comments on the programs.

In the AAAS kindergartens, all classes completed Part One A of the program, while one class moved into the early lessons of Part One B. The two SCIS teachers who responded indicated that they completed the kindergarten program. Since all of the SCIS classes were well into the program by February, it is likely that all completed it. As far as the GCMP program for these classes is concerned, two classes completed the kindergarten program, and two others completed half of it, with the other class in the middle. One of the two SCIS classes for which information is available completed more than half, while the other finished the book.

A majority of the GCMP kindergarten classes completed the program, and none of the remainder completed less than three-quarters.

In the first grade no AAAS class for which information was available finished Part Two B. However, all except one class completed more than two-thirds of it. The range of material these same classes completed in GCMP varied from the entire first grade program, and in the case of a few individuals, beginning of the second grade program, to somewhat less than two-thirds of the program.

84

All of the SCIS classes who had had the kindergarten program completed the first grade program. None of these classes completed the GCMP although three classes finished more than two-thirds of it.

The range of lessons completed was greatest in the first grade classes having GCMP only. Four of these classes completed, or nearly completed, the GCMP first grade program, but one class finished less than a fifth. In connection with this program the teachers commented on the diversity of ability among the groups of children they had, noting that the program was "too abstract," or inappropriate for disadvantaged youngsters. One teacher noted that the parents claimed the concepts were too difficult.

Only one of the SCIS classes that had not had the program in kindergarten completed all the SCIS lessons. However, all of the classes completed at least 24 lessons. One teacher noted that the fine distinctions required in the lessons were too difficult for the slow children in the group.

Although the number of spontaneous comments of this sort were too few in number to develop any generalizations, they do give the reader some sense of the complexities of the teacher's job. Faced with the necessity of guiding a group of youngsters through a particular program, she must make innumerable decisions, even when the program is highly prescriptive. Which youngsters need individual help, and shall that help be given in the total group, in small groups or individually? Is it better to stay with a given lesson until a majority of the class have grasped it, or to move ahead at a steadier pace? If an innovative program seems to be neglecting a skill the teacher thinks important, shall she provide practice anyway? Is the class lethargic in a particular lesson because they have not understood an earlier one? Or is today just a "bad" day for them? The strategies the teacher uses for handling these and similar problems, and their appropriateness to a particular group of children, very likely determine the relative success of an innovative program. Clearly, however, only the most gross evidence about such strategies can be derived from a brief questionnaire.

The questionnaires do provide evidence that with very few exceptions, the differences in the teaching as well as the attitudes and convictions were probably as great within the classes representing a particular instructional program as they were between the groups. It is clear that, as a group, the teachers in the classes having no prescribed lesson had more Master's degrees and were more experienced than the teachers in the other groups. Although this group included several teachers who expressed reservations about the efficacy of early instruction, they could be matched by teachers in the other groups. In all the groups, a majority of the teachers believed that more subject matter in kindergarten was likely to lead to more progress in first grade, expressed some satisfaction with the programs in which they were involved, but, by and large, would have been more confident to be involved in an innovative program in reading. The amount of time the teachers provided for the prescribed programs, or in the classes having

no prescribed lessons, to mathematics and to science, varied from class
to class, but there is no evidence that the children in any one program
consistently spent more hours per week in special instruction than did
the children in any other program. Nor is there much evidence of differences among the groups in the progress made through the programs.
The exceptions are to be found in the SCIS classes that did not begin
the program until first grade, and did not complete all of the first
grade program, and in GCMP group, where the variation in the number of
lessons completed in first grade was quite wide.

The Experts' Views of the Teaching

Although the teachers' reports suggested considerable similarity in
the teaching of the various programs, it is not unlikely that an observer, well versed in the subject matter and cognizant of the aims of a
particular program, could detect important differences in the strategies
used by different teachers. Precise specification and measurement of
these differences would, however, take considerably more time than was
available for observation by the experts in the present study.
(Chapter V, dealing with tape-recorded observations of some of the SCIS
lessons, suggests the direction an attempt at such specification might
take.)

With few exceptions, most of the classes in the study were observed
at least twice by someone who could be regarded as an expert in the
experimental program being taught, or, in the case of the classes having
no prescribed lessons, an expert in the observation of children.

Qualifications of the Experts

As far as possible the observers were individuals who were closely
associated with the program of instruction they observed. In the case
of AAAS, the observer during the kindergarten year was a professor at
Teachers College, Columbia University, who was serving as AAAS consultant in the Pelham schools. In the first grade, the observer was a graduate
student who had been a member of the AAAS writing conference from its in-
ception. The California AAAS kindergarten classes were observed by the
AAAS consultant, a professor of mathematics at the University of California. A graduate student who had been a member of the AAAS writing
conference did the first grade observations.

Members of the SCIS staff at the University of California, who had
assisted in the development of the lessons, observed the California SCIS
classes. Each of the SCIS first grade classes was also tape-recorded once.

The observer for the SCIS program which was initiated only in the
first grade was a graduate student closely associated with the inservice
training program for SCIS. Tape-recordings were also made for each of the
same four lessons in the four classes participating in the study.

The expert who observed the GCMP classes in kindergarten was a
mathematics instructor who had been a consultant for the GCMP. The first
grade observations were done by a professor of mathematics at Teachers
College, Columbia University.

Observations for the classes having no prescribed lessons in kindergarten and beginning a diversified mathematics program in first grade were carried on by an experienced supervisor of elementary mathematics who was completing her doctorate in mathematics education.

It was understood that the teachers having no prescribed lessons in mathematics and science might not be able to specify, particularly at the kindergarten level, the time mathematics and science could be observed. Nevertheless, they were informed that the observers were interested in these areas. In the kindergarten year the senior investigator and her research associate served as observers. In the first grade a graduate student with many years of experience in teaching and in the observation of children served as the observer.

Content of the Observations

The form for reporting on the observations was developed with the help of AAAS and SCIS experts in the kindergarten year. It varied slightly from program to program to conform with the particular goals and format of the program.

The two pages included space to record: the time during which the observer was present; the number of children present; a brief description of the lesson he observed; an indication as to whether the activity was one prescribed in the program, and whether or not its intent was to introduce a particular concept, or develop a concept previously introduced, or to appraise previous learning. In addition the observer was asked to judge whether or not the activity, if it were prescribed by the manual, conformed to or departed from it. In the case of departure or an innovation by the teacher, he was asked to specify its nature and whether or not it enhanced or confused the learning intended by the program. Another judgment concerned whether or not the teaching of the activity indicated an understanding of the entire program. Another question related to the number of children who followed directions and appeared attentive, the number of children who answered questions and the number who asked questions. Finally, where possible, the observer recorded "typical teacher questions" verbatim.

Variation among the Experts

The senior investigator instructed each of the experts in carrying on the observations. She stressed the importance of the judgments regarding the congruence of the observed lesson with the total program. She also gave some emphasis to the observation of the attentiveness of the children but recognized that it would be difficult to appraise this. Somewhat less emphasis was placed on the recording of the number of questions responded to and asked by the children or the kinds of questions posed by the teacher. No attempt was made to assess inter-observer reliability.

The observers consistently responded to each item on the observation schedule. But they varied in the ways they responded to particular items. One observer recorded in detail, submitting what amounted to a comprehensive running record for each lesson he saw. Others made their judgments in telegraphic style. Somewhere in the middle of these extremes was the person who made succinct judgments bolstered with brief bits of the classroom interaction.

Each observer's style appeared to be consistent from one class to another. To the extent that two, or in a few cases, three lessons represent an adequate sample for a particular class, his judgments may approximate the differing amounts of conformity to and understanding of the program that characterized the teaching. Obviously, however, each observer had his own standards for that kind of congruence. Accordingly, it is impossible, with the possible exception of the SCIS program in California, where the same observers were SCIS staff members, to make any comparison between the kindergarten and the first grade in a given program.

In less than a third of the classes observed, the observers' judgment of the second lesson departed from the judgment made during the first lesson. When, for example, a lesson that was judged to conform to the experimental program in the first observation tended to be followed in the second observation by another lesson also judged to be congruent, or when a lesson judged incongruent in the first observation, tended to be followed by one that was also judged incongruent, one might conclude that the teachers were consistent. Unfortunately since the study provides no other check on the observers, one can equally well conclude that once having viewed a class in a particular way, the observers were prone to see it similarly at a second viewing.

Congruence of Observed Lessons with Experimental Programs

The observers' judgments as to whether or not an observed activity conformed to the intent of the program, and as to whether the teaching appeared to reveal understanding of it, may be taken together as an estimation of congruence between the lessons as taught, and the lessons as intended.

Considering the judgment of these particular expert observers, and on the shaky assumption that the lessons they saw were representative, it appears that among the groups having instruction from kindergarten on, AAAS classes came closer to having the program intended than did either SCIS or GCMP. In this connection it should be remembered that the AAAS program is decidedly more prescriptive than is SCIS. GCMP is also prescriptive. However, GCMP is not presented as an experimental program, and the teachers may have felt more free to impose on these lessons their own notions of teaching than was the case for the experimental science programs.

For the two groups not starting instruction until first grade, the SCIS lessons were judged to be rather closely in line with what was expected in that program. Judgment of the mathematics program for these classes was difficult in view of the variety of texts being used.

Judgments made for the classes having no prescribed lesson are not directly comparable to judgments of the other classes in the study. The observers in these classes had to use as a basis for judgment the global objectives set forth in curriculum guides that were relatively unstructured and not at all prescriptive. At both the kindergarten and first grade level, a substantial majority of the observations gave only positive indications of being congruent with the general objectives.

Attentiveness of the Children

If an observer is not required to make any other judgments, he can fairly easily keep account of the number of children who appear, at any one moment, to be attentive to what is going on in a lesson. When, however, he is also required to make other judgments, the task is more difficult. Furthermore, as one observer commented, it is the rare child, in the rare lesson, whose attention fails to wander. The attentiveness that the observer hoped to capture was that stemming from genuine intellectual interest. The observers' comments made it evident, however, that some apparent interest represented little more than good discipline. On the other hand, lessons were observed that seemed to be correctly presented, but that, due perhaps to the makeup of the group, or to the teacher's inability to create the appropriate atmosphere, never sparked the children's interest.

In view of these uncertainties about the actual significance of what was reported as attention, it is unwise to attempt any comparison of the various programs. The only safe generalization is that in all of the programs, some of the lessons observed seemed to capture most of the children's interests, and in all of the programs, some lessons apparently lacked appeal for most of the youngsters.

Any statements about the number of youngsters who answered, and perhaps more important, asked questions, is also inappropriate. Clearly the teachers differed in how many and what kinds of questions they posed the children, and in their expectations for the children's responses. Clearly also they, and the programs as well, differed in the extent to which the children were expected to ask questions. But the different styles of the observers and the fact that they did not observe the same lessons in all the classes limit the usefulness of their reports except for the purpose of illustration.

Manipulative Activity with Objects

Just as only tentative conclusions about the nature of the questioning in the various programs can be drawn from the observations of the experts, considerable caution must also be exercised in considering the amount of manipulative activity with objects that characterized the various programs. It will be recalled that the manuals for SCIS and GCMP suggested that about a third of the responses from the children would involve such manipulation, while in the AAAS program the proportion would be about a fourth.

In the particular lessons that were observed, the AAAS classes provided somewhat more opportunity for the children to handle objects in the first grade lessons than in the kindergarten. At both levels, however, the teachers rotated materials around the class and provided opportunities for individual children, or in some instances groups, to carry out certain manipulative activities on their own.

Although the SCIS program calls for the children to have direct access to objects as often as possible, in the particular lessons observed the teachers varied widely in their procedures. While it is clear from the records that some teachers arranged the objects so that the children, either individually or in small groups, did have an opportunity to handle them, others merely showed them to the children and had them talk about them.

The most obvious shortages, as far as opportunities for the physical manipulation of objects are concerned, came in the GCMP group, at least in the lessons observed. Here more often than not the experiences provided the children were predominantly visual. The children were shown pictures, or the flannel board was used, or they followed directions for marking pictures in their own workbook. In general, in this program, responses were less often individualized, that is the teacher showed the picture, posed the question, and the children chorused a response.

Further Consideration About Teaching

Exploration of the teaching in the various instructional programs was not the primary objective of this study. Yet the teaching may be one of the crucial variables as far as the effectiveness of the programs is concerned.

In any study comparing instructional programs in the realistic setting of the classroom, teachers, even though adhering to the obvious prescriptions of the program, can be expected to vary in ways that may affect the outcomes. In the present study, some of those who did not use prescribed lessons may have planned and carried out the science and mathematics experiences for their classes in ways as inherently logical as those prescribed in the manuals. Conversely, some of those who did use the prescribed lessons may not have grasped their logic, or conveyed it to the children.

On the basis of the available data, it can be said that the teachers differed somewhat in the amount of education and experience they had, a difference favoring the classes with no prescribed lessons. It is also possible that the AAAS lessons were more often taught in accord with the intent of the program than were the other lessons.

In Chapter V, where the transcripts of several SCIS lessons are analyzed, the complexities of the classroom interaction are made more apparent. It seems likely that only through such close scrutiny can the possible contributions of the teaching to the children's thinking be adequately appraised.

CHAPTER V

A CLOSER LOOK AT TEACHING: THE SCIS PROGRAM[1]

Chapters III and IV have emphasized the importance of an examination of the activities of the teachers and children in the classroom for a thorough evaluation of the relationship of a curriculum and the development of logical thinking. A manual might suggest that a preponderance of the teaching should require manipulative activities by the children, but it is the teacher who arranges the lessons so that this does or does not occur. It is the teacher who can transform the learning of science vocabulary and terminology from an exercise in memorizing into a tool for organizing the environment. And it is only by observing the teacher and students in the classroom that the cognitive interaction of the participants may be evaluated.

Background for the Observational Study

With the conviction that an observational study of the teachers and pupils involved in the study would provide a valuable supplement to the other data collected in the overall study, SCIS science lessons taught by four first grade teachers to their regular classes were tape-recorded for further study. The teachers and children were all from one of the schools participating in the larger study. Although it would have been desirable to include teachers and schools from some of the other programs, for practical reasons involving personnel, money, and equipment, this was not feasible. Since the recording had to be limited, it seemed reasonable to select SCIS classes because the designers of the SCIS programs incorporated into their curriculum many of the ideas of Piaget, from whose writings were derived the theoretical underpinnings of the entire study presented in these eight chapters.

Characteristics of the Classes Studied

The mean Peabody Picture Vocabulary Test I.Q. scores for the children in the four participating classes ranged from 105 to 113.

Class	Mean PPVT I.Q.	Standard Deviation	No. of Children
1	105.33	17.06	21
2	105.47	9.26	17
3	105.53	9.69	17
4	113.41	15.34	17

The mean in Class 4 is higher than the means in the other classes, and in Classes 1 and 4 there was more variability in the scores. The mean PPVT I.Q. score for all children completing the overall study was 106.19, so that the children in the four classes studied are not unrepresentative of the larger population in this respect.

---

[1]This chapter was prepared by Felice Gordis with the assistance of Paula Jean Martin.

According to information given by the teachers in the self-report questionnaires administered in the larger study, one teacher was less experienced than the others in teaching first-graders. This teacher also had not obtained the same level as the others in terms of degrees achieved through formal schooling. The total number of years these teachers had spent in classroom teaching ranges from 12 to 35 years, so that they were all alike in being very experienced teachers.

Obtaining Tape Recordings of Classroom Teaching

Making a permanent record of the lessons which can be analyzed later at some leisure greatly facilitates making a detailed study of the classroom interaction. The most important step in securing the needed records was to obtain the cooperation of the teachers. These four teachers were most helpful in this regard, consenting to the intrusion of the tape-recording[1] equipment and some rearranging of schedules. Without their consent and help in securing the cooperation of the children in their classes, it would not have been possible to conduct this study. A second step in obtaining recorded records of teaching sessions is to try out the procedures before beginning the recording of the lessons intended for analysis. Such preliminary recording sessions were also made during times when SCIS lessons were being taught and served to acquaint both the investigators and their classes with the recording equipment.

For purposes of this study four teaching sessions from each of the four classes were recorded, producing 16 tapes. For each class the sessions covered Lessons 20, 21, and 22 from the first grade SCIS Manual, Material Objects, Chapter III, "Comparison and Serial Ordering of Objects." These lessons were recorded during one two-week period in May, 1967.

Each teacher was asked to conduct lessons of at least twenty minutes and to end them at any point after that deemed appropriate by her. In general because of scheduling problems, it was decided to stop recording after about forty minutes, even though a lesson might continue.

Recording Procedures

Recording was accomplished by placing one wireless lavaliere microphone and transmitter on the teacher and one such set on one child in each classroom. In addition to these "live" microphones, five "dead" mock-ups were placed on five other children in each classroom so that it would appear that a microphone was in the vicinity of all the children. Each of the two "live" microphones transmitted via FM receivers to a four-track stereophonic tape recorder.[2] On the parallel track of the

---

[1] Since this study was planned, a number of investigators have filmed classrooms using video tape. However, the costliness of video tape equipment prohibited its use for this study.

[2] The recording system was designed by Dr. John Swayze.

tape in the recorder receiving from the teacher's microphone, a running commentary of the teacher's non-verbal behavior, relevant student behavior, and other previously specified activities was recorded. Two observers who had previously practiced observing these teachers and classes during preliminary taping sessions alternated in describing each session so that each observer described half the sessions of each teacher. The kinds of behavior to be described and the format to be used were specified in advance.

The teacher's speech was transmitted by the microphone she wore as was the speech of children in her vicinity. Since classroom noise level affected the clarity of the recordings, when a class discussion type lesson involving the entire class was being taught, the tape recorder was put on the setting that allowed it the greatest sensitivity. When activity was group centered with the teacher moving about from group to group and classroom noise level consequently higher, the tape recorder was put on the setting which tended to limit its sensitivity to voices in the teacher's immediate vicinity. This reduced interference from noise and conversation from other parts of the room. In order to further reduce noise, flannel cloths were placed on tables and desks during the recording periods.

The advantage of using a wireless microphone setup is that the recording equipment in no way restricts the teachers' or pupils' freedom of movement. In fact during a preliminary recording session, one of the teachers, still wearing the microphone and transmitting to the recorders, left the room for six or seven minutes to collect some wandering children.

Typed transcripts of the teacher-student dialogue and of the observer's comments were prepared from the tapes. (The tapes from the microphone on the child in each class were used to clarify the teacher transcript.)

Reliability of Observers' Commentary on Non-Verbal Behavior

After some practice, both observers independently described the same teacher at the same time in order to provide an indication of the reliability of the observations.

A modified version of the episode as described by Wright (1967) was used to code the observations involved in the reliability check. Episodes were coded as centering around actions with science materials and non-verbal behaviors with cognitive significance. An example of the first is sanding a piece of wood and of the second, making an illustrating gesture of an incline. Two coders reached a 93 per cent level of agreement in using this episode system. Comparing episoded transcripts of the observations of the two observers independently describing the same classrooms at the same time, the observers were found to be in agreement 79 per cent of the time.

The commentaries were an invaluable supplement to the taped

dialogue. The following excerpt from a transcription of dialogue and the corresponding observer commentary is presented to demonstrate their usefulness:

The teacher has asked one child to order four red colored rectangular-shaped cards that vary in brightness. The word "dark" is in a card holder on the table and the child is to place the red cards in holders using the property of color brightness. There are also inequality signs on the table to be inserted between the cards. The other children are watching the child who is working at a table in front of the classroom.

Observer Commentary

Teacher now turns to child arranging materials on the table. He moves around (missing). Teacher holds up frame with the word "dark" and one hand on little boy's shoulder. He points to two of them. The darkest. The two in the middle. The one on the right is darker than the one on the left and he has the sign with open arrow in front of one of them. Teacher makes comparison motion, illustrating motion of balance. She still has the frame with "dark." Holds it up in front of him. He looks at the frames and holds arrow in his hand and places arrow between the two he was talking about. Points to the lighter and the darker and he has arrow between them in the correct direction. He goes to sit down.

Dialogue

T: Now this is the word. This is the property. What is it?

C: Dark.

T: And what did you find out?

C: This is darker than that one.

T: Point really to it. Show us which ones you mean.

C: These two are the ones I'm talking about and this one is darker than that--this red is darker than that red.

T: Well where's the sign that tells us? There has to be one sign between the two. If you're comparing two things, you know, like a balance or an imbalance. This is the word. Now find something for us that tells us the story. That makes the story. Find the one you think is--what's the word?

C: Dark.

T: All right. Want to read it?

C: This is less dark than this one.

T: All right and read it the other way. This is----

C: This is darker than that one.

T: More dark. All right. Anyone else want to come up and perhaps put the signs between all four rectangles? You might have to move them around. What is the property we're thinking of?

Analyzing the Cognitive Interaction

Although there has been a renaissance of naturalistic studies of classroom interaction, very little attention has been turned to cognitive variables, and systematic studies of cognitive aspects of the early elementary school class are very few.

Because of the lack of comparable studies at the first or second grade level, the findings in this study will have to be viewed in relation to studies of older children.

The objectives of this part of the study were to find out what cognitive acts the teachers required of the children, the extent to which manipulative activity was requested, and what information was presented. A system was devised which drew upon Piaget for analyzing cognitive acts and upon the work of Arno Bellack (1966) for obtaining interaction units.

Interaction Units

Bellack has described four interactional units which classify the discourse in the classroom according to the pedagogical function it serves. The units thus obtained are appropriate to the nature of classroom give and take, and also allow the isolation, for further analysis, of utterances with similar functions. There are four "moves" in the system developed by Bellack. Two of these "moves" or units are initiatory (soliciting and structuring), and two are reflexive (responding and reacting).

By initiatory is meant that in terms of the four moves, solicitation and structuring moves begin discussions, move them forward and elicit responses and reactions. Reflexive moves come in response or reaction to the initiatory moves. Responses and reactions are considered reflexive because they refer to and occur in relation to the moves that came before.

These moves describe the function or effect of a speaker's utterance vis-à-vis the expectancies and roles of the persons participating and in the light of the social structure of the classroom. Bellack views the classroom interaction as an example of verbal activity that is governed by certain rules of the classroom context. Each utterance directed to others is consequently a "move" in a metaphorical game.

95

A solicitation (coded SOL) is a move which is intended to elicit a response from the person(s) addressed.

Examples:

T/SOL: Now this word says what?

T/SOL: Now who can show us that this was more dark than this?

T/SOL: I wonder if anyone could read this to us first. Just tell us what these signs tell you.

Structuring moves (coded STR) set the context for subsequent activity but do not elicit an immediate response.

Examples:

T/STR: Boys and girls, let's begin this lesson by speaking about some of the things that we did last week.

T/STR: All right. Now this morning, I'm going to show you four different rectangles. And let's see if we can put these in order from the shortest to the longest.

Responding moves (coded RES) occur only in relation to soliciting moves and are considered to be elicited by a particular solicitation.

Examples:

T/SOL: You were picking out what?

P/RES: The darkest.

T/SOL: How many agree with Heather?

P/RES: I don't agree 'cause that's light.

T/SOL: And Jonathan, the next one? You don't have much choice, do you?

P/RES: No, 'cause that's the last one.

Reacting moves (coded REA), while occasioned by any of these moves, are not directly elicited by them. Rather they modify, rate, or comment upon any move (including another reacting move).

Examples:

T/REA: Oh I don't see too many hands.

T/REA: Oh you're going to the lightest.

T/REA: And when we say more, we could just say more long, if we wanted to, or longer by itself.

A more detailed description of the moves accompanied by additional examples may be found in Appendix B, which contains a copy of the analysis system.

Having divided the data into moves, it was then possible to look at certain groups of utterances. For example, soliciting moves could be counted for the number requiring manipulative behavior.

SCIS Information

Each move was analyzed for the SCIS information which formed the context of the utterance. To accomplish this a content analysis of the informational and conceptual aspects of the Material Objects manual was prepared. The information presented in the manual was organized into five major concept classes plus one grouping entitled "scientific procedures." The five concept classes are: concept of objects, concept of properties, concept of materials, concept of change, and concept of variation in properties. Each of the five contains four sub-categories which range from general to specific and includes a category for inaccurate, or in one instance, very concrete, representations of the concept. For the purposes of this report the sub-categories were used only for the concept of "variation in properties."

For this concept, the sub-categories were:

1) The meaning of serial ordering   Coding symbol: (V)

   Example: A serial ordering is when you make them into
             stairsteps.

2) Discussing actual serial orderings   (V-)

   Example: How did you order your dowels?

             From highest to lowest.

3) Quantifying properties   (VV-)

   Example: This rasp is more rough than the vinyl.
             These are equal height.

4) Failure to quantify   (VVV-)

   Example: The rasp is rough and the vinyl is smooth.

Cognitive Actions

To determine which cognitive actions were required of the children, a list of such actions, related to the concept areas tested in the interviews conducted in the overall study, was prepared. The cognitive actions listed were drawn primarily from the writings of Piaget and organized into groups according to his theoretical discussion of the formation of operational structure. The cognitive acts were organized

97

into groupings relevant to the achievement of operational structure of class relations, conservation, seriation, ordination, and transitivity.

Examples:

Seriation   (S)

    Order your dowels from shortest to longest.
    Which is rougher, the rasp or the vinyl?

Class Relations   (C)

    What properties do these objects have?
    This ball is red.
    These are both the same color.

Conservation   (Q)

    I rubbed the dust off this piece, but it's still the same wood.

Ordination   (O)

    This is the third tallest.

Transitivity   (T)

    I used my finger to measure, and this is longer than this.

Manipulations and Explanation

Each solicitation was examined to determine if it required a response involving manipulation of material in a cognitively significant manner. Giving out or collecting materials, for example, was not considered a cognitively significant manipulation of material. Asking a child to make a serial ordering or arrange two objects with inequality signs was.

The SCIS manual emphasizes the importance of the teacher requesting the child to give evidence for a classification or conclusion or identification of scientific materials. Therefore the coder marked each solicitation requesting an explanation and each other move which itself was an explanation.

Excerpt from Coded Protocol

The coders listened to the tapes as they coded. The following excerpt is taken from the selection quoted on page 94.

Teacher:	(Move #1)	Now this is the word. This is the property. What is it?
Pupil:	(Move #2)	Dark.
Teacher:	(Move #3)	And what did you find out?
Pupil:	(Move #4)	This is darker than that one.

Code

Move #1:   T/SOL/VC/C/2
Move #2:   P/RES/VC/C/1
Move #3:   T/SOL/VC/S/1
Move #4:   P/RES/VVC/S/1

Interpretation

Move #1: The teacher solicits for two half-lines expecting
a class relations response dealing with the property, color
brightness, used in the serial ordering. Move #2: The pupil responds referring to the serial ordering by making a class relations response about the property used in the ordering, color
brightness. Move #3: The teacher asks for a seriation response
again referring to the ordering by color brightness. Move #4:
The pupil makes a seriation response that deals with the SCIS
content of quantifying a property. (Appendix B explains the
coding system fully.)

Reliability of the Analysis System

The reliability of the analysis system was estimated by comparing,
for each part of the system, coded sections of protocols independently
analyzed by two different coders. One seven-page section of transcript
was randomly chosen from the transcripts from each of the four classes,
producing a sample of 28 pages of dialogue to be used for the reliability check. This sample was used to calculate the reliability
for the pedagogical moves. Another 28-page sample, similarly obtained,
from each of the four classes was coded to check the remaining parts
of the system.

In calculating the various reliability figures, two different formulas were used. One is the standard per cent of agreement formula, and
the second is taken from Wright (1967, p. 96):

$$\text{Estimate of Accuracy} = \frac{\text{Episodes Marked by X Marked Also by Y}}{\frac{\text{Episodes Marked by X} + \text{Episodes Marked by Y}}{2}}$$

The estimate of accuracy is .96 for identifying units in the data.
The coders agreed in 92 per cent of the cases when classifying them as
either responses, solicitations, structuring or reacting moves. In
selecting the SCIS context, they agreed in 82 per cent of the cases, and
in identifying the kind of cognitive tasks required, 93 per cent of the
time. The per cent of agreement for the reference medium, involving the
category of "solicitations requesting manipulative responses," was
91 per cent. The estimate of accuracy in recognizing moves involving
explanations is .93.

Findings

The findings presented here should be viewed against the information presented in Table 9. In this table the utterances that were not codable, either because transmission was inadequate or the coder was unable to assign them to any category, are presented as per cents of the total number of moves for each class.[1] This is being done even though it is quite possible that a single noncodable utterance would not correspond to a single move. Expressing the amount of noncodable speech in this manner, however, gives an approximation of the amount of data that is excluded from the analysis. As may be seen, for the teachers, this is a negligible amount, while for the pupils, it is more substantial. While bearing in mind this limitation of the data, the number of noncodable utterances will not be included in the calculations.

The four sessions in Class 1 averaged 28 minutes in length, those of Class 2, 34 minutes in length, Class 3, 35 minutes, and in Class 4, the average length of sessions was 32 minutes. The shortest lesson, lasting 22 minutes, was taught by the teacher of Class 1, and the longest, lasting 47 minutes, by the teacher of Class 2.

Table 9

Noncodable Utterances Expressed in Terms of Per Cent of
Moves for Teachers and Pupils for Each Class

Class	Total Number[a] of Teacher Moves	Per Cent of Teacher Utterances Not Codable	Total Number[a] of Pupil Moves	Per Cent of Pupil Utterances Not Codable
1	962	2.1	540	14.4
2	1335	1.6	844	11.1
3	1398	.2	862	10.2
4	915	2.2	590	17.6

[a]This figure is the total number of moves coded plus the number of noncodable utterances. In all other calculations the total number of moves coded is used and the noncodable utterances are not included.

---

[1]Findings are presented for all four sessions of each class combined, unless otherwise specified.

A total of 7,021 moves were made during the sixteen taping sessions, ranging from approximately 1,400 moves for two of the classes to about 2,100 per four sessions for the other two classes. This yielded an average of 439 moves per session. During the sixteen sessions, 12,586 lines were spoken, the range for the four classes being approximately 2,500 to 3,700 lines. The average number of lines per session was 786.

Role of the Teacher and Pupils

The results concerning the respective proportion of the verbal activity by teacher and pupil as represented in moves are presented in Table 10. As this table demonstrates, the teachers did more talking than did the pupils in each of the four classrooms. The teachers spoke between 63 and 67 per cent of the moves, consisting of 71 to 79 per cent of the lines. This yields a teacher-pupil ratio of approximately 3 to 2 for moves and 3 to 1 for lines. (The per cents for the individual sessions from each class are similar to those presented here.)

Table 10

Per Cent of Lines and Moves for Teachers and Pupils
in Each Class and for All Classes Combined

Class	Teacher	Pupil
1		
Moves	67.1	32.9
Lines	79.0	21.0
2		
Moves	63.7	36.3
Lines	73.1	26.9
3		
Moves	64.3	35.7
Lines	71.5	28.5
4		
Moves	64.9	35.1
Lines	72.3	27.7
Classes Combined		
Moves	64.8	35.2
Lines	73.7	26.3

These findings are strikingly similar to those reported by Bellack (1966), Fey (1968), and Hoetker (1969) who also analyzed recordings of classroom lessons for pedagogical moves. They found approximately the same per cents of teacher/pupil moves and lines even though they studied

101

senior high school social studies, junior high math, and junior high English classes, respectively. In each of these studies, the ratio of teacher to pupil moves was found to be about 3 to 2, and teacher to pupil lines about 3 to 1. At least in this very basic aspect of division of verbal activity, these first grade classes are very similar to classes of much older pupils.

In Table 11 are presented the distribution of moves according to pedagogical category for each class and all classes combined. The predominant activity is soliciting, both in moves and line count, with approximately equal amounts of responding and reacting, and a substantially smaller amount of structuring. As compared to Fey (1968), a larger amount of speech is devoted to soliciting in the first grade classes than in junior high school classes.

Table 11

Per Cent of Moves in Each Pedagogical Category for Teachers and Pupils Combined for Each Class and for All Classes Combined

Class	SOL	RES	STR	REA
1				
Moves	44.6	19.7	3.9	31.8
Lines	48.3	13.6	11.5	26.6
2				
Moves	45.0	26.6	3.9	24.5
Lines	52.0	20.5	7.0	20.5
3				
Moves	45.2	24.9	3.7	26.2
Lines	46.3	21.0	9.2	23.5
4				
Moves	43.4	28.1	5.3	23.3
Lines	46.7	22.9	9.6	20.8
Classes Combined				
Moves	44.7	24.9	4.1	26.3
Lines	48.4	19.6	9.2	22.8

Aside from differences in amount of verbal activity performed by teacher and pupils, there are differences in the pedagogical roles of the teacher and pupil as evidenced by the pedagogical moves each is most likely to make. In Table 12 are presented the per cents of each category of pedagogical move made by teacher and pupil. Initiatory moves are almost always made by the teacher. These teachers make from 84 to 93 per cent of the solicitations and 91 to 100 per cent of the structuring moves. Pupils, in turn, do most of the responding; 87 to 96 per cent of the responses were made by them. Teachers' reflexive moves are primarily confined to reacting. As Bellack has observed, the pupil and teacher do indeed play complementary roles in the classroom. Although there are slight differences in the per cents among the teachers studied here, particularly in the per cents of responses, what is most striking is the similarity among them in overall division of the classroom roles.

As before, these results are quite similar to those reported by investigators who studied junior high and high school classes, the teachers playing the role of initiator and reacting to the pupils' responses (Bellack, 1966; Fey, 1968). Others, such as Marie Hughes, using a very different approach for analyzing classroom dialogue, have also found teacher dominance of the classroom to be typical (Hughes, 1959).

Table 12

Per Cent of Moves by Teachers and Pupils
in Each Pedagogical Category for Each Class

Class	Number of Moves	Per Cent of Moves by Teachers	Per Cent of Moves by Pupils
Solicitations			
1	626	84.3	15.7
2	929	92.1	7.9
3	980	84.7	15.3
4	600	93.7	6.3
Responses			
1	276	13.0	87.0
2	548	3.5	96.5
3	539	10.9	89.1
4	388	5.2	94.8
Structurings			
1	55	100.0	0
2	81	91.4	8.6
3	81	95.1	4.9
4	73	94.5	5.5
Reactions			
1	447	72.3	27.7
2	506	72.1	27.9
3	569	75.4	24.6
4	322	76.4	23.6

Tables 13 and 14 present the per cent of moves in each pedagogical category for teachers and pupils. Of the moves made by the teacher, 60 per cent are devoted to soliciting, and approximately 30 per cent to reacting. For the pupils, 57 per cent of their moves are responses, and reactions, 17 per cent with almost no structuring moves. Although there were some variations among the teachers studied, again, the similarities far override any differences in the distributions of the moves.

Table 13

Per Cent of Teachers' Moves and Lines in Each
Pedagogical Category for All Classes Combined

Pedagogical Move	Per Cent of Teachers' Total Moves	Per Cent of Teachers' Total Lines
Solicitations	61.0	61.1
Responses	2.9	2.1
Structurings	6.0	12.1
Reactions	30.0	24.7

Table 14

Per Cent of Pupils' Moves and Lines in Each
Pedagogical Category for All Classes Combined

Pedagogical Move	Per Cent of Pupils' Total Moves	Per Cent of Pupils' Total Lines
Solicitations	14.6	12.9
Responses	65.4	68.7
Structurings	.6	.9
Reactions	19.5	17.5

Pedagogical Role and Substantive Content

The remaining findings to be presented are restricted to those moves that focused on SCIS content and that involved the cognitive actions being studied here.

Example of move with substantive content:

T/SOL: Order your sticks by length.

Example of move without substantive content:

T/SOL: Would everybody please sit quietly?

In Table 15 are given the per cents of moves that contained such substantive material. As can be seen, in terms of both lines and moves,
the majority of the moves were devoted to the material to be covered.

Table 15

Per Cent of Moves and Lines in Each Pedagogical Category
Referring to Substantive Content[a] for All Classes Combined

Pedagogical Move	Per Cent of Moves Substantive	Per Cent of Lines Substantive
Solicitations	67.0	70.5
Responses	84.3	85.2
Structurings	74.8	78.8
Reactions	69.3	74.0
All Moves	72.2	74.9

[a]By substantive content is meant moves with SCIS context and
involving cognitive tasks.

A closer analysis of this is presented in Table 16. Here the per cent of
total moves in each pedagogical category that are substantive is given
separately for the teacher and pupils in each class. What is of interest here is that for all classes, only a minority of teacher responses
and pupil solicitations deal with substantive material. Only 15 per cent
of all pupil moves are solicitations to begin with, and of these less
than a third deal with substantive matters. Apparently when these
pupils did solicit, it was in reference to either procedural matters or
other matters not related to the lesson. Except for pupil solicitations
and teacher responses, most of the classroom discourse does deal with
the lesson material to be presented. Despite some variation, the
teachers are alike in the per cents of moves devoted to substantive material.

In Table 17 are presented the number of lines per move for the four
classes for each pedagogical category. As could be expected, teachers'
moves tend to be longer than their pupils'. Teacher solicitations are
longer than pupil responses and the teachers' structuring moves are the
longest moves of all. The teachers and pupils in each class are similar
in the length of their moves, but Teacher 1 spoke longer soliciting,
structuring, and reacting moves than did the other three teachers.
Teacher 1's structuring moves were particularly notable for their
greater length when compared to structuring moves made by the other teachers.
For all classes combined and teacher and pupil moves combined, there were
1.86 lines per move.

Table 16

Per Cent of Total Number of Moves in Each Pedagogical Category Referring to Substantive Content[a] for Teacher and Pupil in Each Class

Class	Per Cent of Total Teacher Moves Substantive	Per Cent of Total Pupil Moves Substantive
Solicitations		
1	76.6	33.7
2	73.1	28.8
3	69.5	24.7
4	69.2	36.8
Responses		
1	11.1	89.6
2	21.1	88.1
3	8.5	90.4
4	30.0	91.0
Structurings		
1	80.0	0
2	74.3	71.4
3	72.7	75.0
4	73.9	75.0
Reactions		
1	80.8	61.3
2	70.4	48.9
3	78.6	42.9
4	67.5	66.2

[a] By substantive content is meant moves with SCIS context and involving cognitive tasks.

Table 17

Average Number of Lines Per Move by Pedagogical Category
for Moves Referring to Substantive Content
by Teacher and Pupil for Each Class

Class	SOL Teacher	Pupil	RES Teacher	Pupil	STR Teacher	Pupil	REA Teacher	Pupil
1	2.37	1.21	1.75	1.36	6.11	---	1.91	1.12
2	2.11	1.19	1.00	1.35	3.44	2.20	1.56	1.29
3	1.93	1.08	1.40	1.46	4.52	1.33	1.70	1.23
4	2.02	1.29	2.00	1.53	3.51	1.00	1.79	1.18

Cognitive Processes

One of the major tasks posed for this analysis was to provide some direct evidence about the cognitive processes actually used in the classroom. Table 18 presents the per cent of moves referring to each category of cognitive process. For all classes, the largest per cent of moves dealt with seriation processes followed by class relations processes. Since the lessons to be taught involved the comparison and serial ordering of objects, this might be expected. The analysis of the SCIS program presented in Chapter III had found a preponderance of suggested responses dealing with the logic of classes. The large number of moves in this category suggests that some of the emphasis in the program is reflected in the classroom discourse. Despite the lack of emphasis in the curriculum on number, in three of the classes, 2 to 4 per cent of the moves involved numerical content.

Table 18

Per Cent of Moves Referring to Each Category of Cognitive
Process for Each Class, Teacher and Pupil Combined[a]

Class	Total No. of Moves	Cognitive Tasks Class Relations	Conservation	Seriation	Ordination	Transitivity	(Conservation)[b]
1	766	36.2	0	60.1	0.3	0.5	3.0
2	1181	44.1	0.7	50.6	0.4	0.3	3.8
3	1235	27.6	1.5	68.3	0.4	0.2	2.0
4	775	39.7	0	58.6	0	1.4	0.3

[a]SOL-A's and REA-A's are excluded (see Appendix B, Pedagogical Moves, 2.5 and 2.15).
[b]Although these moves involve actions relevant to conservation, their context was simply evaluating the number of objects in a set.

Table 19 presents the per cent of moves referring to the various
SCIS concept categories. Here again the classes are more alike than
different in the distribution of the moves. The concept of "variation
in properties" and the concept of "properties" dominate the discourse.
Taken together with the predominance of moves relating to seriation
and class relations, it would seem that class relations processes
were used in connection with the property category, and seriation
with the concept of variation category. The category of science procedures for these lessons involved primarily discussion about the meaning
of inequality signs and their use.

Teachers 2 and 3 each conducted one lesson in which there were many
moves for which SCIS concepts of "properties," "objects," and "variation"
were applied to non-SCIS materials such as ordinary classroom objects.
The other two teachers did not pursue this kind of extension of the
concepts presented.

Table 19

Per Cent of Moves[a] Referring to Each SCIS Category
for Each Class, Teacher and Pupil Combined

		SCIS Categories					
Class	Total Moves	Object	Property	Material	Change	Variation	Science Pro
1	921	10.7	14.3	3.8	.3	64.5	7.4
2	1308	10.6	26.9	2.5	.9	51.8	7.3
3	1421	9.1	17.5	.6	1.3	65.5	6.1
4	923	4.3	26.7	3.0	.4	58.7	6.8

[a]
SOL-A and REA-A pedagogical moves are excluded.

Within the "variation of properties" category, a finer analysis of
the distribution of the moves was made. They were categorized as to the
level of generality at which they presented the concept of variation as
described on page 93. Table 20 presents the per cent of moves at these
levels for each class. As can be seen, discussing actual orderings and
quantification of properties received the largest per cents, and these
two concepts were emphasized in the manual. Two of the teachers,
3 and 4, devoted a greater per cent of moves to the more general level
discussions about what serial orderings are than did the other two
teachers. These two classes also produced comparatively fewer failures
to quantify responses than did the other two classes. Despite such
relatively small differences, the data tend to highlight the similarities
among the four classes. This can be further seen in Table 21 which orders

the properties involved in serial orderings and quantified relations for each class by the frequency of moves pertaining to them. For all classes, length/height, global size, and color brightness are the three properties most frequently involved in the discourse. The kinds of materials provided, dowels and cards varying in color brightness, would lead one to expect such a result. The extensive use of the size category, however, might reflect a more global approach to identifying properties than the SCIS curriculum would prefer. In addition to the properties presented in Table 21, less frequently mentioned properties that were discussed in almost every class were diameter size, width, shape, heaviness, and in two classes, hardness.

Table 20

Per Cent of Moves for Each Sub-Category Dealing With Variation in Properties for Each Class, Teacher and Pupil Combined

	Categories			
Class	Nature of Serial Ordering	Actual Serial Ordering	Quantifying Properties	Failure to Quantify
1	3.9	67.7	27.1	1.4
2	4.5	58.2	35.4	1.9
3	7.5	51.8	39.9	0.8
4	10.2	58.2	31.2	0.4

Table 21

Rank Ordering of Properties Serialized and/or Quantified in Each Class

	Class			
Rank	1	2	3	4
1	Length/Height[a]	Length/Height[a]	Size	Length/Height[a]
2	Color Brightness	Color Brightness	Length/Height[a]	Size
3	Size	Size	Color Brightness	Color Brightness
4	Bounciness	Bounciness	Other[b]	Texture-Other[c]
5	Texture	Form	Hardness	

[a] Length and height were used interchangeably.

[b] This category includes miscellaneous properties not readily classified into the more common property names, and usually not suggested by the manual.

[c] The same number of moves focused on the categories of "texture" and "other" in Class 4.

Manipulation of Material

According to the analysis in Chapter III, one-third of the responses were to require direct manipulation of physical objects by the children. In Table 22 are presented the per cents of cognitive solicitations that directed manipulative responses. For the teachers there was quite a wide range in the per cents, from a low of about 12 per cent to a high of 29 per cent. Only Teacher 1 solicited manipulative responses approaching the number recommended by the manual as revealed in Chapter III of the report. Of course the number of manipulative responses actually made by the children is unknown, and it may be that the per cent of solicitation directing manipulative activity is not a good indication of the amount of manipulative activity that actually occurred.

Table 22

Per Cent of Substantive Solicitations[a] Requesting
Manipulation of Material for Each Class

Speaker	Class			
	1	2	3	4
Teacher	28.8	21.2	16.2	11.7
Pupil	15.2	0	13.5	21.4

[a]SOL-A's excluded

Explanations

Another emphasis in the SCIS program was in having the child give evidence or reasons or explanations for his statements. Therefore the data were analyzed for the number of explanations the teachers requested from their pupils. These data are presented in Table 23 along with the per cent of explanations made by the pupils (in terms of moves) in each class. Only between 11 and 16 per cent of the teacher solicitations called for explanations and between 10 and 15 per cent of the pupils' moves are explanations.

There were only two pupil requests for explanations, one such pupil solicitation occurring in Class 3 and the other in Class 4.

110

Table 23

Per Cent of Substantive Moves Involving Explanations
for Each Class for Pupil and Teacher

Moves Involving Explanations	Class			
	1	2	3	4
Requesting Explanations				
Per Cent of Teacher Substantive Solicitations[a]	10.8	13.6	12.0	16.2
Giving Explanations				
Per Cent of Pupil Substantive Moves[b]	12.7	9.6	10.7	14.6

[a] SOL-A's excluded.

[b] This includes Pupil STR, RES, and REA moves.

Discussion and Summary

What emerges from the findings presented in this chapter is that the four teachers studied were very similar to each other in the ways they structured the activity in their classes, and the pupils were similar in their responses to the teachers. Despite variation in the actual number of moves and lines involved, approximately the same per cents of moves and lines were devoted to teacher and pupil roles in all four classes although Teacher 1 tended to speak longer moves than did the other teachers. What is also clear is that the teachers dominated the discourse not only by speaking the majority of lines and moves, but also by the kind of pedagogical moves they made. The teachers did by far most of the soliciting and structuring, thus acting as the initiators of the discourse. The pupils were left to respond and react. The tendency is heightened for discourse involving substantive material. This was so despite the guidance of a curriculum which sought to encourage experimentation in the presentation of activities. Whatever the SCIS program intended, the teachers did not adopt different pedagogical roles from those of teachers studied by other investigators. Whether or not the recording procedures had any effect on the teachers and pupils is not known. The teachers were presenting lessons they had never taught before and which they considered difficult; perhaps this affected their teaching.

The four teachers were similar in their way of handling the SCIS material. The concepts the manual emphasized were the ones emphasized in the discourse. As initiator, the teacher directed a substantial portion of the discourse to certain substantive categories, and in the role of responding, the pupils followed the teacher's lead. The four teachers studied did spend the most substantial amount of their time in terms of moves and lines on developing content, rather than on housekeeping or non-science matters.

Fewer manipulative responses were required of the children than were proposed by the manual, and only a small per cent of responses were expected to involve explanations.

Young children are thought to be very curious about their environment and prone to ask many questions. Yet the children studied here rarely directed questions of substantive content to the teacher, and almost never requested explanations. Except for the large number of properties in the "other" category, there was little evidence in the analysis prescribed here of the spontaneity the program had hoped to create. The teachers taught as did teachers with much older pupils. For example, the SCIS program did not emphasize vocabulary learning. Yet informal observations made during preliminary taping sessions indicated that some of the teachers spent a good deal of time in teaching material names such as polystyrene, vinyl, oak, balsa, lead and brass. It was clear, however, that the children found the materials provided by the SCIS program for them for playing and working fascinating. They could be observed applying many different schemas in an effort to assimilate them to their world, perhaps a more informal and richer one than could be revealed by the kind of analysis attempted here. In a number of sessions, in fact, the children asked that the science materials, including the word frames and inequality signs, be left out so that they could use them between lessons.

These first grade classes were strikingly similar to junior and senior high school classes in the division of teacher-pupil verbal activity and in the pedagogical roles assumed by teacher and pupil. To what extent these first grade classes are typical of first grade classrooms in general is not known. The small size of the sample dictates caution in interpreting the findings. However, the similarity of these classes to the other classes studied by other investigators suggests that the patterns of roles in the classroom are established very early in the child's school career, and are resistant to change. Many of the researchers in classroom learning seem to assume that there is too much teacher domination of the classroom activities, particularly verbal. However, there is no hard evidence as to the most desirable ratio of teacher to pupil discourse. It is not known if pupils generally learn more or less with a more or less permissive or dominating teacher in terms of the substantive material taught, or in terms of other less easily measured outcomes of classroom teaching and learning. It is quite probable that the age of the students, their past formal educational experience, their level of achievement in the subject, the nature of the subject itself, and certainly not least of all, the personality and other characteristics of the teacher will determine the most effective teaching strategy.

It should be noted that this analysis has focused on the teacher-pupil interaction and pedagogical roles. The pupil-pupil interactions and pupil self-activity also deserve study, and are probably equally as significant as the teacher-pupil interaction. No analysis has as yet been made of the child tapes, but casual reading indicates these are a fascinating source of material for the researcher able to capture the richness these tapes offer. Analysis was accomplished in this study only for the verbal interaction in the classroom. Non-verbal responses of pupils, such as their groupings of materials and the actual steps they used to form serial orderings were not analyzed. Such behavior was described only when it was relevant to the teacher-student dialogue. Obviously a comprehensive study of such non-verbal but cognitively significant behavior would prove most revealing. Another kind of unknown in this kind of analysis is the covert response made by a pupil to the teacher's salutations and covert reactions to classroom activities. Presumably these also play a role in the learning process and in the development of operational intelligence. Other interesting aspects of classroom learning such as the playful quality of many of the pupils' actions in relation to the material is missed by this kind of analysis, and perhaps it is here that the children's curiosity and creativity is most likely to be expressed.

The congruity or lack of it between teacher solicitations and pupil responses would also provide another avenue for analysis. Indeed, teachers attempting to analyze their own remarks in terms of this kind of coding system might be surprised at the difficulties caused by vagueness and ambiguity in their questions and reactions.

In final comment, despite the program emphasis on exploration and discovery, the pattern of the teacher's dominating the discourse prevailed. This finding might disappoint those who expect a revolution in teaching to occur in response to new curricula. However, research findings suggest that the traditional teacher-pupil roles are pervasive and well established. It is probably unrealistic to expect changes in style of teaching to accompany the introduction of improved academic content.

CHAPTER VI

THE RESULTS: EFFECTS OF INSTRUCTION

The major question in this study has to do with the effects of early instruction on the logical thinking abilities of young children. Four groups were studied from kindergarten. For two of these, instruction included prescribed programs in both science and mathematics. A third group had only the mathematics program. The fourth group had no program of prescribed lessons. In the first grade two additional groups, neither of which had had prescribed lessons in kindergarten, joined the study. The two additional groups had a mathematics program closely resembling, but not identical to, the mathematics program used in the groups that had entered the study earlier. One of these additional groups had a prescribed program in science. The other did not.

Table 4 in Chapter II shows for each group the number of children who remained in the study to its completion. The thinking of the children beginning in kindergarten was assessed in the fall of 1965, again in the fall of 1966, and finally in the fall of 1967, while those beginning in the first grade were assessed only in the fall of 1966 and the fall of 1967. In this chapter reference is made only to the longitudinal groups, that is, those children in the six groups who were present for all the interviews for their particular groups.

The measure of logical thinking, used in the fall of second grade when the average age of the children was seven years and four months, consisted of a series of Piaget-derived tasks. This chapter first describes the overall performance of the children in these post-test tasks, taking into account certain related variables. Then, addressing the major questions of the study, the performance of the groups with differing kinds of instruction is examined, again with consideration of related variables. In the succeeding chapter, the specific tasks are examined in more detail and some of the relationships among them explored, and interpreted in the framework of Piagetian theory.

The Post-Test Measure of Logical Thinking

Initially each kind of task included in the post-test was scored or coded in such a way that partial credit could be given. For example, in the conservation tasks a child could receive credit for conserving number even if he did not conserve quantity. Or in the class inclusion tasks a child could be given variable credit depending on whether he responded correctly in one, two, three or four of the tasks. Such partial credit identifies the child who in that particular type of task can be regarded as transitional. He is beginning to use an operational mode of thought, but he is misled when a problem is posed him in a slightly different way, or when confronted with a request for an explanation, he assumes himself to be wrong and changes his view. In some instances he begins to catch on to the logic of the problem as the questioning proceeds, but the interviewer using a standard procedure has no way of knowing whether the child would maintain the apparent insight if the questioning proceeded further.

Evidence from other studies indicates that the typical seven-year-old would be transitional rather than operational in most of the tasks of the post-test. However, it seemed appropriate to use a stringent test of the effectiveness of the programs of instruction, requiring that the child show a preponderance of operational responses before he was credited as an operational thinker. For this purpose no partial credit was given. Each kind of post-test task, except the matrix, was rescored on a 0 (not operational) and 1 (operational) basis as follows:

> Conservation of number and quantity. One (1) for conservation in all three tasks. Zero (0) for all other combinations.
>
> Conservation of weight. One (1) or zero (0) as originally scored for overall performance.
>
> Class-inclusion. One (1) for correct solutions in all four tasks. Zero (0) for all other combinations.
>
> Seriation. One (1) for a combined score of 30 in all four tasks. Zero (0) for all other scores.
>
> Ordination. One (1) for a combined score of six (6) in tasks A and B. Zero (0) for all other scores.
>
> Reordering. One (1) for a combined score of two (2) in tasks A and B. Zero (0) for all other scores.
>
> Transitivity. One (1) or zero (0) as originally scored for overall performance.

Figure 1 shows the number of children whose scores clearly showed that they were thinking on an operational level in dealing with the tasks used in this study. Obviously the tasks differ in level of difficulty. Over half of the children succeeded in the least difficult task—conservation of number. In contrast, less than 10 per cent were operational in the reordering and class inclusion tasks. Ordination is more difficult than conservation, but easier than conservation of weight or transitivity.

The data were next examined to see whether any overall patterns could be detected. The tasks represent three different kinds of operations that are essential for logical thinking: conserving, classifying, and serial ordering. For each operation Piaget has shown a typical sequence of development, into which the tasks included here might be expected to fall. Thus children would be expected to conserve number and quantity before they would be able to conserve weight, to arrange a series before they could solve the problem of ordination, and to accomplish both these before they could reorder a series that has been scrambled. The transitivity problem may be regarded as a problem of the seriation type, successful solution following seriation and ordination and possibly reordering. The transitivity problem may also be

115

regarded as an extension of the conservation problems involving the conservation of length. Successful solution of the inclusion problems, representing the most advanced sort of classification, would be expected to follow after solution of the less difficult classification problems represented in the matrices. (The analysis of the matrix problems is separated from the analysis of the other tasks for reasons suggested in Chapter II and elaborated in this chapter.)

On a theoretical basis, then, one might expect to find an ordering of the conservation and seriation kinds of tasks, and then be able on an empirical basis to combine these orders with each other and with the class inclusion task in such a way that the performance of the children could be classified according to predominant patterns.

Overall Performance, All Programs Combined

For seven kinds of tasks, each kind receiving a score of 0 or 1, 128 patterns are possible. Actually, among the children in the study for whom complete data were available,[1] 73 different patterns appeared. Of these patterns, the 1 1 1 1 1 1 1 (clear evidence of logical thinking in all seven kinds of tasks) appeared only three times, and the pattern 0 0 0 0 0 0 0 (no evidence of operational thinking) appeared 136 times. Three other frequent patterns were 1 0 0 0 0 0 0 (operational only in conservation of number and quantity) shown by 55 children, 0 0 0 0 1 0 0 (operational only in ordination) shown by 31 children, and 1 1 0 0 0 0 0 (operational in both conservation of number and quantity and weight) shown by 26 children. No other patterns appeared as frequently as these.

In 314 cases the patterns conformed to what might have been expected on the basis of the sequences described above. In the remainder of the patterns children were scored operational in theoretically more difficult tasks when they had not been scored as operational in less difficult tasks. As is suggested in Figure 1, ordination did not prove to be more difficult than seriation. Transitivity tasks also were less difficult than might be anticipated on the basis of the theory. Twelve children were scored operational in the transitivity task and in no other. Class-inclusion, clearly the most difficult task, was scored operational for another sixteen children whose performance in a majority of the other tasks was not operational. These and other variations rendered attempts to order the patterns on the basis of theory unsuccessful. Attempts to order them empirically on the basis of the apparent difficulty of the tasks were also unsuccessful.

Considering the narrow age range of the group, the general unreliability of performance of children under the age of eight, and the inclusion of four kinds of operations in the patterns, the expectation of ordering them was, perhaps, unwarranted. As Table 24 indicates, the

---

[1]The reader will note that the total number of children varies in some of the tables. This is because some protocols had missing information and could not be used in all of the analyses.

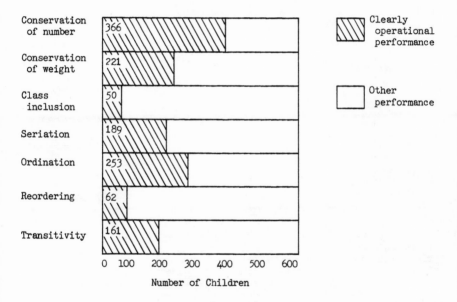

Fig. 1.   Proportion of 629 second grade children with clearly operational performance in seven kinds of post-test tasks.

117

correlations between the tasks are low. This suggests that for seven-year-olds, the prediction of an operational response from one task to another is hazardous even when the tasks bear as close a theoretical relationship to one another as do the two conservation tasks or the seriation and ordination tasks.

Table 24

Intercorrelations (Phi Coefficients) for Performance
on Post-Test Tasks of 629 Children at
Beginning of Second Grade, Based on
0-1 Scores for Evidence of Operational Thinking

	Conservation of Number 1	Conservation of Weight 2	Class Inclusion 3	Seriation 4	Ordination 5	Reordering 6	Transitivity 7
1. Conservation of Number	-	.32	.18	.26	.20	.11	.21
2. Conservation of Weight		-	.13	.20	.20	.32	.18
3. Class Inclusion			-	.20	.11	.22	.15
4. Seriation				-	.21	.21	.13
5. Ordination					-	1.4	.19
6. Reordering						-	.09
7. Transitivity							-

It may be argued that items with correlations of similar size are sometimes combined in tests of achievement, thus justifying a summation of the number of tasks in which each child was clearly operational as a total score for operational thinking. This argument is rejected on two counts. First, such pooling masks the individuality in development which is so characteristic of the young child. Second, it may mask the differential effects of particular programs of instruction. The extent of such effects is apparent in Table 25.

This table shows for all programs combined, and for each program separately, the per cent of children who were scored operational in the seven kinds of post-test tasks. Before the extent of the differences among the programs is considered, the performance of the children in all the programs combined will be examined, giving attention to some of the variables that may affect it.

Table 25

Per Cent of Children in Six Programs Clearly Operational
in Seven Post-Test Tasks at Beginning of Second Grade[a]

	Per Cent Operational							
	Conservation of		Class Inclu-sion	Serial Ordering			Transi-tivity	No. of Chldrn.[b]
Program	No.	Wt.		Seria-tion	Ordina-tion	Reorder-ing		
All Programs	58	35	8	30	40	10	26	628
Initiated in Kindergarten								
AAAS (GCMP)	70	41	9	24	35	6	40	93
SCIS (GCMP)	68	40	13	35	37	13	13	79
GCMP Only	55	38	11	34	49	15	19	122
No Pre-scribed Lessons	67	39	4	38	48	6	37	136
Initiated in First Grade								
SCIS (Math)	45	27	7	23	32	12	19	113
Math Only	45	25	5	25	34	7	22	85

[a] Based on 0-1 scoring procedures. Per cents given represent the number of children in each task scoring 1.

[b] Total, including those not operational, who attempted each of the seven kinds of tasks.

Sex

On an overall basis, the performance of the boys and the girls (see Appendix C) is strikingly similar.

PPVT I.Q.

In considering the possible relations between performance on the Peabody Picture Vocabulary Test and performance in the post-test tasks, the nature of the PPVT and the conditions of its administration need to be borne in mind. It is essentially a test of auditory comprehension. Hence, I.Q.'s obtained with it are at best only roughly comparable with other measures of mental maturity. The groups who began instruction in kindergarten were tested at the beginning of the kindergarten year, so that the results for them are likely to be less reliable than the results for the groups who began instruction in first grade and were not tested until then.

Table 26 shows three I.Q. groups: 110 and above, 90 to 107, 89 and below. The top group includes the PPVT classification of "rapid learners" (110-124) and "very rapid learners" (125 and above), and the lowest group includes "very slow learners" (below 75) as well as "slow learners" (75-89).

In preliminary analyses of the post-test tasks, the performances of 47 children who were in the PPVT I.Q. group of 125 and above were examined separately from those of the 214 children with PPVT I.Q.'s from 110 to 124. They were sufficiently similar to warrant combining them with the adjacent group. So few children scored in the PPVT I.Q. range below 89 that no attempt was made to differentiate the "very slow" from the "slow" learners in the post-test tasks.

Examination of Table 26 shows that for each task the per cent of children who are clearly operational is largest for the group with the highest PPVT I.Q.'s and lowest for those with the lowest PPVT I.Q.'s. The differential effects as related to the programs of instruction are considered later.

Socioeconomic Status

Information regarding socioeconomic status was available for 558 of the 628 children for whom there were PPVT I.Q.'s and is also shown in Table 26. The overall post-test performance of the two groups is similar although the breakdown into three groups by socioeconomic status is not completely parallel to the breakdown by PPVT I.Q. The Pearson product moment correlation between PPVT I.Q. scores and S.E.S. scores is .28. As Table 26 indicates, larger per cents of the children in the upper socioeconomic group are clearly operational in all tasks than is the case for those in the lower groups.

Table 26

Per Cent of Children in All Groups Combined, Categorized by
I.Q.[a] and S.E.S.,[b] Clearly Operational in Post-Test Tasks
at Beginning of Second Grade

Task	Per Cent Operational							
	PPVT I.Q.				S.E.S.			
	All I.Q.'s	110+	90-109	89-	All Levels[c]	80+	40-79	39-
Conservation of Number	58	70	54	35	60	69	43	50
Conservation of Weight	35	49	29	10	37	43	28	17
Class Inclusion	8	14	5	0	8	12	3	2
Seriation	30	40	27	9	31	39	17	13
Ordination	40	47	40	16	41	45	32	33
Reordering	10	13	8	4	9	12	3	4
Transitivity	26	32	24	10	27	31	17	22
Total Number of Children	628	260	289	79	558	363	149	46

[a] Peabody Picture Vocabulary Test, Form A.

[b] Based on U.S. Bureau of the Census, Methodology and scores of socioeconomic status. Working Paper No. 15, Washington, D. C., 1963. (Occupations transformed to socioeconomic status: Levels above 80, professionals and managers; between 40 and 79, skilled workers; below 39, largely unskilled.)

[c] Includes only those children for whom information concerning socioeconomic status was available.

Initial Conservation Status

Table 27 shows the second grade performance in post-test tasks of the children who entered the study in kindergarten in relation to their conservation status at that time. It also shows the second grade performance in post-test tasks of all the children in the study, including both those who entered in kindergarten and those who entered in first grade, in relation to their status in conservation in the first grade.

As far as the children are concerned, for whom kindergarten status is available, it is clear that the per cents of children who are operational in the second grade tasks are higher among those who conserved in all three tasks in kindergarten than among those who were not conserving at all in kindergarten. The differences between those children who conserved in only the easiest task (number after counting), and those who also conserved in the more difficult conservation of number task are not great, nor are they consistent. This is in line with previous findings (Almy, Chittenden and Miller, 1966) regarding the relative difficulty of the conservation tasks at the kindergarten level and their relationships to later performance.

In contrast, when the performance of all the children in the post-test tasks is viewed against their first grade conservation status, the increases in the per cent of children who are clearly operational appears to be more consistently related to the earlier status. The trend is for the group who achieved conservation in three tasks to perform better than those who were correct in only two, those who achieved in two better than those in only one, and all these better than those achieving in none. As in the case of kindergarten status, the differences are greatest between those correct in all three tasks and those who had none correct.

The performance in the post-test tasks of the children in the various groups can now be viewed against the overall performance described above.

Major Comparisons

The major questions raised by this study require the pooling of the data from one or more of the programs. Thus all of the classes having one or more programs with prescribed lessons beginning in kindergarten may be examined in relation to the classes in which such programs did not begin until first grade. Similarly the three groups of classes that had prescribed lessons may be examined against the group of classes that had none. For these two major comparisons the numbers of children involved are large enough so that differences in the per cent of children whose performances in a particular kind of task are operational are generally meaningful even after the breakdown for PPVT I.Q., socioeconomic status, and initial conservation pattern. On the other hand, when fine comparisons involving only two or three groups of classes are made, the numbers become too small to permit one to draw safe conclusions. Where differences fit the theory on which the study is based and are either congruent or strikingly incongruent with the emphasis in the

122

Table 27

Per Cent of Second Grade Children in All Groups Combined
Who Were Clearly Operational in Post-Test Tasks
in Light of Their Earlier Performance
in Conservation Tasks

	Per Cent with Indicated Conservation Status							
	In Kindergarten[a]				In First Grade[b]			
Task	No Tasks	Task A Only	Tasks A & B	All 3 Tasks	No Tasks	Task A Only	Tasks A & B	All 3 Tasks
Conservation of Number	51	72	76	81	29	38	61	80
Conservation of Weight	27	41	54	65	12	16	41	49
Inclusion	2	13	20	15	2	2	5	15
Seriation	19	41	34	58	13	18	28	43
Ordination	31	55	54	46	16	30	46	48
Reordering	4	11	22	15	2	2	10	16
Transitivity	21	37	27	27	11	17	20	37
Total Number of Children	170	148	41	26	83	128	105	227

[a] Conservation status in kindergarten was not known for the two groups entering the study in first grade.

[b] Per cents related to conservation status in first grade include children who entered study in kindergarten as well as those who entered in first grade.

123

instructional program, attention will be called to them. Differences of this sort suggest hypotheses for further testing, but they cannot be taken as conclusions.

In Table 24, the reader may compare the performance of the groups of classes as they actually occurred, that is, with the variability that characterizes typical classes of second graders. Tables 26 and 27 provide a means of viewing several important sources of such variability successively. In the tables that follow, when the numbers are appropriately large, groups having different kinds of programs are also examined according to these variables. (The reader who is interested in finer details than are included in this chapter is referred to Appendix C.)

Information is also presented comparing the performance of four matched groups of children. Representing the four kinds of instructional programs that were studied from kindergarten, these groups were matched on the basis of sex, chronological age, PPVT I.Q., and status in conservation in kindergarten. This comparison provides the clearest information about the efficacy of the four programs.

Instruction Initiated in Kindergarten and Continued in First Grade vs. Instruction in First Grade Only

How does the performance in the post-test tasks of all of the children who had prescribed lessons in science and mathematics (AAAS-GCMP and SCIS-GCMP) or in mathematics alone (GCMP) beginning in kindergarten compare with the performance of all of the children who had no prescribed lessons until they reached first grade, at which time some classes had SCIS-Math and others had Math only? As Table 28 shows, the performance overall of those who had early instruction is better than of those who did not have it. The direction of these differences holds in the top PPVT I.Q. group and in the middle I.Q. group, and generally in the two top socioeconomic groups.[1] (See Appendix C.)

When the comparisons between the group having prescribed lessons in kindergarten and those having such lessons only in first grade are made on the basis of their status in conservation when they were in first grade (see Appendix C), the differences favor the group beginning in kindergarten, the numbers are small and there are several reversals.

---

[1]Although no prediction was made regarding the differences, the data were subjected to chi square analysis. Overall, differences in the per cents of operational performances were significant at the .05 level or better for the five tasks: conservation of number, conservation of weight, class inclusion, seriation, and ordination. When the groups were divided according to PPVT I.Q. level, significant differences were found for children in the 90-109 range for four tasks: conservation of number, conservation of weight, seriation, and ordination. For children in the range of PPVT I.Q.'s above 110, differences were significant for the conservation of number and class inclusion tasks. Differences for children with PPVT I.Q.'s below 89 were not significant. Differences among the groups when divided according to socioeconomic status were also not significant.

Table 28

Per Cent of Second Grade Children in Different I.Q.[a] Groups Having
Prescribed Lessons Initiated in Kindergarten or First Grade Who
Were Clearly Operational in Post-Test Tasks

Program Initi- ated in	Conservation of		Class Inclu- sion	Serial Ordering			Transi- tivity	No. of Chldrn.
	No.	Wt.		Seria- tion	Ordina- tion	Reorder- ing		
				Per Cent Operational				
				All PPVT I.Q. Groups				
Kinder garten	63	39	11	31	41	12	24	294
First Grade	45	26	6	24	33	10	21	198
				PPVT I.Q. 110 and Above				
Kinder- garten	74	53	19	37	44	15	30	118
First Grade	59	42	9	35	42	13	24	79
				PPVT I.Q. 90-109				
Kinder- garten	61	36	7	33	46	10	23	135
First Grade	39	19	5	18	31	10	20	94
				PPVT I.Q. 89 and Below				
Kinder- garten	41	15	0	7	20	5	10	41
First Grade	20	4	0	8	12	4	12	25

[a] Peabody Picture Vocabulary Test, Form A.

In considering the extent to which these results favor the groups having early instruction, and the children in the upper and middle PPVT I.Q. groups, two facts need to be kept in mind. First, relatively little is known about the nature of the kindergarten experience of the children for whom prescribed instruction was begun in first grade. Conceivably, had that experience been of a different sort, whether or not prescribed lessons were involved, the children's performances in the post-test tasks might more nearly have approximated those of their counterparts who began participation in the study when they were in kindergarten. Second, the number of children with PPVT I.Q.'s below 89 is too small for meaningful conclusions.

Prescribed Programs Beginning in Kindergarten vs. No Prescribed Lessons in Kindergarten or First Grade

For those children participating in the study from kindergarten, post-test performances of those who had prescribed programs may be compared with those who had no prescribed lessons (see Table 29). Overall, the children having no prescribed lessons in kindergarten did about as well as those who had them. None of the differences in per cent of children who were clearly operational is large, although five of the seven comparisons favor the group with no prescribed program. Four of these differences are maintained in the high I.Q. group. In the two lower I.Q. groups, the per cent of children who performed operationally is about the same for those having no prescribed lessons as for those having such instruction.

When socioeconomic status is taken into consideration (see Appendix C), the differences, in contrast to those in the PPVT I.Q. breakdown, tend to favor the children having special programs in the top socioeconomic group, and those having no prescribed lessons in the next socioeconomic group.

The comparisons of the group having no prescribed lessons with that having prescribed programs (see Appendix C) is particularly interesting when made according to kindergarten conservation status. Except for the two kinds of tasks in which operational thinking was least likely to appear--class inclusion and reordering--the differences in per cents among those children who were not conserving at all in the kindergarten pre-tests or who were conserving in only the easiest task, favor the group having no prescribed lessons. Among those children who in kindergarten were conserving in the two easier tasks, or in all three tasks, the direction of the differences is reversed. Unfortunately, the numbers of children are too small for generalization. The discrepancy in performance between those who conserved in the two easiest tasks and those who conserved in all three tasks can only be attributed to unknown selective factors affecting the small numbers of children involved.

One may speculate that a relatively unstructured but active kindergarten experience provides the less mature children an opportunity to develop spontaneously the ability to conserve and some degree of operational thinking. It should be noted that of those children who did not

126

TABLE 29

Per Cent of Second Grade Children in Different I.Q.[a] Groups
Having or not Having Prescribed Lessons in Kindergarten
Who Were Clearly Operational in Post-Test Tasks

	Per Cent Operational							
	Conservation of		Class Inclu-sion	Serial Ordering			Transi-tivity	No. of Chldrn.
Programs	No.	Wt.		Seria-tion	Ordina-tion	Reorder-ing		
All PPVT I.Q. Groups Combined								
Prescrbd.	63	39	11	31	41	12	24	294
Lessons not Prescrbd.	67	39	4	38	48	6	37	136
PPVT I.Q. 110 and Above								
Prescrbd.	74	53	19	37	44	15	30	118
Lessons not Prescrbd.	75	52	10	51	60	11	44	63
PPVT I.Q. 90-109								
Prescrbd.	61	36	7	33	46	10	23	135
Lessons not Prescrbd.	63	32	0	28	43	2	35	60
PPVT I.Q. 89 and Below								
Prescrbd.	41	15	0	7	20	5	10	41
Lessons not Prescrbd.	46	8	0	15	15	0	8	13

[a] Peabody Picture Vocabulary Test, Form A.

127

conserve at all in the kindergarten interviews, more in the program
without prescribed lessons became operational in the second grade interviews than was the case for their counterparts in the prescribed programs. However, they did not do as well as their fellows in the program
with no prescribed lessons who did conserve in kindergarten.

When performance in the post-test tasks is viewed according to
first grade conservation patterns (see Appendix C), there are several
differences favoring the group with no prescribed program but they are
not consistent over conservation patterns.

Comparisons of Matched Groups

To gain a picture of the effects of the programs on children of
equivalent ability and background, matched groups were set up. Matching
was done on the basis of sex, a range of three months in chronological
age, and six points in PPVT I.Q., and an equivalent number of conservation tasks correct at the kindergarten interviews. With these con-
straints, 26 children from each of the four instructional programs
(AAAS, SCIS, GCMP, No Prescribed Lessons) studied from the beginning of
kindergarten were selected.

The comparability of the socioeconomic status of each set of four
children was also examined. In the majority of cases the children were
in adjoining if not the same levels. In three cases, however, one of
the four children matched on sex, PPVT I.Q., and conservation status
differed from his counterparts by four or more levels in socioeconomic
status. Since the information regarding socioeconomic status had been
derived from school records that were sometimes subject to misinterpre-
tation, these discrepancies were disregarded.

Consideration was also given to the extent to which each of the
groups of 26 children represented the classes in its instructional program. Each of the kindergarten classes in the prescribed programs was
represented by at least one child. Two of the kindergarten classes not
having prescribed lessons were, however, not represented. The available
information for these classes gave no indication that they differed in
any important way from the classes that were represented.

Table 30 shows the number of children in each of the four matched
groups whose responses in the post-test tasks were operational. This
table indicates clearly that the children in the program where there
were no prescriptions for mathematics and science lessons were as competent in the post-test tasks as their counterparts in prescribed programs.

Comparisons Between Programs

The possibility that different prescribed programs may have different effects may be examined by comparing them one by one, or in groups
of two. The data for these comparisons are presented in Table 25 for
single programs. Data for combined programs, AAAS (GCMP) considered
together with SCIS (GCMP), are presented in Appendix C. Appendix C also
shows the data grouped on the basis of related variables.

Table 30

Number of Children in Four Instructional Programs,
Matched for Sex, C.A.,[a] I.Q.[b] and
Initial Status in Conservation,[c]
Giving Operational Responses in Post-Test Tasks

Program	N	Conservation of No. Wt.		Class Inclu- sion	Serial Ordering			Transi- tivity
					Seria- tion	Ordina- tion	Reorder- ing	
				Initiated in Kindergarten				
AAAS (GCMP)	26	19	15	2	6	12	1	14
SCIS (GCMP)	26	20	13	2	9	12	3	4
GCMP Only	26	10	8	2	9	12	4	4
No Pre- scribed Lessons	26	19	13	1	11	15	2	9

[a]Within three-month range.

[b]Within six-point range on Peabody Picture Vocabulary Test, Form A.

[c]Number of tasks correct.

Science and Mathematics vs. Mathematics Only

Both the AAAS and the SCIS groups who entered the study in kinder-garten had the GCMP mathematics program as well. To what extent was participation in both science and mathematics rather than only in mathe-matics associated with increased evidence of operational thinking in the post-test tasks?

Initial inspection of the data suggested that more children who participated in programs involving both science and mathematics were operational in the conservation and transitivity tasks than was the case for those who had had only mathematics. These differences tended to hold when related variables were considered. In contrast, the group having only the mathematics program appeared to do somewhat better on the serial ordering tasks. In the matched groups (see Table 30), as far as the conservation tasks are concerned, the superiority of the groups having both mathematics and science over those having only mathematics parallels the findings for the larger groups. The AAAS (GCMP) programs show a larger number of operational responses in the transitivity tasks,

as in the larger groups. However, the differences in the serial ordering tasks are less marked.

Another comparison of science and mathematics with mathematics only
may be made by examining the performances in the post-test tasks of
children who participated in the SCIS science program and in a mathematics program beginning in first grade and their counterparts who had
only the mathematics program. In this case the mathematics program
varied somewhat. Either the Greater Cleveland or the Addison-Wesley
program served as the text when one was used. Overall the differences
are minimal.

AAAS (GCMP) vs. SCIS (GCMP)

Since the two science programs had somewhat different emphases, it
may be asked whether or not the children participating in them differed
in their performances in the post-test tasks. Overall, the differences
are small except for the transitivity tasks, where a larger per cent of
children in the AAAS program are operational. The direction of the differences in the three kinds of serial ordering tasks favors the SCIS
program and tends to be maintained over the breakdowns by PPVT I.Q.

SCIS Initiated in Kindergarten vs. SCIS Initiated in First Grade

With the exception of their performance in the transitivity tasks,
the per cents of children who were operational in their thinking are
greater for those children who had the program in both kindergarten and
first grade. These differences tend to hold over the different PPVT
I.Q. groups.

GCMP Initiated in Kindergarten vs. Mathematics Initiated in First Grade

With the exception of their performance in the transitivity tasks,
larger per cents of children in the group that had a mathematics program
from kindergarten are operational in the post-test. The differences
tend to hold over PPVT I.Q. groups.

No Prescribed Lessons vs. Mathematics Only Beginning in First Grade

If more information were available regarding the kindergarten program of the children entering the study in 1966 who had a mathematics
program beginning in first grade, they might provide an interesting comparison group to those children who had no prescribed lessons in either
kindergarten or first grade. The direction of the differences between
the groups tends to favor the children having no prescribed lessons in
either kindergarten or first grade, even when PPVT I.Q. is taken into
account.

Program Emphases

The reader will recall that the analysis of the content of the
teacher's manuals for the prescribed programs (Chapter III) tentatively
suggested that the post-test performances of children who had the AAAS

program might be superior in the conservation, serial ordering and transitivity tasks, while those who had SCIS might excel in the class inclusion tasks. No prediction was made as to whether children in SCIS or GCMP would rank second in conservation, serial ordering and transitivity. However, the likelihood that those in AAAS would do better than those in GCMP in the class inclusion tasks was suggested.

The analysis of the manuals also suggested that the SCIS program and the GCMP programs emphasized the manipulation of objects somewhat more than did the AAAS program. However, observation in the classrooms (see Chapter IV) raised the possibility that in the GCMP program the children often observed the manipulation of objects or of pictured objects rather than actually handling them individually. Whether there were appreciable differences in the total amount of opportunity for action on objects in the various programs is not known. Piaget's theory suggests that those programs having greater opportunity for such action should, other things being equal, make more progress in logical thinking. On this basis one might predict that SCIS (GCMP) would be more effective than AAAS (GCMP), and it in turn better than GCMP alone. Whether the effects might be different for different tasks is also a matter for conjecture.

The fact that, on the whole, the children who had no prescribed lessons can be described as performing neither better nor worse than those who had one or more of the prescribed programs makes suspect any assertion of differences in specific tasks. Nevertheless, certain trends in the data may be noted.

On an overall basis, and in the matched groups, the children having both science and mathematics did somewhat better in the conservation tasks than those who had only mathematics. More children who had the AAAS program were operational in the transitivity tasks than was the case in the other prescribed programs. There is a slight tendency for more of the children who had SCIS and GCMP, or GCMP alone, to be operational in the serial ordering tasks than is the case for the children who had AAAS and GCMP. The number of children in any of the programs who were operational in the class-inclusion tasks is so small that the slight difference tending to favor the SCIS (GCMP) program deserves only passing mention.

Other Results

Matrix Tasks

The matrix tasks, according to Piaget, may be solved either perceptually or logically. The procedures used in the present study required the child to indicate verbally, after an opportunity for deliberation, which of several designs would appropriately complete the matrix. He was not permitted to place any of the cards into the matrix, but there is no way of ascertaining whether this may have guarded against a tendency to perceptual solution. In any case, the results of the matrix tests were not pooled with the measures of operational thinking.[1] They do, however, provide some interesting supplementary information, particularly as it relates to the relative emphasis on classification in the various programs.

The matrix tasks were scored in two different ways. A total score was given for the sum of the number of correct attributes the child had chosen in each of the eight tasks. A second score was given for the maximum number of attributes used in any of the tasks. Thus a child who correctly used three attributes in at least one task could be distinguished from the child who never used more than one or two attributes.

The means and standard deviations for total scores on the matrix tasks of children in various programs initiated in kindergarten are as follows:

Program	Mean	S.D.
AAAS (GCMP)	12.45	3.79
SCIS (GCMP)	13.02	4.11
GCMP only	13.34	3.96
No Prescribed Lessons	12.51	3.72

As in the other tasks, the performance of the children in prescribed programs is statistically not significantly different from that of the children who had no prescribed lessons.

The means and standard deviations of the total scores of the children who did not begin prescribed programs until the first grade are:

SCIS (Math)	11.67	3.75
Math only	11.53	3.49

As in most of the other tasks, the performance of these children is significantly poorer than that of the children beginning prescribed programs in kindergarten.

Table 31 shows for each of the matrices the per cent of children all of whose choices were correct. It will be noted that the number of children who can handle all of the matrices correctly is small. The differences between children in the various programs are also small. However, mention may be made of the fact that slightly more SCIS children are correct in all their choices, a finding that parallels the tendency for slightly more of them to be correct in all the class inclusion tasks.

The second score, maximum number of attributes in any of the matrix

---

[1]This decision accords with the judgment of Piaget's collaborators at Geneva. Personal communication from Hermione Sinclair, March, 1968.

Table 31

Per Cent of Second Grade Children Selecting All Correct Attributes
in Each of Eight Matrix Tasks

Programs	A Form, Color	B Form, Shading	C Form, Number	D Color, Dirctn.	E Form, Color, Dirctn.	F Form, Color, Dirctn.	G Form, Color, Dirctn.	H Form, Color, Size	All Tasks	No. of Chldrn.
				Initiated in Kindergarten						
AAAS (GCMP)	66	29	37	51	27	20	20	24	1	94[a]
SCIS (GCMP)	77	39	38	51	27	23	29	38	4	79
GCMP only	80	44	43	64	30	15	21	26	2	122
No Prescribed Lessons	72	29	36	54	27	18	20	23	1	136
				Initiated in First Grade						
SCIS (Math)	61	30	34	63	23	12	16	11	1	114
Math only	72	28	22	49	17	8	15	17	0	87
All Programs	71	33	36	56	25	16	20	23	2	632

[a]Includes six children who did not have AAAS program consistently.

tasks, gives some indication of the child's ability to handle complex information. Table 32 shows the number and per cent of children in each program using only one attribute in all the tasks, together with those who in at least one task used two, and those who at least once used three. As will be apparent in Chapter VII, certain trends in the data suggest that children who are able to use three attributes are most adept in the other post-test tasks as well.

Table 32

Number and Per Cent of Second Grade Children Using
Maximum of One, Two, or Three Attributes in the Matrix Tasks

Program	One Attribute		Two Attributes		Three Attributes	
	Number	Per Cent	Number	Per Cent	Number	Per Cent
Initiated in Kindergarten						
AAAS (GCMP)	6	6	47	50	41	44
SCIS (GCMP)	6	8	32	40	41	52
GCMP only	6	5	62	51	54	44
All Prescribed Programs	18	6	141	48	136	46
No Prescribed Lessons	11	8	62	46	62	46
Initiated in First Grade						
SCIS (Math)	10	9	69	60	35	31
Math only	5	6	52	60	30	34
Both Prescribed Programs	15	7	121	60	65	32

Performance of the children in the four groups that were matched for chronological age, PPVT I.Q., and conservation status in the kindergarten follows the direction found in the larger groups. The means and standard deviations for the matrix scores of these groups are as follows:

Program	Mean	S.D.
AAAS (GCMP)	12.62	2.46
SCIS (GCMP)	13.73	2.51
GCMP only	12.81	2.50
No Prescribed Lessons	11.08	2.46

The maximum number of attributes handled in the matrices follows the trend found in the analysis of the data from the larger groups. As Table 33 indicates, slightly more children in the SCIS program were able to use the maximum number of attributes correctly than was the case in the other programs.

Table 33

Maximum Number of Attributes Used Correctly in Matrix Tasks
by 26 Children in Each of Four Instructional Programs
Matched for Sex, Chronological Age,[a] I.Q.,[b]
and Initial Conservation Status[c]

	Number of Children Correctly Using		
Program	One Attribute	Two Attributes	Three Attributes
AAAS	2	12	12
SCIS	0	10	16
GCMP	1	16	9
No Prescribed Lessons	3	15	7

[a]Within 3-month range.

[b]Within 6-point range, on Peabody Picture Vocabulary Test, Form A.

[c]Number of tasks correct.

Longitudinal Data

Previous sections of this chapter have referred to the children's status in the conservation tasks in either kindergarten or first grade as a variable related to their performance in the post-test tasks. The repetition at successive interviews of the conservation and the class inclusion tasks also provided some measure of the progress the children made as they moved through kindergarten and first grade. This section considers the nature of the progress of the groups representing the various instructional programs, and also the progress made by individual children within those groups.

Conservation Tasks. Previous studies (Almy, Chittenden and Miller, 1966) had shown that the three tasks involving conservation of number after counting (task B), conservation of number without counting (task A), and conservation of a quantity of liquid (task C), were ordered in difficulty. In the main, children who were successful in task C, were also successful in tasks A and B, and those who were successful in task A, but not in task C, were successful in task B. A sequence of this sort conforms to the theory of Piaget.

Tables 34 and 35 show the number and per cent of children in each of the six programs whose performances fell into one of the four patterns, conserving in no task, conserving only in task B, conserving in both task A and task B but not in task C, and conserving in all three tasks, A, B, and C. These tables also show the number and per cent of the children whose performance did not fit these expected patterns.[1]

To the extent that the ability to conserve number is, as Piaget indicates, basic to the understanding of other concepts in mathematics and science, Tables 34 and 35 provide a picture of the different levels of understanding confronting the teachers in each of the groups at the initiation of the programs. They also provide a measure of the development of such understanding as the groups moved from kindergarten into first grade, and from first grade into second.

When the distributions of the children's performances according to the four regular or other patterns in each of the instructional programs are compared, differences are apparent. For example, in the beginning of kindergarten, fall 1965, the program having no prescribed lessons had more children who conserved in no tasks than did the other groups. However, this difference is not statistically significant. Nor are the differences significant at the first grade level. However, when the distributions of the patterns of performance for all six groups are examined at the first grade level, a chi square test (x^2 = 41.61 d.f. 20, $p < .005$) indicates that the distributions are not homogeneous. In comparing the first grade performance of those who entered the study in first grade with those who had participated since kindergarten, it is interesting to note that the performance of the former at first grade is less good than the performance of the latter. It is, however, clearly better than the kindergarten performance of those children who were initially interviewed in kindergarten. A year's increment in chronological age evidently makes a difference in performance.

The differences between the groups in which the study was initiated in kindergarten and those in which it did not begin until first grade are maintained at the second grade level. Again, there are no significant statistical differences among the distributions of patterns in the four groups beginning at kindergarten, nor between the two groups beginning in first grade, but a chi-square test applied to the distributions in the six groups indicates that they are not homogeneous (x^2 = 39.45 d.f. 20, $p < .01$). It appears that the groups who began the instructional programs at the first grade level made slower progress toward conservation in all the tasks than did their counterparts for whom participation in the study began earlier.

---

[1] In the previous study, where more longitudinal data were involved, these irregular patterns (12% of the total) were altered to fit the theoretical sequence. In the present study, for calculation of x^2, the irregular pattern of conservation in tasks B and C, but not A, was retained, other irregulars were omitted.

Table 34

Number and Per Cent of Children Studied in Kindergarten
and Again in First and Second Grades Revealing
Conservation in Three Tasks[a] in Successive Interviews

Tasks in which Children Conserved	Instructional Program							
	AAAS (GCMP)		SCIS (GCMP)		GCMP Only		No Prscrbd. Lessons	
	N	%	N	%	N	%	N	%
	Kindergarten Fall 1965							
None	32	36	33	42	48	39	58	44
Only B	34	38	20	25	48	39	46	35
Only B & A	10	11	10	13	10	8	11	8
B, A & C	7	8	6	8	8	7	5	4
Other Patterns	6	7	10	13	8	7	13	10
	First Grade Fall, 1966							
None	3	3	9	11	16	13	18	14
Only B	19	21	14	18	22	18	19	14
Only B & A	14	16	10	13	26	21	16	12
B, A & C	43	48	34	43	43	35	61	46
Other Patterns	10	11	12	15	15	12	19	14
	Second Grade Fall, 1967							
None	3	3	2	3	3	3	3	2
Only B	8	9	9	11	17	14	8	6
Only B & A	10	11	6	8	14	11	10	8
B, A & C	63	71	54	68	67	55	89	67
Other Patterns	5	6	8	10	21	17	23	17

[a] Task A: Conservation of the equality of two sets of blocks through two transformations.

B: Conservation of the number of a set of blocks that have been counted through two transformations.

C: Conservation of the equality of two quantities of water through one transformation.

137

Table 35

Number and Per Cent of Children First Studied in First Grade
and Then Again in Second Grade Revealing
Conservation in Three Tasks[a] in Successive Interviews

Tasks in which Children Conserved	Instructional Program			
	SCIS (Math)		Math only	
	N	%	N	%
	First Grade Fall, 1966			
None	20	17	16	18
Only B	30	26	22	25
Only B and A	21	18	17	20
B, A and C	26	23	20	23
Other Patterns	18	16	12	14
	Second Grade Fall, 1967			
None	4	4	4	5
Only B	21	18	20	23
Only B and A	20	17	14	16
B, A and C	52	45	39	45
Other Patterns	18	16	10	11

[a]
Task A: Conservation of the equality of two sets of blocks
through two transformations.

B: Conservation of the number of a set of blocks that
have been counted through two transformations.

C: Conservation of the equality of two quantities of water
through one transformation.

In contrast to Tables 34 and 35, showing the performances of the
same groups of children at successive time intervals, Tables 36 and 37
group the children according to the way the pattern in which an individual's performance falls at one interview is related to the pattern of
his performance at the succeeding interview. For example, the top
matrix in Table 36 shows that at the kindergarten interview there are
32 children in the AAAS group who are not conserving in any task. At
the first grade level the performances of these 32 children are spread
over the four regular patterns. Two are still not conserving in any
task, 16 only in task B, 4 in both task B and task A but not in any
other. Seven have reached pattern 4 and are conserving in all tasks.
Three fall into "other" patterns, perhaps conserving in B and C, or in
A alone, or even in C but not in B or A.

Again, using the AAAS group as an example, it is clear that the most typical transitions from kindergarten to first grade are from pattern 1, no conservation, to pattern 2, conservation only in task B (for 16 children), and from pattern 2 to pattern 4, conservation in all 3 tasks (for 20 children). Obviously, the fact that so many children move into the most advanced level in first grade limits the amount of movement (at least in these tasks) that can be made in second grade. Note that of the 43 children who have moved into pattern 4 in first grade, 38 remain there at the second grade interview, and 5 regress.

On the assumption that the effectiveness of a program may be measured by the rates of progress made in conserving, the distributions of changes from one pattern to another were examined. The distributions in the four regular patterns in first grade of those who had been in pattern 1 (no conservation) in kindergarten appeared rather similar. (Compare the first rows of the kindergarten-to-first-grade matrices of the four programs in Table 36.) A chi square test for homogeneity was not significant. However, the distributions of children whose performance started with pattern 2 appeared less similar. (Compare the second rows for each of the kindergarten-to-first-grade matrices in Table 36.) In the AAAS program, of the 34 children who were in pattern 2 in kindergarten, 20 (60%) reached pattern 4 in first grade. Similarly, 12 out of 20 (60%) of SCIS, and 27 out of 46 (58%) of those in the program with no prescribed lessons reached pattern 4. However, in the GCMP program only 20 out of 48 (42%) made similar progress. The number of children originally in pattern 3 in first grade was small in all programs. (Compare the third rows for each of the kindergarten-to-first-grade matrices in Table 36.) Accordingly, they were combined with the children who were originally in pattern 2 for purposes of a chi square analysis. For this analysis, children whose performances fell into patterns other than the four regular ones were not included. The differences in the two distributions were not significant (x^2 = 7.15, d.f. 3, p < .10).

Similar comparisons may be made for the distribution of performances in the second grade of children who had been in patterns 2 or 3 in first grade. (Compare the second and third rows of each of the first-to-second-grade matrices in Tables 36 and 37.) It will be noted that with the exception of the GCMP group the number of children in each of these patterns in first grade is quite similar. In the second grade a smaller per cent of the GCMP group have moved from patterns 2 and 3 to pattern 4 than is the case for the other programs. Chi square analysis of the distributions of the patterns of performance in second grade of the children who were in patterns 2 and 3 in the first grade (omitting those in patterns other than the four regular ones) showed a significant difference (x^2 = 12.77, d.f. 5, p < .05).

Table 38 shows the performance of children in the four matched groups. At the first grade interview it appears that children in the AAAS (GCMP) group and the group having only GCMP are moving somewhat more slowly than the children in the other groups. By second grade,

Table 36

Patterns of Conservation Abilities Revealed by Children
in Four Instructional Programs in Interviews
Repeated at Yearly Intervals from
Beginning Kindergarten to Beginning Second Grade

Markov Matrices

AAAS (GCMP) 89 Children						
Kindergarten	First Grade					
Pattern[a]	1	2	3	4	Other	Total
1	2	16	4	7	3	32
2	1	3	6	20	4	34
3	0	0	2	6	2	10
4	0	0	0	6	1	7
Other	0	0	2	4	0	6

First Grade	Second Grade					
Pattern[a]	1	2	3	4	Other	Total
1	2	0	0	1	0	3
2	0	5	3	10	1	19
3	0	1	3	9	1	14
4	0	0	3	38	2	43
Other	1	2	1	5	1	10

SCIS (GCMP) 79 Children						
Kindergarten	First Grade					
Pattern[a]	1	2	3	4	Other	Total
1	3	11	6	8	5	33
2	4	2	0	12	2	20
3	0	0	3	6	1	10
4	1	0	1	3	1	6
Other	1	1	0	5	3	10

First Grade	Second Grade					
Pattern[a]	1	2	3	4	Other	Total
1	0	3	2	3	1	9
2	1	4	2	7	0	14
3	1	0	1	7	1	10
4	0	0	1	29	4	34
Other	0	2	0	8	2	12

Table 36, Continued

	GCMP 122 Children					
Kindergarten	First Grade					
Pattern[a]	1	2	3	4	Other	Total
1	13	12	7	11	5	48
2	2	9	10	20	7	48
3	1	1	2	4	2	10
4	0	0	3	4	1	8
Other	0	0	4	4	0	8

First Grade	Second Grade					
Pattern[a]	1	2	3	4	Other	Total
1	1	5	2	5	3	16
2	2	9	2	6	3	22
3	0	1	2	16	7	26
4	0	1	6	29	7	43
Other	0	1	2	11	1	15

	No Prescribed Lessons 133 Children					
Kindergarten	First Grade					
Pattern[a]	1	2	3	4	Other	Total
1	13	11	10	15	9	58
2	3	7	3	27	6	46
3	1	0	1	8	1	11
4	0	0	1	3	1	5
Other	1	1	1	8	2	13

First Grade	Second Grade					
Pattern[a]	1	2	3	4	Other	Total
1	2	3	5	4	4	18
2	0	4	1	12	2	19
3	0	1	1	12	2	16
4	0	0	2	52	7	61
Other	1	0	1	9	8	19

[a] Pattern 1: Conservation in no task.
2: Conservation in task B only.
3: Conservation in only task B and task A.
4: Conservation in tasks B, A and C.

141

Table 37

Patterns of Conservation Abilities Revealed by Children
in Two Instructional Programs in Interviews
at Beginning of First Grade
and Beginning of Second Grade

Markov Matrices

	SCIS Math 115 Children					
First Grade			Second Grade			
Pattern[a]	1	2	3	4	Other	Total
1	2	5	5	6	2	20
2	2	9	6	9	4	30
3	0	4	4	8	5	21
4	0	1	2	21	2	26
Other	0	2	4	7	5	18

	Math Only 87 Children					
First Grade			Second Grade			
Pattern[a]	1	2	3	4	Other	Total
1	3	5	1	5	2	16
2	1	10	5	3	3	22
3	0	1	5	10	1	17
4	0	1	2	14	3	20
Other	0	3	1	7	1	12

[a] Pattern 1: Conservation in no task.
         2: Conservation in task B only.
         3: Conservation in only task B and task A.
         4: Conservation in tasks B, A and C.

however, only the GCMP group looks different from the others. This
corresponds to the overall trends for the programs.

Class Inclusion Tasks

In these four tasks the child was confronted with the problem of
judging the quantitative superiority of a superordinate class to its
subclasses under circumstances in which the two subclasses were unequal
in number (tasks using plastic fruit and wooden blocks), or originally
equal and then unequal in number (metal cars). The tasks were known to
be difficult for second-graders, but it was also known that second-
graders (but not kindergarten children) significantly improved their
performance after a period of training in classification (Miller, 1966).

Table 38

Number of Children in Matched Groups Studied in Kindergarten
and Again in First and Second Grades
Revealing Conservation in Three Tasks[a] in Successive Interviews.
(Groups Matched for Sex, Chronological Age,[b]
I.Q.,[c] and Initial Status in Conservation[d])

Tasks in Which Children Conserved	Kindergarten Fall, 1965	First Grade Fall, 1966	Second Grade Fall, 1967
AAAS (GCMP)			
None	11	1	1
Only B	11	6	1
Only B and A	3	7	4
B, A, and C	0	9	19
Other Patterns	1	3	1
SCIS (GCMP)			
None	11	2	1
Only B	9	2	0
Only B and A	4	5	3
B, A and C	0	15	20
Other Patterns	2	2	2
GCMP Only			
None	11	3	1
Only B	11	7	8
Only B and A	3	5	1
B, A and C	0	10	10
Other Patterns	1	1	6
No Prescribed Lessons			
None	11	2	0
Only B	11	2	1
Only B and A	3	5	3
B, A and C	0	13	19
Other Patterns	1	4	3

[a]Task A: Conservation of the equality of two sets of blocks through two transformations.

B: Conservation of the number of a set of blocks that have been counted, through two transformations.

C: Conservation of the equality of two quantities of water through one transformation.

[b]Within three-month range.

[c]Within six-point range on Peabody Picture Vocabulary Test, form A.

[d]Number of tasks correct.

Since the instructional programs included practice in classification it seemed likely that children who had had such practice would do better in the post-tests than those who had not, and possibly would begin to show improvement at the first grade level. It also seemed likely that a sequence of acquisition such as that found for the conservation tasks might appear.

The results were not as anticipated. Even at the second grade level half of the children were unable to succeed in the first and easiest task (see Appendix C). While at each of the three interviews there was some tendency for those who were correct in only one task to be successful in the first task, the other successes appeared to follow no particular pattern.

Discussion

The results of this study appear to pose a paradox. On the one hand, the children who participated in programs where prescribed instruction in mathematics and science was initiated at the kindergarten level performed somewhat better in the logical thinking tasks in the second grade than did the children whose participation in prescribed programs did not begin until first grade. Little is known about the latter children's kindergarten experience except that it has been described as "typical." On the other hand, the children participating in prescribed programs beginning in kindergarten did no better than their counterparts who participated in the study from the beginning of kindergarten but who had no prescribed lessons in kindergarten or in first grade.

These equivocal results suggest that the comparability of the groups of children, and more especially the comparability of their school experience, apart from the prescribed programs, needs further examination. If it can be demonstrated that the groups differ in ways not yet taken into account, or that the school experience provided for those who had no prescribed lessons had certain unique characteristics, the hypotheses may be generated for further testing and eventual resolution of the paradox.

Comparability of the Groups

Although it is true that the groups representing the various programs were drawn from different communities, and that the distribution of ability as measured by PPVT I.Q., and of socioeconomic status as measured by occupational level differed somewhat from group to group (see Tables 4 and 6 in Chapter II), the results that are cited also tend to hold when PPVT I.Q. is taken into consideration.

Since the measure of verbal ability was administered at the beginning of the kindergarten year to the children beginning the prescribed programs in kindergarten, and not until the beginning of the first grade to those children who did not begin the prescribed programs until first grade, there is no way of knowing whether the two groups were strictly comparable in kindergarten. However, their mean PPVT I.Q.'s did not differ significantly. On the other hand, it should be noted that the group beginning the prescribed programs in first grade presented a wider range in parental socioeconomic status than was the case for the group beginning the prescribed program in kindergarten.

The case for the comparability of the group that had no prescribed lessons in kindergarten or first grade to the group having prescribed programs beginning in kindergarten is less good. The mean PPVT I.Q. was significantly higher for the former, the range of socioeconomic status was limited. But in initial conservation status they gave no evidence of being advanced over the other groups.

Differences in socioeconomic status might affect performance in the post-test measures fairly directly, with children in the upper levels having more opportunity within the context of the family for experiences leading toward a logical view of the world. In addition, differences in socioeconomic status and differences in the distribution of verbal ability might also affect performance indirectly through the medium of the classes in which the children were taught. If these differences had these effects, then one would expect better performances overall from the groups with the largest proportion of parents having middle and high socioeconomic status. On this basis, the groups beginning the prescribed programs in kindergarten should do better than those beginning it in first grade, and the group with no prescribed lessons should do at least as well or possibly better than those with the prescribed program.

Although the results of the study do appear to follow these trends, they must be interpreted with great caution. The socioeconomic measure, derived from the reported occupations of the parents, provides only the roughest approximation of their status. As indicated in Chapter II, it gives no clue as to the intellectual climate of the homes, or the kind of teaching carried on there.

Comparability of Classes Within the Programs

None of the school systems involved in the study customarily engaged in any kind of intelligence or achievement testing prior to second grade, and as far as is known, no attempt was made to group children in any way homogeneously. Nevertheless, the constitution of neighborhoods, the bussing of children in some schools and not in others, underlines the possibility that the mixture of abilities and attitudes in some classes differed from that in others. It seems likely, moreover, that some programs, notably the one that had no prescribed lessons, and possibly AAAS, had less such variation than the others.

There were no marked variations in the number of children enrolled in the classes, nor in the length of the school day. However, some of the first grade classes in Englewood, where children did not participate until first grade, were organized in clusters so that one teacher might handle the mathematics or the science lessons for more than one group of children. Also, in Garden City, where there were no prescribed lessons, the first grade children, except when they were invited to return in the afternoons in small groups, ordinarily had a school day lasting four hours, instead of the four and a half that was typical in the prescribed programs. If an extra half hour of schooling were to have any effect, it would seem to weigh in favor of the classes having the prescribed lessons.

Reports from the classroom observers, from the interviewers, and from the teachers themselves (see Chapter IV) indicated that there was at least as much variation in classroom structure and atmosphere within the prescribed programs as between them. Classes in which there were no prescribed lessons also varied considerably in this regard.

As was noted earlier, no detailed information was available for the kindergarten classes for the children who did not enter the study until they were in first grade. Their kindergarten classrooms were never visited.

The Garden City kindergartens differed from all the others in the study in ways that may have influenced the outcome. First, they were identified as kindergartens that gave specific attention to science and mathematics concepts, although they had no prescribed lessons. Their teachers knew that they were involved in a study comparing the effects of prescribed instruction with the child-centered, loosely structured, informal activities they customarily included in their curriculum. Second, the teachers themselves were, by and large, more experienced and had more years of education, than the teachers in the kindergartens with prescribed programs. Third, the children in these classes had somewhat better verbal ability, and were more homogeneous socioeconomically.

Resolution of the Paradox

Some ways out of the paradox confronted in the beginning of this discussion may now be proposed. First the introduction of mathematical and scientific concepts in the curriculum of early childhood tends to facilitate the development of logical thinking. Such introduction is more efficacious when it occurs in kindergarten than when it is post-poned to first grade. However, experienced teachers familiar with and interested in the elementary concepts, planning activities around the children's interests, are as effective as teachers who use prescribed lessons.

This resolution of the paradox assumes that the kindergarten program will have intellectual content. It does not resolve questions having to do with the relative effectiveness of experienced teachers with prescribed programs versus experienced teachers with little familiarity with the concepts. (In the present instance it appears that those who taught the classes having no prescribed lessons had had considerably

146

more opportunity to familiarize themselves with modern mathematics programs than with comparable science programs.) Nor does it throw any light on the question of the effectiveness of the inexperienced teacher with or without a good knowledge of mathematics and science.

This proposed resolution assumes that the experience and education of the teachers is a primary factor in the outcome in the second grade. It overlooks another factor that may have more significance than is immediately apparent. Considering that only a small portion of the kindergarten-first grade curriculum is modified by the introduction of prescribed lessons, it is perhaps unrealistic to expect any major effects on the children's thinking. When there are no prescribed lessons, the teacher has, if she chooses to take advantage of the situation, both more freedom and more time to follow the individual interests of the children. If she takes advantage of this, any problem she poses, or whatever explanation she makes, is more likely to have the full attention of the child than is the case when there is a lesson that must be covered. The notion that the competence and interest of an experienced teacher is essential to the development of logical thinking in the young child has considerable appeal.

The apparent paradox in the finding that children having prescribed lessons in kindergarten did better than those starting in first grade, but no better than those who had no prescribed lessons but were studied from kindergarten may be resolved another way. This resolution views the apparent kindergarten-first grade differences as spurious. It takes account of the fact that the children studied from the time they were in kindergarten had additional opportunity to accustom themselves to being interviewed, and consequently were better able to adapt to the interviewers in the post-test tasks at the second grade level. It will be recalled, however, that the first grade performances of the children being interviewed for the second time was clearly better than the initial performance of the latter. Furthermore, they were interviewed somewhat later in the fall semester than was the case for the other children. Accordingly, it seems unlikely that the kindergarten-first grade differences can be attributed primarily to familiarity with the interview procedures.

A third resolution of the paradox, one that might be espoused by proponents of Piaget's theories, suggests that the kindergarten-first grade difference is an artifact, not of the familiarity of the children with the procedures, but rather of the timing of the post-test tasks. According to this view, the standardization of the tasks and their administration when the operations of conservation, classification, and serial ordering are not firmly established but still in formation inevitably increase the probability of falsely designating a child as operational in a particular task when he has not yet really achieved that level. To a lesser extent one may also err in the opposite direction. This resolution of the paradox will be discussed at the end of Chapter VII, where the relationships among the post-test tasks are examined.

147

THE RESULTS: FROM THE VIEWPOINT OF PIAGETIAN THEORY

The analysis of the post-test performance of the children in the various instructional programs has highlighted their variability. At least for the seven-year-old, who is just beginning the shift into operational thinking, the ability to think logically in one kind of task is no guarantee of such ability in another.

According to Piaget, progress toward operational thought comes with "articulated intuition" in which the consequences of action can be anticipated and previous states reconstituted. But there is not yet reversibility. If a spatial arrangement is changed, the child does not mentally put the elements back in their original order. "However, the beginnings of anticipation and reconstitution prepare for reversibility. They constitute a regulation of the initial intuition and this regula- tion prepares for the operations" (Piaget, 1967, p. 33).

The protocols of the present study are replete with instances of this kind of intuitive thinking. They provide far fewer examples of intuitions transformed to the systems of operations or "groupings" than Piaget postulates for the age of seven.

> It is remarkable to see the formation of a whole series
> of these groupings by children at about age seven. They
> transform the intuitions into operations of all kinds
> and explain the transformation of thinking described
> earlier. Above all, it is striking to see how these
> groupings are formed, often very rapidly, through a sort
> of total reorganization. No operation exists in an iso-
> lated state; it is always formed as a function of the
> totality of operations of the same kind. For example, a
> logical concept of class (combination of individuals) is
> not constructed in an isolated state but necessarily
> within a classification of the grouping of which it forms
> a part. A logical family relation (brother, uncle, etc.)
> is constituted only as a function of a set of analogous
> relations whose totality constitutes a system of relation-
> ships. Numbers do not appear independently of each other
> (3, 10, 2, 5, etc.); they are grasped only as elements
> within an ordered series: 1,2,3...,etc. Likewise,
> values exist only as a function of a total system or "scale
> of values." An asymmetric relationship such as $B < C$ is
> intelligible only in relation to the possible seriation
> of the set $0 < A < B < C < D...$, etc. What is even more
> remarkable is that these systems of sets are formed only
> in the child's thinking in connection with the precise
> reversibility of the operations, so that they acquire a def-
> inite and complete structure right away. (Piaget, 1967, p. 49)

In several of his books (for example, <u>The Child's Conception of Number</u>, <u>The Early Growth of Logic</u>, <u>The Psychology of Intelligence</u>), Piaget has discussed the interrelatedness of the four kinds of operations investigated in the present study--conservation, serial ordering, classification and transitivity. Using clinical methods, and not necessarily using the same children to investigate each kind of operation, he has established a sequence of stages for the order of acquisition of each operation. It should be noted that most of his data have been cross-sectional rather than longitudinal.

The procedures in the present study were standardized rather than clinical. The tasks, with the exception of the matrices, were not exact replicas but they were clearly comparable to those used by Piaget. Since each of the children in the study was presented with all the tasks, the data provide good opportunity to investigate the interrelationships among the developing operations. The children's performances in tasks such as those used for conservation and serial ordering can be arranged according to the difficulty of the tasks to see whether or not the stages described by Piaget emerge. While most of the data are not longitudinal the fact that the conservation and also the class inclusion tasks were presented in kindergarten (to a majority of the children) and in first grade as well as in second grade permits study of the development of those operations.

In Chapter VI, we dealt with the question of the relationships among the tasks and to some extent also with the question of sequence. In the present chapter the data from all the groups are pooled. The relationships among tasks that represent similar operations are examined in greater detail. The comprehensive view of the thinking processes of the young second-grader that emerges from this examination puts the results reported in Chapter VI in a new perspective.

Conservation

As indicated in Chapter VI, the children's performance in the conservation tasks involving number and quantity suggested considerable orderliness in the acquisition of the operation. When the data from Tables 34 and 35 in Chapter VI are pooled, two findings are highlighted. One is the extent of variation, as indicated by instances where the child handles a difficult task correctly but misses an easier one, or where he appears to have the concept at one interview and misses it at the next. Such variation may be regarded, at least in part, as a concomitant of the standardized procedure.

Contrasting with the variation is the obvious regularity of most of the patterns of performance, and the shifts from one pattern to another at subsequent interviews. The process is clearly not deterministic. The fact that the child has arrived at pattern three, conserving in both number tasks, is no guarantee that at the next interview he will have arrived at pattern four, conserving in both the number and the quantity of liquid tasks. Rather the process may be described as stochastic. If at first grade his performance falls in pattern three, the chances are only 6 in 10 that he will move to pattern four at the next, second grade interview. If, on the other hand he has reached pattern four at first grade, the chances of his remaining there at the next interview are 8 in 10.

According to Piaget's theory, children who are able to conserve number and quantity may or may not be able to conserve weight. Children who can conserve weight should, however, be able to conserve number and quantity. Thus it should be possible to extend the patterns of conservation to include the weight task. The reader may recall from Chapter VI (Table 24) that second grade performance in the conservation tasks used in the longitudinal parts of the study as related to performance in the conservation of weight showed a higher correlation (phi coefficient, .32) than was found for any other two tasks. Prior to discussion of this relationship, however, the nature of the conservation of weight tasks needs consideration.

In order to have his performance in the weight tasks classified as operational, the child had not only to assert that the weight had not changed in each of the three transformations, but he also had to give at least one clear explanation in response to the question, "How can you tell?" Further, he did not receive credit for such an explanation if either of his other two explanations indicated non-conservation or uncertainty.

Examination of the content of the children's responses indicates that the successive transformations are disruptive to continuous understanding of the equality of the two balls of clay. The following example of a youngster whose answer seems to arrive at conservation _after_ the third transformation indicates why a conserving answer is meaningless without a clear explanation.

Task A
    First transformation. "The red is more....It's rolled like a hot dog, it's heavier because it's thick and long."
Task B
    Second transformation. "The blue is more....It's skinnier now, when it's skinny it gets lighter."
Task C
    Third transformation. "They are the same....The blue is taken apart and once it's taken apart it is lighter and the red is the same thing."

Table 39 reflects the difficulty the seven-year-old has in maintaining a concept in the face of perceptual change and repeated questioning. The number of children giving _clear_ evidence of conservation in both answers and in explanations decreases after the second and third transformations.

Table 39

Number[a] and Per Cent of Second Grade Children Giving Evidence
of Conservation in Answers[b] and Explanations[c]
in Conservation of Weight Tasks[d]

Conservation in		Task A		Task B		Task C	
Answer	Explanation	N	%	N	%	N	%
None	None	181	29	231	37	216	34
Clear	None	31	5	23	4	40	6
Clear	Uncertain	11	2	5	1	79	13
Clear	Probable	102	16	87	14	100	16
Clear	Clear	301	48	283	45	193	31
All Tasks		627	100	630	99	630	100

[a] Children who failed to respond in a particular task are not
included in the totals.

[b] "Does one of these weigh more?"

[c] "How can you tell?"

[d] Equality of weight of two balls of PlayDoh when in Task A one is
elongated, in Task B it is further elongated, and in Task C the other
ball is broken into smaller pieces.

The three-fold repetition of the question, "How can you tell?"
placed a considerable demand on the child's ability to justify his own
thinking. In this respect the procedure somewhat resembles the clinical
inquiry of Piaget. However, the interviewer in the standardized procedure is not free to vary the objects used in the tasks, or to pose the
questions differently. When a child starts out with a conserving answer
and explanation and shifts to an inadequate explanation in one or both
of the ensuing tasks, the interviewer assumes that he is responding to
the transformation that confuses him. The child, of course, may change
his explanation in the belief that it is for some reason unsatisfactory
to the adult.

To return to the question of whether the patterns of conservation
obtained from the longitudinal data can be extended to include the conservation of weight, Table 40 shows performance in the weight tasks in
relation to the conservation patterns for number and quantity. Seventy-
nine per cent of the 212 children who were scored as "operational" in the
weight tasks conserved in all the other conservation tasks. Of the 412
children who were not scored as "operational" in the weight tasks,
47 per cent did conserve in all the other conservation tasks.

Table 40

Conservation of Weight[a] Performance for
624 Second Grade Children Revealing Different Patterns
of Conservation Ability in Number Tasks[b]

Tasks in Which Children Conserved	Performance in Weight Tasks			
	Not Operational (65%)		Operational[c] (35%)	
	N	%	N	%
None	20	5	0	0
Only B	83	20	4	2
Only B and A	58	14	16	7
B, A and C	192	47	176	79
Other Patterns	59	14	26	12
All Patterns	412	100	212	100

[a] Equality of weight of two balls of Play-Doh through three transformations.

[b] Task A: Conservation of the equality of two sets of blocks through two transformations.
B: Conservation of the number of a set of blocks that have been counted, through two transformations.
C: Conservation of the equality of two quantities of water through one transformation.

[c] "Operational" defined as three conserving answers and at least one conserving explanation.

Considering that 176 of the 368 children who were operational in all three number tasks were also conserving in weight, one might say that at the beginning second grade level the probabilities are not quite five out of ten that children conserving in all number tasks can also conserve weight.

This sort of substantiation of Piaget's theory intrigues the educator, for it suggests that a development order can be placed on the presentation of at least some of the concepts children must acquire. It also suggests the feasibility of assessment procedures designed to reveal when a particular concept is likely to be acquired with the least instructional effort. Conceivably, however, conservation concepts may be unique in the ease with which they can be ordered and assessed. Information regarding the sequence of acquisition of other concepts is much needed.

The Serial Ordering Tasks

Three kinds of tasks were involved in serial ordering. In seriation tasks (A, monkeys, and B, balloons) the child arranged first six, and then eight items in order according to their size. In the first set of ordination tasks he identified which balloon belonged to a particular monkey after the perceptual correspondence between the balloons and the monkeys had been displaced. The second set of ordination tasks posed the same problem but with sets of items (knives and forks) that had both been put into serial order and correspondence by the interviewer. The reordering tasks applied first to the balloons and later to the knives. In both instances one series (monkeys, forks) was left intact, while the other (balloons, knives) was scrambled, and the child was required to identify the proper correspondence for a specified item.

The expectation that children might find the seriation tasks easier than the ordering tasks, and the ordering tasks easier than those involving reordering, arose from Piaget's discussion of the transition from "serial correspondence to ordinal correspondence." He notes that three stages appear:

> In the first, the child loses all idea of correspondence as soon as one of the series is displaced and merely chooses the elements that are opposite one another. In the second stage, he tries to discover the correct correspondence either by empirical means or by counting, but he constantly confuses the right position with that of the preceding term. In the third stage, however, he solves the problem by coordinating his estimate of the required position with that of the cardinal value of the sets in question. (Piaget, 1941, Conception of Number, pp. 106-107)

The child who can consistently respond at the level of the third stage in tasks involving reconstruction considers each element "both as an element of a class and of a relationship, not alternatively and separately . . . but simultaneously, forming one and the same operational whole" (Piaget, 1941, p. 120). Numerically, the operations of classes and relations are represented in cardination and ordination.

Piaget warns, however, that the sequence he describes may not always hold.

> It is obvious that in each test a considerable number of heterogeneous factors intervene, e.g., the words used, the length of the instructions given, their more or less concrete character, the relationship between the instructions and the individual experience of the child, the number of elements involved, the intervention of numbers the child knows, etc. We noticed wide differences in the results of the various tests of cardinal correspondence,

showing that we never succeed in measuring understanding
of this correspondence in its pure state and that the
understanding is always with respect to a given problem
and given material. The calculation of the correlation
between the levels of cardination and ordination, without
the accompaniment of an extremely thorough qualitative
analysis, could therefore give only misleading results,
unless our experiments were transformed into "tests" in
which statistical precision could no doubt easily be
obtained, but at the cost of no longer knowing exactly
what was being measured.(Piaget, 1941, p. 149)

Relationships Among the Tasks

In the present study, as has been noted, the children performed
somewhat better in the ordination tasks than in the seriation tasks.
The reordering tasks were clearly the most difficult. Despite Piaget's
caveat against attempts at correlation, it is interesting to examine the
extent to which individual children revealed operational thinking in the
three kinds of tasks.

In Table 41 only those children whose solutions were correct
throughout each of the kinds of tasks are classified as operational.
As indicated earlier, this kind of scoring eliminated children whose
responses were transitional. Each of the kinds of tasks may also be
examined separately to see how extensive such responses were.

Table 41

Patterns of Operational Performance in
Serial Ordering Tasks of Second Grade Children

Tasks in Which Operational Thinking Was Revealed	No. of Children	Per Cent
None	282	53
Only Ordination	133	25
Only Seriation	70	13
Ordination and Seriation	82	15
Ordination, Seriation and Reordering	24	5
Other Patterns	38	7
All Tasks	629	100

Seriation Tasks

The maximum score possible for the first seriation task was 12, and for the second, 18. The scores in the first task (A, six items) ranged from 5 to 12, and in the second task (B, eight items) from 5 to 18. In both cases the scores tended to cluster toward the top. The median score for task A was 11.71 and for task B, 16.71. Sixty-two per cent of the children received the top score in task A, 37 per cent the top score in task B, and 30 per cent had top scores in both tasks.

Ordination Tasks

The ordination tasks called for three responses for each of the corresponding series of monkeys and balloons and knives and forks. Table 42 shows the number of correct responses given for each of the two sets. The slightly better performance on the second series may reflect familiarity with the task. The differences in the ordinal position of the items in the two series (3, 6 and 9 for the first series; 4, 7 and 8 for the second) seem insufficient to account for any differences in performance.

Table 42

Number and Per Cent of Correct Responses Given by
Second Grade Children in Six Ordination Tasks

Number of Correct Responses	Series			
	Monkeys-Balloons		Knives-Forks	
	No. of Children	Per Cent	No. of Children	Per Cent
None	63	10	22	3
One	85	13	54	9
Two	154	24	160	25
Three	331	52	397	63
All Responses	633	99	633	100

Table 43 relates performance in the seriation tasks to performance in the ordination tasks. The children have been arranged in groups according to the number of correct responses they gave to the six ordination questions. For each group the median seriation score is presented. For this purpose the ordination responses made in the monkey-balloon series were pooled with those in the knife-fork series. The seriation tasks were treated separately. The development of the two abilities is not precisely parallel, but close.

155

Table 43

Median Scores in Each of Two Seriation Tasks
of Second Grade Children Giving Different Numbers
of Correct Responses in Six Ordination Tasks

Ordination Tasks			Seriation Tasks	
No. of Correct Responses	No. of Children	Per Cent	Task A (Six Items) Median Score (Range 5-12)	Task B (Eight Items) Median Score (Range 5-18)
Zero	8	1	11.8	15.0
One	23	4	10.6	13.4
Two	33	5	11.1	14.6
Three	54	9	11.6	14.7
Four	90	15	11.7	16.7
Five	149	25	11.5	16.5
Six	250	41	11.8	17.5
All Responses	607	100	11.7	16.8

Some children did rather well in the seriation tasks and performed rather poorly in the ordination tasks. In these instances the seriation task was probably solved intuitively rather than operationally. Such an intuitive or global approach, as Piaget has demonstrated, breaks down when applied to the ordination problem. It also breaks down when applied to a more difficult seriation task. The median scores for the second and more difficult seriation problem are spread further apart than is the case for the easier seriation task.

Reordering Tasks

The reordering tasks were more demanding than the ordination tasks. After a series that had been placed in one-to-one correspondence with another series was scrambled, fewer children were able to identify correctly items that were in correspondence than was the case when one of the series was merely moved in space. Similarly, the fact that a child can form a series and set up a correspondence with another series gives no sure guarantee, at the ages tested, that he can make a correct identification of corresponding items after one series has been scrambled. There was, however, some evidence that performance in these tasks improved with practice. In the first reordering task, 116 children, or 18 per cent, responded correctly. In the second task, however, 258, or 41 per cent, responded correctly. But only 62 children, or 9 per cent, responded correctly in both tasks.

To examine the relationships between performance in the reordering tasks and the seriation tasks, median seriation scores were calculated for children who were successful and for those who were unsuccessful in each of the reordering tasks. In both tasks the median scores were only slightly higher for those who succeeded than for those who did not.

In Table 44, the performance of children in the reordering tasks is related to their performance in the ordination tasks. The children have been grouped according to the number of correct responses in ordination, and the number and per cent who responded correctly in each of the reordering tasks is presented for each group. It can be seen that overall the per cents of children succeeding in the reordering tasks increase as the scores in ordination increase.

Table 44

Number and Per Cent of 629 Second Grade Children
Responding Correctly in Reordering Tasks
Who Had Different Numbers of Correct Ordination Responses

Ordination		Reordering			
No. of Correct Responses	Children Number	Task A (Monkeys) Chldrn.Rspdg.Correctly		Task B (Knives) Chldrn.Rspdg.Correctly	
		Number	Per Cent	Number	Per Cent[a]
Zero	9	1	11	3	33
One	25	1	4	7	28
Two	36	4	11	10	28
Three	60	6	10	20	33
Four	92	13	14	37	40
Five	154	26	17	70	45
Six	253	65	26	111	44

[a] Based on total succeeding and not succeeding for the specified number of correct performances in ordination.

Table 44 also suggests the necessity for caution in interpreting data such as these. On the basis of the figures for the first reordering task alone, the probability that a child succeeding in all of the ordination tasks will succeed in reordering appears small but is greater than if he succeeds in only four or five of the ordination tasks. However, the additional information provided by the second reordering task indicates that those who succeed in four and five ordination tasks are as likely to succeed in reordering as those who succeed in six.

Clearly, as Piaget contends, a variety of factors influence each child's performance in the serial ordering performance. Experience with the interview procedures is one such factor. Experience in and out of school may also be important in the age period covered in this study. A child may become quite adept at a particular task, using the number line, for example, but his demonstrated success in that provides no guarantee that he may not fumble when he confronts the problem of ordering in a new context.

In this connection it may be worth noting that in preparing the various analyses of the data, the investigators often had the impression that the children's performance in the serial ordering tasks and also in the transitivity tasks was somewhat less consistent and less predictable on the basis of PPVT I.Q. or conservation level or program of instruction than was the case in the other tasks.

Transitivity Tasks

When the post-tests were being constructed, the transitivity tasks were thought to tap abilities similar to but more advanced than those involved in the serial ordering tasks. The transitivity tasks involve the logic of relations, as do the serial ordering tasks. Since the comparisons were to be made on the basis of length, they were similar to the comparisons made in the serial ordering tasks. But there are other important elements in the tasks.

One such element is the fact that the child must maintain his grasp of the relationships between the two sticks, A and C, and the measuring stick, B, against an illusion that distorts those relationships. From this point of view the task is not dissimilar to that involved in the conservation tasks. A second important element is that after each statement of his judgment, the child was asked, "How can you tell?" The scoring allowed full credit if the child made the correct judgment each time but justified it only once. Interviewers in the present study suggested that from the child's point of view, the repetition of the request for justification may challenge his understanding of the relationship among the sticks as the conservation questions challenge his understanding of the effects of transformation.

It may be argued that the appropriate conservation tasks to be compared with these transitivity tasks would be ones involving the conservation of length. This is certainly true. However, Piaget in discussing the transitivity of equivalence (A= B, B = C: A = C) notes: "Broadly speaking, it can be said that children who fail to understand composition of relations of equivalence also fail to grasp one-one correspondence, whereas those who understand one-one correspondence are at once able to compose several relations" (Piaget, 1941, pp. 204-205). In the present instance the transitivity tasks deal with inequalities, and in line with current findings related to the conservation of inequalities (Brison, 1966 ; Davol et al., 1967), are perhaps easier than tasks involving equalities. Accordingly, it seems reasonable to expect that children who have achieved conservation of number, an operation based on an understanding of one-one correspondence, will be more likely to be operational in the transitivity tasks.

The method of scoring the transitivity tasks used in the present study may be regarded as stringent. In the Smedslund (1963) study, from which the testing procedures of the present study were derived, the scoring was somewhat less stringent. Credit for transitivity was given in that study if the child gave four correct judgments and/or at least one correct explanation. In the present study, one explanation as well as all judgments had to be correct. Table 45 shows the performance of the children in each of the four tasks. The number of children making correct judgments and giving correct explanations increases as the tasks proceed. But study of the individual performances indicates that the number of children who are consistent across all the tasks is not as large. Of 160 children who were scored clearly operational (four correct judgments and one adequate explanation), only 90 gave correct judgments and explanations in all four tasks. The remainder, although they gave four correct judgments, gave from one to three correct explanations. Another 84 children, who were not scored as operational, gave judgments in each of the four tasks, but no correct explanation.

Table 45

Performance of 633 Second Grade Children
in Each of Four Transitivity Tasks

| Task | Number of Children with Designated Performance | | |
	Incorrect Judgment and Explanation	Correct Judgment and Inadequate Explanation or No Explanation	Correct Judgment and Adequate Explanation
A	336	152	145
B	283	203	147
C	263	213	157
D	254	203	176

Relationship of Transitivity to Serial Ordering

About half of the children (347 out of 629) were operational in at least one of the serial ordering tasks, while only 160 children were scored operational in the transitivity tasks. However, as may be seen in Table 46, 29 per cent of the children who were operational in the transitivity tasks were not operational in any of the serial ordering tasks. It is also interesting to note that while relatively few (24) children were operational in all three of the serial ordering tasks,

they were divided about equally on the transitivity tasks, 13 being
operational and 11 not operational.

Table 46

Patterns of Performance in Three Kinds of Serial Ordering
Tasks for 629 Second Grade Children
Who Were Scored Operational and Not Operational
in Transitivity Tasks

| Performance in Serial Ordering | Performance in Transitivity Tasks | | | |
| | Operational | | Not Operational | |
	No. of Children	Per Cent	No. of Children	Per Cent
Operational in				
No task	46	29	236	50
Ordination only	42	26	91	19
Seriation only	19	12	51	11
Ordination and seriation only	30	19	52	11
Ordination, seriation and reordering	13	8	11	2
Other patterns	10	6	28	6
All Patterns	160	100	469	99

Relationship of Transitivity to Conservation

A somewhat similar picture emerges as far as the relationship with
conservation is concerned. However, the reader may recall (Table 24,
Chapter VI) that the correlation between conservation and transitivity
scores is higher than it is for any of the other tasks. One hundred
twenty-two, or 76 per cent, of the children who were operational in the
conservation of number tasks were also operational in the transitivity
tasks. But there were 24 per cent who did not meet the criterion for
operational thinking in conservation and who did meet it in transitivity.

It is interesting to note that while 122 children were operational
in both the conservation of number and the transitivity tasks, 104 children (Table 46) were optional in both the transitivity tasks and in
one or more of the serial ordering tasks. However, when the patterns of
performance across all three kinds of tasks were examined (see the discussion of overall performance for all programs in Chapter VI), only

55 children who were operational in the transitivity tasks were found to be also operational in both the conservation of number and one or more of the serial ordering tasks. Of these 55, only 16 were also conserving in weight. These findings offer some support for the notion that children might handle the transitivity tasks presented in this study either as problems related to serial ordering or as conservation problems.

Classification Tasks

Two kinds of tasks tapped the children's ability to classify--the matrices and the class-inclusion problems.

Piaget's studies have indicated that the matrix tasks may be solved by four-and five-year-olds. The class-inclusion tasks are difficult even for the older children. Thus it might be said that these measures tap the extremes of classification ability for the age period encompassed by the study. However, the possibility that solution of the matrices at the earlier levels may derive from a perceptual matching procedure not involving a conception of a class of objects somewhat limits the usefulness of the matrix tasks.

Adequate assessment of classification, according to Piaget, would include some means of appraising the child's grasp of both extension (definition of the members of a given class) and intension (the properties common to its members). Coordination of these two aspects of classification involves both retroaction (hindsight), keeping in mind the way in which a collection or class was started, and anticipation (foresight), looking ahead to either more comprehensive classes, or to finer divisions of those already formed (Inhelder and Piaget, 1964, pp. 282-287).

Both the matrix tasks and the class-inclusion tasks furnish evidence on these kinds of processes. In the matrix tasks, the comments the children made in response to the question "How can you tell?" provided supplementary information to the cards they selected. However, since the interviews were rather long, and many of the children not inclined to make explanations, the data in the present study were not as complete as one would like for these tasks. In contrast, the explanations in the class-inclusion tasks may be analyzed for evidence as to the way the child arrived at his conclusion. This kind of analysis has not yet been completed.

Matrix Tasks

The matrix tasks, as Table 47 shows, vary in difficulty. The three-attribute tasks, as one would anticipate, appear to be slightly harder than the two-attribute tasks.

The children's total scores in the matrix tasks may be related to their performance in the seven other kinds of post-test tasks (see Appendix C, Table 2). While there was much variation in performance on

these other tasks, it is clear that a larger per cent of children who
scored at the mean (12.4) or above in the matrices were operational
in their thinking than was the case for those scoring below the mean.

A child could score as much as 16 without ever using three attributes. Accordingly, it seemed that the score representing the maximum
number of attributes used might provide a better clue to the level of
the child's thinking than did the total score. All the children with
scores of 17 or above also had a score of 3 for maximum attributes. But
there are also children with scores of less than 16 who may have a score
of 3 for maximum attributes.

Table 47

Means and S.D.'s of Number of Attributes Correctly Used
in Eight Matrix Tasks by 629 Second Grade Children

Task Attributes		Mean	S.D.
		Two-Attribute Tasks	
A	form/color	1.69	.52
B	form/shading	1.17	.68
C	form/number	1.22	.67
D	color/direction	1.45	.69
		Three-Attribute Tasks	
E	form/color/direction	1.84	.82
F	form/color/direction	1.75	.75
G	form/color/direction	1.78	.91
H	form/color/size	1.78	.81

Table 48 shows the relationships between the level of functioning
in the matrix tasks and success in the other tasks. The relationship to
the two most difficult of the other tasks, reordering and class inclusion, is noteworthy.

Class Inclusion Tasks

The class inclusion tasks, like the conservation tasks, were presented to all of the children in the study at interviews in both the first
and second grades. A majority of the children were also interviewed
in the kindergarten. Table 49 shows the per cent of both groups who were
correct in each of the tasks at each of the successive interviews. The
table emphasizes the difficulty of these tasks for second-graders as well

162

Table 48

Per Cent of 628 Second Grade Children Operational and
Not Operational in Post-Test Tasks
Grouped According to the
Maximum Number of Attributes Used in Matrix Tasks

	Per Cent Using Designated Number of Attributes			
Post-Test Tasks	One Attribute	Two Attributes	Three Attributes	No. of Children
Conservation				
Operational	05	42	53	365
Not Operational	10	63	27	263
Conservation of Weight				
Operational	04	42	54	222
Not Operational	09	56	35	406
Class-Inclusion				
Operational	00	32	68	50
Not Operational	08	53	40	578
Seriation				
Operational	04	34	63	188
Not Operational	08	59	33	440
Reordering				
Operational	03	31	66	62
Not Operational	07	53	39	566
Transitivity				
Operational	04	44	51	171
Not Operational	08	54	38	457

as for kindergartners and first-graders. The findings parallel those of
Kofsky (1966),who found this kind of task to be next to the most difficult of eleven experimental tasks set up to test the developmental sequence for classification as described by Piaget. Nineteen per cent of
the seven-year-olds in Kofsky's study were successful. However, the
number of items in her tasks was smaller than in task D in the present
study and none involved alteration of the relationships as did task D.

163

Table 49

Per Cent of Children Succeeding in Each of
Four Class Inclusion Tasks in Successive Interviews

Task	Fall, 1965	Fall, 1966	Fall, 1967
	Per Cent of 431 Children Interviewed Three Times		
Fruit	20	41	51
Blocks	6	16	25
Cars	6	21	45
Added Cars	3	10	23
	Per Cent of 202 Children Interviewed Twice		
Fruit		32	48
Blocks		7	13
Cars		13	31
Added Cars		6	18

Both the matrix tasks and the class inclusion tasks may be studied
for evidence of what might be called individual style. The interviewers
noted that some children made immediate judgments and revised them,
while others were inclined to stick by their original assertions. In
the class inclusion tasks, the length and the complexity of the answers
also reflected individuality. Inhelder and Piaget (1964) have commented
that "there is bound to be a good deal of variation between individuals
(and much of this variation may well be due to differences of character
rather than cognitive differences)" (p. 287).

Discussion

Although the primary intent of this study is not to uphold or
negate the tenets of Piaget's theory, the results presented in this
chapter shed some light on certain persistent issues. These issues have
some theoretical interest as well as pertinence to pedagogical application.

As the recent volume of research based on Piaget's theory, <u>Logical
Thinking in Children</u>, edited by Sigel and Hooper (1967), points out, two
of the central themes in the theory are the invariance of the stages and
the hierarchical and integrative nature of cognitive growth. The papers
in that volume offer better support for invariance than for integration
(p. 505). This is also true for the results in the present study,
although, as suggested at the end of Chapter VI, those of decided

Piagetian persuasion can argue that the lack of support for integration stems from the nature and the timing of the interviews.

Support for the notion of invariance in the acquisition of operational concepts is strongest in the conservation tasks, where the children, by and large, conserved number in relation to blocks before they conserved quantity in relation to liquid, and both of these before they conserved weight. In the serial ordering tasks, for which there are no longitudinal data, reordering was clearly more difficult than seriation or ordination. The class-inclusion tasks, for which there are longitudinal data, were not clearly ordered, but this is probably an artifact of their difficulty.

Little support is provided for the notion of "a total reorganization" or hierarchical integration at the age of seven. Only three children of the 622 who were included in the study were operational in all seven kinds of tasks. The picture that emerges is clearly that of a child who is, to use Piaget's terms, capable of "individual concentration," "cooperation" and also of a "certain degree of reflection" (Piaget, 1967, p. 39). He is no longer the quite easily distracted preoperational "child of wonder" as described by Flavell (1963), but neither is he yet the sober, systematic bookkeeper of reality that he is, according to the theory, to become when his thought is truly operational.

The seven-year-old of the present study, then, may perhaps best be described as a "transitional" one, who in many respects thinks and acts differently from the way he did at five, but has only begun to achieve the consistent logic that characterizes operational thought. Whether the description might be different had his interview been clinical in nature is not known. Nor is it known whether postponing the interviews for another six months or perhaps a year would have revealed the complete transformation and reorganization in thinking that Piaget has described.

The most fundamental questions, however, have less to do with the timing of the transition, particularly with when it may be regarded as completed, but are more concerned with the nature of the transition and the factors underlying it. Until these are better understood, it will be difficult to prescribe any kind of pedagogical intervention with assurance as to what its ultimate effect may be.

Piaget speaks of maturation, action on the physical world, social experience, including instruction from adults and collaboration with peers, and equilibration, or self-regulation. The first and the last factors cannot easily be manipulated, although it should be possible and certainly interesting to compare the transitions made by children identified as rapid and slow developers on various physical measures. Obviously, also, all four factors are interrelated. Increasing the child's opportunities for action on the physical world, or structuring it in different ways, or providing more adult instruction, or perhaps more contact with peers in an adjoining stage of cognitive development should demand more accommodation, and an eventual assimilation on the part of the child. But it is just here that equilibration theory offers more promise than direction. How is the educator to determine when the cognitive input is sufficient to facilitate the child's learning, when it may be so complex as to serve only to confuse, or when it is so meager as to impede learning?

The gaps in present knowledge are reflected in the results of the present study. The scientists and mathematicians who prepared the lessons prescribed for kindergarten and first grade drew as well as they could on current information regarding learning and concept formation in early childhood, including that provided by Piaget. The programs were tested in classrooms so that something was known about how the children would cope with them. But whatever the effect of the prescribed lessons may have been, there is no evidence that they led to a new integration or total reorganization of the children's thinking as they began second grade.

The picture of the cognitive development of the five-to-seven-year old that has been derived from the findings throws considerable light on the difficulties, given the present state of knowledge, of prescribing a program of instruction to facilitate logical thinking in those years and also on the difficulties of carrying out such programs. We shall return to these matters of practical application in Chapter VIII.

CHAPTER VIII

SUMMARY AND IMPLICATIONS

The major questions addressed in this study concerned the effects of instruction in the basic concepts of mathematics and science beginning in kindergarten, or beginning in first grade, on the logical thinking abilities of second grade children. Groups of children whose mathematics and science lessons were prescribed in teacher manuals and workbooks by representatives of these disciplines were compared with groups of children in classes where the mathematics and science activities were limited to those planned by the teachers. The groups having prescribed lessons in kindergarten were also compared with groups whose prescribed lessons began only in first grade.

The children's performance in tasks derived from the work of Piaget, involving conservation, serial ordering, transitivity and classification, provided the information regarding their abilities in logical thinking. The content of the prescribed lessons as set forth in the teachers' manuals was analyzed to see to what extent the lessons emphasized such abilities. Some of the lessons in each of the prescribed programs were observed in the classrooms by experts competent in judging whether they were proceeding as anticipated by those who had prescribed them. A set of lessons for one program was tape-recorded.

The results are not clear-cut. In the second grade the group of children who had no prescribed lessons in either kindergarten or first grade performed about as well in the Piaget-derived tasks as did the groups who had prescribed lessons beginning in kindergarten. But the latter groups performed better than did the groups whose prescribed lessons began only in first grade.

The ambiguity of the findings precludes the drawing of final conclusions, either as to the major questions of the study, or as to the more subsidiary questions having to do with the relative efficacy of different ways of presenting science concepts to children and also with the relative effectiveness of different kinds of teaching strategies. Nevertheless, they do provide evidence as to the nature of the children's thinking in second grade, and also earlier. Evidence of this sort throws light, as does evidence gathered in the subsidiary study of the teaching of some of the prescribed lessons, on the complex interactions that are involved when early instruction is undertaken.

The lack of satisfactory evidence with regard to the major questions of the study may be attributed to the inability to control adequately in a field setting certain variables relative to the outcome. Conceivably, however, the equivocal nature of the findings is not an artifact of the research design but a true reflection of the recalcitrance of the young child's thought structures to modifications from without.

The findings regarding the nature of the second-graders' thinking are not equivocal. The range of tasks presented and the number of children involved are sufficient to warrant generalization. The child beginning second grade is typically inconsistent and often illogical when confronting the kinds of tasks posed in the study. He has not yet developed, or does not readily bring to bear on the tasks, the coordinated structures that Piaget describes as typical of the child who has reached the operational level of thinking.

These findings, together with the inferences regarding the thinking of the kindergarten and first grade child that can be made from them, and from other data in the study, have implications for the content of the mathematics and science curriculum and also for the kind of instruction necessary if the curricula are to be effective.

Curricular Content and Its Timing

The variation in progress toward operational thinking exhibited among the second-graders in this study raises many questions about the way that progress occurred. In what order were the basic concepts presented in the lessons acquired? Were the children who, in second grade, appeared to be operational in the serial ordering tasks but not in the conservation or class inclusion tasks more alert, in the kindergarten, to differences than to similarities? Why were some early conservers not yet operational in the serial ordering tasks when they reached second grade?

The longitudinal data in this study, and in other studies, indicates that there is an invariant order for the acquisition of conservation. Presumably invariance in sequence also applies to the acquisition of the abilities involved in serial ordering, transitivity, and class inclusion. Then individual variation in the timing of the acquisition depends not only on maturation but also on the timing of the environmental encounters from which the concepts are constructed. Perhaps, however, certain kinds of encounters effect reorganizations that may telescope certain stages. Or cognitive learning in these years may be orderly to the extent that the child has been exposed to and has retained the order imposed on him by adult arrangement, but disorderly to the extent that he has responded to a great variety of physical and social encounters in his own idiosyncratic fashion.

All of these possibilities, but particularly the last two, are clearly fraught with hazards for the curriculum innovator who is intent on imposing his logic on the prelogic of the young child. He must arrange the concepts that are to be taught in some order, beginning with the ones that appear on the basis of intuition or empirical investigation to be easiest for the children to grasp, and teachable through the medium of some specified activities. The adequacy of the match between the activities and the child's interest may be the key to the success or failure of a particular curriculum.

Those who propose prescribed lessons are obviously not unaware that in the classroom they must reach not just one typical child, but twenty to thirty different children. Moreover when the curriculum is being developed for use in many different communities, the classrooms, depending on their socioeconomic and geographical settings, will each present different mixtures of experiential backgrounds to say nothing of personality and attitudinal factors. Those who construct the curriculum may decide to take such diversity into account and to suggest different instructional strategies either to build background or to extend interest. Or they may conclude that they can prescribe the instruction, as well as the content of the curriculum, so specifically that a majority of the children, if not all, can benefit from them. Different groups may, of course, proceed through the lessons at different rates.

In the present study two of the prescribed programs (AAAS and GCMP) were quite explicit about how the instruction was to be conducted, although their pacing and the extent to which certain exercises were to be repeated were left to the teacher's judgment. The SCIS program was less prescriptive and left many more decisions to the teacher. Clearly the nature of the instruction may be an important variable in the effectiveness of any prescribed program.

Instruction and the Assessment of the Individual

The SCIS program, more or less explicitly, based its theory of instruction on Piaget's theory of equilibration or self-regulation. The curriculum for the classes that had no prescribed lessons, but who had a variety of activities related to mathematics and science beginning in kindergarten, was not explicitly committed to the theory of equilibration. The general concepts to be conveyed in this curriculum were also of a different order from those stressed in the other programs. Nevertheless, it may be said that both of these curricula placed relatively less emphasis on the acquisition of concepts through direct instruction, and relatively more emphasis on the child's construction of the concepts from his own experience and at his own pace, than was the case in the other curricula.

Critics of Piaget's theory of equilibration have suggested that it ought not to be applied to instruction. They note that when a child at a certain point in time lacks a particular concept, it cannot, according to Piagetian theory, be taught to him directly. Rather, attempts at training or instruction lead to pseudoconcepts that break down when the questions or the materials representing the concept are changed. The notion that the child must construct the concept from his own experience implies that direct teaching is of no avail.

It is true that Piaget's statements of the factors involved in the transition from one kind of thinking to another (maturation, experience with the physical world, social experience and equilibration) offer the educator no prescription for what to teach, or when, or how. But it does not seem that they rule out the necessity for any kind of instruction.

169

The process of equilibration involves both accommodation and assimilation. Instruction provides new information, and suggests to the child that adults organize information or view the world differently than he does. The child may accommodate to, or imitate the adult's statements without grasping their full significance. However, given sufficient opportunity not only to practice saying them, but to test their applications through his own experiences, the child eventually assimilates the adult's meaning, wholly or in part, and makes it part of his own system of meanings.

In the present study the data from the classroom observations of the experts and more particularly the tape-recorded classroom observations provide many instances where a child's statement or his behavior implies that he has made a verbal accommodation to a concept without grasping its full meaning. For example, when children in a first grade class made an ordering of colored cards on the basis of color brightness, one child questioned whether or not this was a serial ordering since it was not done by size.

This and similar instances underline the importance of the teacher's understanding of the cognitive significance of the child's comments. They also suggest the importance of the teacher's skill in individualizing and diversifying activities. If she fails to adapt these to the level of their understanding, some children may waste time repeating activities of which they have had a surfeit, and others may flounder because they have had an insufficiency.

In retrospect it seems fairly clear that none of the prescribed programs offered the teachers much help in assessing the progress the children were making. Had they had access to the kind of techniques used by Piaget, and had they felt free to use them with individuals in the classroom, they might have viewed the children's thinking differently. Perhaps they would have been better able to ascertain the sources of their confusion and to provide activities to correct them.

The notion that the instruction should match or pace the children's cognitive development appears logical, but much is still to be learned about how to assess such development as well as about pacing instruction to it.

The problem is not only that development appears to be uneven, and that progress as the teacher observes it may be a matter of advance and retreat rather than the forward-moving sequence so often inferred from Piaget's theory; it is also that individual children differ so much not only in cognitive level, but also in their attitudes, their interests and their concerns.

Learning to carry on clinical interviews of the type used by Piaget would give teachers command over an important assessment technique. But many questions as to how such assessment would be done need consideration. Would teachers trained in Piaget techniques replicate his interviews in the classroom? Or would they use his method of inquiry in their discourse with the children? Or would they apply insights derived from his theory to their observation of the ways the children handled materials and equipment and responded to instruction?

Many years ago Susan Isaacs commented that Piaget's interviews (dealing with causality) dug deeper than he realized. She was concerned that he was tapping elements of the child's fantasy rather than appraising his understanding of reality. This comment is not without relevance today. What does repeated assessment come to mean to the child? Here again we may anticipate that the significance of repeated inquiries would vary from child to child. Properly conducted, by an interviewer who respects the child's way of looking at the world, his pace and his style, the Piagetian tasks appear to be intriguing and satisfying to most youngsters. Whether this would continue to be true if they became a regular part of the curriculum is a question not yet much investigated.

Assuming that Piaget techniques were to be incorporated into the repertory of teachers, particularly at the early childhood level, a further question has to do with the use to be made of the information to be gained through such assessment. Several of the studies in which attempts have been made to train children in operational thinking suggest that instruction might reasonably be given to children who were in transitional stages, while it might be postponed for those who gave no indication of being transitional. But what kind of instruction is appropriate and if there is to be postponement, how long should it be? During such a period of postponement is there to be no instruction, or are there activities that should be regarded as prerequisites for later development? It may be argued that more knowledge of the thinking of the individual children and more opportunity to adapt the lessons to their particular ways of thinking was exactly what the prescribed programs in this study needed for full effectiveness. But it may also be argued that the expectation of effecting a major change in the organization of children's thinking through a modification of a fraction of the total curriculum is unrealistic. (Those who wrote the prescribed programs did not specify the accomplishment of such an objective for the beginning of the second grade, although the lessons prescribed for first grade clearly implied an expectation for considerable progress by then.)

The argument that curricular change is unlikely to accelerate, or even to facilitate the transition from preoperational to operational thinking is supported by the tape-recorded lessons. The data from these highlight the fact that not all of the time devoted to prescribed lessons is devoted to cognitive interchange. Procedural matters take up a little more than a fourth of the time. Furthermore, the actual involvement of each child as the lessons proceed is difficult to estimate.

The tape-recorded data also suggest that the usual give and take of the classroom discourse allows little leeway for dealing with other than the expected or "right" answers. Even in the lessons where the teachers were encouraged to allow the children much freedom in exploring and talking about the properties of objects, there were few questions and relatively little searching for explanations on the part of the children. This finding may be an artifact stemming from the teachers' knowledge that they were being tape-recorded and the fact that they were teaching the lessons for the first time. Under these circumstances perhaps they felt safer in following the rules of the classroom game as it is most typically played. However, assuming the finding to be genuine, it suggests that the game must be modified if the instruction is to be cognitively productive for first-graders.

One such modification would encourage more interchange among the children themselves. Piaget has made few pronouncements on pedagogy but they do clearly support the notion that the children have much to gain from each other, particularly when the environment also provides many opportunities for physical as well as social encounters. Such interchange was prescribed although possibly not realized in the SCIS lessons. It may be presumed that such interchange was also emphasized in the classrooms that did not have prescribed lessons.

A second modification would provide for more frequent and more meaningful cognitive exchanges between the adult and the children. To accomplish this, the amount of time the teacher spends working with the class as a total group may need to be reduced and the time she spends with small groups and individuals increased.

The curiosity, imagination, and intuitive thinking that are presumed to characterize the preoperational child may not be necessarily antithetical to the logic of the adult. But capturing and holding the interest of the child so as to shift his view toward that of the adult is not easy. Sometimes the child apparently assimilates a concept the adult has tried to teach him, but in doing so distorts the meaning the adult intended. For example, some of the youngsters in some of the SCIS classrooms carried out serial orderings with alacrity and seeming understanding. Yet their commentary had nothing to do with height, width, texture, or any variable of interest to the scientist. Rather they arranged the objects as a family, beginning with the "Daddy," and continuing through the mother, and various brothers and sisters down to the "tiny baby."

Perhaps the critical problem in developing curriculum for these early childhood years, and also in providing instruction, is to find ways of helping children to invest interest in knowing more and more about their physical and social environment. The organization of such knowledge in a logical, systematic way is a major goal. But it does not appear to be one toward which progress can be greatly accelerated by the usual methods of instruction. Each child needs time to sort out the aspects of his knowledge that are purely personal from those that are shared with others. He needs time to divorce the fanciful and the aesthetic from the scientific. Since science and mathematics draw on imagination and creativity as well as on logic, the time devoted to modes of knowing other than the scientific need not necessarily impede his progress.

Eventually, as any teacher who has covered the grades from kindergarten through third knows, and as Piaget has maintained, children do become able to handle knowledge in ways similar to those of the adult, although they cannot yet process as much complex information. The present study has investigated some of the factors involved in this transition from preoperational to operational thinking. It has examined the complexities involved in instruction designed to facilitate the transition, and it has highlighted the extent to which the transition does indeed seem to be a matter of individual development.

REFERENCES

Almy, M., Chittenden, E., & Miller, P. Young children's thinking. New York: Teachers College Press, 1966.

American Association for the Advancement of Science, Commission on Science Education. Newsletter, 1964, 1, No. 1.

Aschner, M. J. The analysis of verbal interaction in the classroom. In A. Bellack (Ed.), Theory and research in teaching. New York: Teachers College Press, 1963. Pp. 53-78.

Beilin, H. C. & Franklin, I. C. Logical operations in area and length measurement: Age and training effects. Child Development, 1962, 33, 607-618.

Bellack, A. A. The language of the classroom. New York: Teachers College Press, 1966.

Braine, M.D.S. The ontogeny of certain logical operations; Piaget's formulation examined by non-verbal methods. Psychological Monographs, 1959, 73, No. 5.

Brison, D. W. Acceleration of conservation of substance. Journal of Genetic Psychology, 1966, 109, 311-322.

Brodlie, J. An examination of the relevance of Piaget's theory of "logical multiplication" to modern elementary school mathematics. Unpublished doctoral dissertation, Teachers College, Columbia University, 1966.

Bruner, J. S. The process of education. Cambridge, Massachusetts: Harvard University Press, 1960.

Chittenden, E. A. The development of certain logical abilities and the child's concepts of substance and weight: An examination of Piaget's theory. Unpublished doctoral dissertation, Teachers College, Columbia University, 1964.

Churchill, E. Counting and measuring. Toronto: University of Toronto Press, 1961.

Davol, S. H., Chittenden, E. A., Plante, M. L., & Tuzik, J. A. Conservation of continuous quantity as investigated as a scalable development concept. Merrill-Palmer Quarterly, 1967, 13, 191-199.

Deans, E. Elementary school mathematics: New directions. U.S. Department of Health, Education, and Welfare (E2-9042), Bulletin, 1963, No. 13.

Dodwell, P. C. Children's understanding of number and related concepts.
    Canadian Journal of Psychology, 1960, 14, 191-205.

Dunn, L. M. *Expanded manual, Peabody Picture Vocabulary Test*.
    Minneapolis: American Guidance Service, Inc., 1965.

Educational Services Incorporated. *Goals for school mathematics, the
    report of the Cambridge Conference on School Mathematics*. Boston:
    Houghton Mifflin, 1963.

Eicholz, R. E., & Martin, E., Jr. *Elementary school mathematics*.
    Reading, Massachusetts: Addison-Wesley, 1963.

Elkind, D. The development of quantitative thinking. *Journal of
    Genetic Psychology*, 1961, 98, 36-46.

Elkind, D. Discrimination, seriation and numeration of size and
    dimensional differences in young children. *Journal of Genetic
    Psychology*, 1964, 104, 275-296.

Fey, J. Patterns of verbal communication in mathematics classes.
    Unpublished doctoral dissertation, Teachers College, Columbia
    University, 1968.

Flavell, J. H. *The developmental psychology of Jean Piaget*. Princeton,
    New Jersey: D. Van Nostrand, 1963.

Greater Cleveland Mathematics Program. Teacher's Guide for Kindergarten.
    Chicago: Science Research Associates, 1962.

Greater Cleveland Mathematics Program. Teacher's Guide for First Grade.
    Chicago: Science Research Associates, 1962.

Guilford, J. P. The structure of intellect. *Psychological Bulletin*,
    1956, 53, 267-293.

Heath, R. W. *New curricula*. New York: Harper & Row, 1964.

Hoetker, W. J., & Ahlbrand, W. P. The persistence of the recitation.
    American Educational Research Journal, 1969, 6, 145-167.

Hood, B. H. An experimental study of Piaget's theory of the development
    of number in children. *British Journal of Psychology*, 1962, 53, 273-286.

Hughes, Marie M., *A research report: Assessment of the quality of teaching
    in elementary schools*, Salt Lake City: University of Utah, 1959.

Hughes, M. M., & Associates. *A research report: Development of the means
    for the assessment of the quality of teaching in elementary schools*.
    Salt Lake City, Utah: University of Utah Press, 1959.

Hunt, J. M. *Intelligence and experience*. New York: Ronald Press, 1961.

Karplus, R., & Thier, H. D. *A new look at elementary school science*.
    Chicago: Rand McNally, 1967.

Kessen, W., & Kuhlman, C. (Eds.) Thought in the young child. <u>Monographs of the Society for Research in Child Development</u>, 1962, <u>27</u>, No. 2.

Kofsky, E. A scalogram study of classificatory development. <u>Child Development</u>, 1966, <u>37</u>, 191-204.

Kohn, M. Analyses of two kindergarten settings. In A. Bellack (Ed.), <u>Theory and research in teaching</u>. New York: Teachers College Press, 1963. Pp. 102-112.

Laurendeau, M., & Pinard, A. <u>Causal thinking in the child: A genetic and experimental approach</u>. New York: International Universities Press, Inc., 1962.

Lockard, J. D. Joint Project of the American Association for Advancement of Science and the Science Teaching Center, University of Maryland, March 1965.

Lovell K. <u>The growth of basic mathematical and scientific concepts in children</u>. London: University of London Press, 1961.

Matthews, G. The Nuffield Mathematics Teaching Project. <u>The Arithmetic Teacher</u>, 1968, <u>15</u>, 101-102.

Medley, D., & Mitzel, H. E. A technique for measuring classroom behavior. <u>Journal of Educational Psychology</u>, 1958, <u>49</u>, 86-92.

Miller, P. The effects of age and training on children's ability to understand certain basic concepts. Unpublished doctoral dissertation, Teachers College, Columbia University, 1966.

Piaget, J. <u>Judgment and reasoning in the child</u>. New York: Harcourt, Brace & World, 1926.

Piaget, J. <u>The moral judgment of the child</u>. New York: Harcourt, Brace & World, 1932.

Piaget, J. <u>Le développement de la notion de temps chez l'enfant</u>. Paris: Presses Université de France, 1946.

Piaget, J. <u>The child's conception of the world</u>. London: Routledge & Kegan Paul, 1951.

Piaget, J. <u>The child's conception of number</u>. New York: Humanities, 1952.

Piaget, J. <u>The psychology of intelligence</u>. London: Routledge & Kegan Paul, 1959.

Piaget, J. Cognitive development in children: Development and learning. <u>Journal of Research in Science Teaching</u>, 1964, <u>2</u>, 176-186.

Piaget, J. Foreword to Almy, M. <u>Young children's thinking</u>. New York: Teachers College Press, 1966.

Piaget, J. <u>Six psychological studies</u>. New York: Random House, 1967.

Piaget, J., & Inhelder, B. Le développement des quantités chez l'enfant. Neuchâtel: Delachaux & Niestlé, 1941.

Piaget, J., & Inhelder, B. The child's conception of space. London: Routledge & Kegan Paul, 1956.

Piaget, J., & Inhelder, B. The growth of logical thinking from childhood to adolescence. New York: Basic Books, 1958.

Piaget, J., & Inhelder, B. The early growth of logic in the child. New York: Harper & Row, 1964.

Piaget, J., Inhelder, B.,& Szeminska. The child's conception of geometry. New York: Basic Books, 1960.

Ripple, R. E., & Rockcastle, V. N. (Eds.) Piaget rediscovered: A report of the Conference on Cognitive Studies and Curriculum Development. School of Education, Cornell University, March, 1964.

Rosenthal, R., & Jacobson, L. Pygmalion in the classroom. New York: Holt, Rinehart & Winston, 1968.

Science--A process approach. Parts IA, IB, IIA, IIB. Prepared by Commission on Science Education. Third Experimental Edition. American Association for the Advancement of Science, 1965.

Science Curriculum Improvement Study. Teacher's Manual for SCIS Kindergarten. Trial Edition, October, 1964. Berkeley: University of California, 1964.

Science Curriculum Improvement Study. Teacher's Guide--Material Objects. Preliminary Edition. Boston: Heath, 1966.

Senesh, L. Our working world, families at work, resource unit. Chicago: Science Research Associates, 1963, 1964.

Sigel, I. E., & Hooper, F. E. Logical thinking in children: Research based on Piaget's theory. New York: Holt, Rinehart & Winston, 1968.

Smedslund, J. The acquisition of conservation of substance and weight in children. Scandinavian Journal of Psychology, 1961, 2, 11-19.

Smedslund, J. The acquisition of conservation of substance and weight in children, IV. An attempt at extinction of the visual components of the weight concept. Scandinavian Journal of Psychology, 1961, 2, 153-155.

Smedslund, J. Development of transitivity of length in children. Child Development, 1963, 34, 389-495.

Smedslund, J. Concrete reasoning: A study of intellectual development. Monographs of the Society for Research in Child Development, 1964, 29, No. 2, Serial No. 93.

Smith, B. O. Toward a theory of teaching. In A. Bellack (Ed.), Theory and research in teaching. New York: Teachers College Press, 1963. Pp. 1-10.

Stanley, J. C. Measurement in today's schools. Englewood Cliffs, New Jersey: Prentice-Hall, 1964.

Steiner, G. L. A developmental study of children's concepts of life and death. Unpublished doctoral dissertation, Teachers College, Columbia University, 1965.

Sullivan, E. E. Piaget and the school curriculum. Ontario, Canada: The Ontario Institute for Studies in Education. Bulletin 2, 1967.

Taba, H. Thinking in elementary school children. Cooperative Research Project No. 1574, San Francisco State College, 1964.

Teaching elementary school mathematics: Tentative guide, kindergarten through sixth grade. New York: Division of Instruction, Garden City Public Schools Board of Education, 1961.

Teaching elementary school science: Tentative Guide, kindergarten through sixth grade. New York: Division of Instruction, Garden City Public Schools Board of Education, 1960.

Thoburn, T., & Dye, J. (Coordinators) Key topics in mathematics. Chicago: Science Research Associates, 1962.

Tuddenham, R. D. New ways of measuring intelligence. American Educational Research Association Convention, Chicago, February 9, 1968.

U.S. Bureau of the Census. Methodology and scores of socioeconomic status. Working paper no. 15. Washington, D. C.: U.S. Bureau of the Census, 1963.

Wohlwill, J. F. A study of the development of the number concept by scalogram analysis. Journal of Genetic Psychology, 1960, 97, 345-377.

Wohlwill, J. F. & Lowe, R. C. An experimental analysis of the development of the conservation of number. Child Development, 1962, 33, 153-157.

Wolf, R. The measurement of environments. In Proceedings of the 1964 Invitational Conference on Testing Problems, Educational Testing Service, Princeton, New Jersey.

Wright, H. F. Recording and analyzing child behavior. New York: Harper & Row, 1967.

Zaccharias, J. R. The requirements for curricula revision. In R. W. Heath (Ed.), New curricula. New York: Harper & Row, 1964.

Schedule for Final Interview
(Includes Tasks Used for Kindergarten and First Grade)

CODE _____   DATE _____

NAME OF CHILD _____

SCHOOL _____   GRADE _____

SEX _____

INTERVIEWER _____

CONSERVATION - BLOCKS

Orientation

FIRST I WANT TO SHOW YOU SOME BLOCKS. HERE ARE SOME RED ONES. (11)
I'M GOING TO PUT THEM ON THE TABLE... LIKE THIS ...(line up)
NOW HERE ARE SOME YELLOW ONES. (8)
I'M GOING TO PUT THEM ON THE TABLE TOO.

____ A. ARE THERE JUST AS MANY YELLOW ONES AS RED ONES?

____ B. YOU TAKE SOME MORE YELLOW ONES, AND MAKE IT SO THERE ARE
         JUST AS MANY.

____ C. (remove one red) NOW I'M GOING TO PUT A RED ONE IN THE BOX.
         WHAT ABOUT NOW?
         (ARE THERE JUST AS MANY RED ONES AS YELLOW ONES?)
         (ARE THERE MORE YELLOW ONES?)

____ D. (return the red one) WHAT ABOUT NOW?
         (ARE THERE JUST AS MANY RED ONES?)

. . . . (Continue only if child has not succeeded above.)

____ E. (remove two yellow)   Comment on Orientation
                                     Understood throughout ____
____ F. (return two yellow)   Prompting needed _____
                                     Doubtful if ever understood ____
                                     Other _____

Testing

____ 1. (bunch red) NOW I'M GOING TO DO THIS TO THE RED ONES.
         WHAT ABOUT NOW?
              More red   More yellow   Same _____

____   (ARE THERE MORE RED BLOCKS, MORE YELLOW BLOCKS, OR ARE THEY
         THE SAME?)

____ 2. (spread yellow) NOW I'M GOING TO DO THIS TO THE YELLOW ONES.
         WHAT ABOUT NOW?
              More red   More yellow   Same_____

Testing (#2, Continued)

____ (ARE THERE MORE RED BLOCKS, MORE YELLOW BLOCKS, OR ARE THEY
THE SAME?)

3. WHY DO YOU THINK SO? _____

CONSERVATION WITH COUNTING

(Return all red blocks to box; put all yellow blocks back into original
row)

1. CAN YOU COUNT? Yes ____ No ____ Other _____

2. CAN YOU FIND OUT HOW MANY YELLOW BLOCKS THERE ARE? YOU COUNT THEM.
(Indicating with finger, interviewer may help child count if neces-
sary)
Number _____

3. SO, HOW MANY BLOCKS ARE THERE? _____

4. (spread blocks) HOW MANY NOW? _____
(If he starts to count, CAN YOU TELL WITHOUT COUNTING?)

No attempt to count ____
Wanted to count but was deterred ____
Counted ____

5. (bunch blocks) HOW MANY NOW? _____

No attempt to count ____
Wanted to count but was deterred ____
Counted ____

(Return all blocks to box)

CONSERVATION - LIQUID

(Put full pitcher and two empty glasses on table)

I'M GOING TO POUR SOME WATER INTO THIS GLASS (fill to 2/3)
NOW I'M GOING TO POUR SOME WATER INTO THIS GLASS (fill to 1/3)

____ A. WHICH HAS MORE?

____ B. CAN YOU MAKE THEM SO THEY ARE THE SAME?

____ C. (pour some from one glass into the pitcher) WHAT ABOUT NOW?
(IS THERE MORE WATER IN THIS GLASS, THIS GLASS, OR ARE THEY
THE SAME?)

____ D. (pour water back so they are the same) WHAT ABOUT NOW?

CONSERVATION - LIQUID, Continued

Comment on orientation
Understood throughout _____
Prompting needed _____
Doubtful _____
Other _____

Testing

1. NOW I'LL PUT THIS INTO HERE (pour one glass into bowl)

_____ WHAT ABOUT NOW?

More in glass   More in bowl   Same _____

_____ (IS THERE MORE WATER HERE OR MORE HERE, ARE THEY STILL
THE SAME?)

2. WHY DO YOU THINK SO? _____

_____

CLASS INCLUSION

I. FRUIT - Use 4 bananas and 6 grapes.

A. HOW ARE ALL OF THESE OBJECTS ALIKE . . . WHAT DO YOU CALL THEM?
Fruit _____   Other _____

B. CAN YOU FIND SOME WAY TO PUT THESE OBJECTS INTO TWO GROUPS
WHICH BELONG TOGETHER?
Correct _____   Incorrect _____

C. PUT ALL OF THE FRUIT INTO ONE GROUP.

Testing

1. SUPPOSE I WANTED ALL THE GRAPES, AND YOU WANTED ALL THE FRUIT.
WHO WOULD HAVE MORE PIECES OF FRUIT?

Experimenter More _____   Child More _____

2. HOW CAN YOU TELL? _____

_____

II. WOODEN BLOCKS - Use 6 blue and 3 orange blocks.

A. CAN YOU FIND SOME WAY TO PUT THESE OBJECTS INTO TWO GROUPS
WHICH BELONG TOGETHER?

Correct _____   Incorrect _____

B. PUT ALL OF THE WOODEN BLOCKS INTO ONE GROUP.

181

Appendix A, Continued

<u>Testing</u>

1. WOULD A TOWER MADE OF ALL THE <u>WOODEN</u> BLOCKS BE TALLER OR SHORTER
   THAN A TOWER MADE OUT OF ALL THE <u>BLUE</u> BLOCKS?

         Taller   Shorter _____

2. HOW CAN YOU TELL? _____

_____

III. METAL CARS - Use 8 blue cars and 4 red cars.

  A. HOW ARE ALL OF THESE ALIKE . . . WHAT DO YOU CALL THEM?

         Cars   Other _____

  B. CAN YOU FIND SOME WAY TO PUT THESE OBJECTS INTO TWO GROUPS
     WHICH BELONG TOGETHER?

         Correct   Incorrect _____

  C. WHY DO THESE THINGS BELONG TOGETHER? WHAT ARE THE NAMES OF
     THE GROUPS? _____

  D. PUT ALL OF THE METAL CARS INTO ONE GROUP.

  E. ARE THERE MORE RED CARS, MORE BLUE CARS, OR ARE THEY THE SAME?

         More red   More blue   Same _____

  F. HOW CAN YOU TELL? _____

_____

<u>Testing</u>

1. ARE THERE MORE <u>BLUE</u> CARS, MORE <u>METAL</u> CARS, OR ARE THEY THE SAME?

         More blue   More metal   Same _____

2. HOW CAN YOU TELL? _____

_____

(Add 4 red cars)

1. ARE THERE MORE <u>RED</u> CARS, MORE <u>METAL</u> CARS, OR ARE THEY THE SAME?

         More red   More metal   Same _____

2. HOW CAN YOU TELL? _____

_____

SERIATION

I. <u>Monkeys and Balloons</u>

  A. HERE ARE SOME PICTURES OF MONKEYS. THIS IS THE BIGGEST MONKEY
     (C), AND WE'LL PUT IT HERE. THIS IS THE SMALLEST MONKEY (E) AND
     WE'LL PUT IT HERE (about 20 inches apart). HERE IS THE NEXT TO
     THE BIGGEST MONKEY (O) AND IT GOES HERE, AND THIS IS THE NEXT TO

182

SERIATION, #IA, Continued

> SMALLEST MONKEY (V) AND IT GOES HERE. (Then, handing the S the remaining 6 cards in standard order, SUMLIP)...) CAN YOU ARRANGE THE REST, PUTTING THEM IN ORDER GOING FROM THE SMALLER ONES TO THE BIGGER ONES? (point). TELL ME WHEN YOU HAVE FINISHED.

(When S indicates that he has finished, record order of his series
here)

   <u>C</u> <u>O</u> __ __ __ __ __ __ <u>V</u> <u>E</u>

(If correct, proceed with B. If incorrect, the interviewer corrects S saying, THAT'S ALMOST RIGHT, BUT THIS MONKEY IS JUST A LITTLE BIGGER THAN THIS ONE, ...)

B. NOW HERE ARE SOME BALLOONS FOR THE MONKEYS. THE BIGGEST BALLOON (R) BELONGS TO THE BIGGEST MONKEY, SO WE'LL PUT IT HERE. THE SMALLEST BALLOON (T) BELONGS TO THE SMALLEST MONKEY, SO WE'LL PUT IT HERE. (Balloons are placed above the corresponding monkeys.) (Then, handing S the remaining 8 cards in standard order, HIMNASEV. . .) CAN YOU ARRANGE THE REST OF THE BALLOONS SO THAT EACH MONKEY WILL HAVE THE RIGHT-SIZED BALLOON, THE BALLOON THAT BELONGS TO HIM? TELL ME WHEN YOU HAVE FINISHED.

   (Record order of S's series here)

   <u>R</u> __ __ __ __ __ __ __ __ <u>T</u>

(If correct, proceed with C. If incorrect, interviewer corrects order saying, THAT'S ALMOST RIGHT, BUT THESE GOT MIXED UP, . . .)

C. WATCH WHAT I DO. (The interviewer pushes the row of monkeys closer together and spreads out the row of balloons, and moves them to the left so that balloon T is above and slightly left of monkey U. Pointing to each monkey in turn, he asks:) WHICH BALLOON BELONGS TO THIS MONKEY?

   ____ 1. monkey (P)
   ____ 2. monkey (S) AND THIS ONE?
   ____ 3. monkey (I) AND THIS ONE?

D. (Leaving the series of monkeys intact, the interviewer scrambles the balloons.) THE BALLOONS ARE MIXED UP AGAIN. CAN YOU FIND THIS MONKEY'S BALLOON NOW?

   ____   monkey (L) <u>Comment on S's method of solution</u>:
                     Reorders through card H _____
                     Reorders series completely ____
                     Visual estimate _____
                     Apparently random choice _____
                     Other _____

(Interviewer picks up monkeys in order, CEOVSUMLIP, and balloons in order, RTHIMNASEV.)

SERIATION, Continued

II. Knives and Forks

A. HERE ARE SOME KNIVES. THIS TIME I'M GOING TO PUT THEM IN ORDER, GOING FROM THE LARGEST TO THE SMALLEST. (Interviewer lays out in order, EDUCATIONS.) NOW HERE ARE SOME FORKS THAT GO WITH THE KNIVES. I'LL PUT EACH FORK ABOVE THE KNIFE IT GOES WITH. THIS BIGGEST FORK (C) GOES HERE ABOVE THE BIGGEST KNIFE, AND THE SMALLEST FORK (Y) GOES HERE ABOVE THE SMALLEST KNIFE. AND THE REST OF THEM GO THIS WAY (Interviewer lays out remaining forks in order, OMPLEXIT.)

B. NOW, WATCH WHAT I DO. (Interviewer pushes the row of forks closer together and he spreads out the row of knives, and moves them to the right so that knife E is below and slightly right of fork L.) (Pointing to each knife in prescribed order, he says:)

_____1. WHICH FORK GOES WITH THIS KNIFE? (U)

_____2. AND THIS ONE? (T)

_____3. AND THIS ONE? (N)

C. HOW DID YOU DO THESE? (Interviewer checks appropriate choice)

Ordination (counting) _____

One to one correspondence _____

Other _____

D. (Leaving the series of forks intact, the interviewer scrambles the knives saying:) NOW THEY ARE ALL MIXED UP AGAIN. CAN YOU FIND THE KNIFE THAT GOES WITH THIS FORK, ...)

_____ (X)

Comment on S's method of solution:

Reorders through card I _____
Reorders series completely ____
Visual estimate _____
Apparently random choice _____
Other _____

(Interviewer picks up knives in order, EDUCATIONS, and forks in order, CYOMPLEXIT.)

TRANSITIVITY

PRACTICE I

(Interviewer indicates two sticks on Practice I cloth and asks:) WHICH ONE OF THESE TWO STICKS IS LONGER? DON'T COUNT THE ARROWS. JUST LOOK AT THE STICKS.

Correct   Incorrect

184

TRANSITIVITY, #I, Continued

_____ Prompting: (If S doesn't choose the correct stick, interviewer
may prompt by measuring the shorter stick with his fingers and
transferring them to the longer stick, saying:) SEE, THIS STICK
IS SO LONG AND IT ONLY COMES UP TO HERE ON THIS STICK. NOW
WHICH STICK IS LONGER?

                    Correct   Incorrect

PRACTICE II

(Interviewer indicates two sticks on Practice II cloth and asks:)
NOW, WHICH ONE OF THESE TWO STICKS IS LONGER? REMEMBER NOT TO
COUNT THE ARROWS BUT JUST THE STICKS.

                    Correct   Incorrect

_____ Prompting: (If S doesn't choose the correct stick, interviewer
may prompt by measuring the shorter stick with his fingers and
transferring them to the longer stick saying:) SEE, THIS STICK
IS SO LONG AND IT ONLY COMES UP TO HERE ON THIS STICK. NOW
WHICH ONE IS LONGER?

                    Correct   Incorrect

Test
A. (Interviewer displays Cloth A saying:) NOW, LET'S TRY ONE THAT
IS HARDER. BEFORE YOU TELL ME WHICH IS LONGER, I WILL PLACE THE
BLUE STICK LIKE THIS. (Places Blue Stick B next to left-hand
stick with the ends toward himself coinciding.) THE ENDS ARE
EQUAL (E's end) AND YOU CAN SEE THE DIFFERENCE HERE (S's end).

        1. WHICH IS LONGER: THE BLUE OR THE BLACK?

                    Blue   Black

(Interviewer moves the Blue Stick B next to the right-hand
stick with the ends toward himself coinciding.)

        2. WHICH OF THESE TWO IS LONGER: THE BLUE OR THE BLACK?
                    Blue   ′   Black

(After S responds, quickly remove Blue Stick B saying,)

        3. WHICH OF THE BLACK STICKS IS LONGER?

                    Correct   Incorrect

        4. HOW CAN YOU TELL? _____

B. (Interviewer turns cloth around to the Cloth B side.)
LET'S TRY IT ONCE MORE. (Moves Blue Stick B next to the right-
hand test stick with the ends toward himself corresponding and
asks:)

TRANSITIVITY, #IIB., Continued

      1. WHICH IS LONGER? THE BLUE OR THE BLACK?

           Blue   Black

(Interviewer moves the Blue Stick B next to the left-hand stick with the ends toward himself coinciding.)

      2. WHICH OF THESE TWO IS LONGER: THE BLUE OR THE BLACK?

           Blue   Black

(Quickly remove Blue Stick B and ask:)

      3. WHICH OF THE BLACK STICKS IS LONGER?

           Correct   Incorrect

      4. HOW CAN YOU TELL? _____

           _____

C. (Interviewer displays Cloth C saying:) LET'S TRY IT WITH THESE STICKS. (Place Blue Stick Y next to left-hand stick saying:)

      1. WHICH STICK IS LONGER?

           Blue   Black

(Move Blue Stick Y to the right-hand test stick and ask:)

      2. AND WHICH OF THESE STICKS IS LONGER?

           Blue   Black

(Quickly removing Blue Stick Y)

      3. NOW, WHICH OF THE BLACK STICKS IS LONGER?

           Correct   Incorrect

      4. HOW CAN YOU TELL? _____

           _____

D. (Interviewer turns cloth around to the Cloth D side.) LET'S TRY IT AGAIN. (Moves Blue Stick Y next to the right-hand test stick and asks:)

     1. WHICH IS LONGER: THE BLUE OR THE BLACK?

           Blue   Black

(Move Blue Stick Y next to left-hand test stick and ask:)

      2. AND WHICH OF THESE STICKS IS LONGER?

           Blue   Black

(Quickly remove Blue Stick Y and ask:)

TRANSITIVITY, #IID., Continued

     3. WHICH OF THE BLACK STICKS IS LONGER?

         Correct   Incorrect

     4. HOW CAN YOU TELL? _____

MATRIX

PRACTICE I

I AM GOING TO SHOW YOU SOME CARDS WITH PICTURES DRAWN ON THEM.
HERE IS A CARD WITH SOME RACING CARS. THERE IS A PLACE FOR ONE
MORE CAR... (pointing to the blank space).

A. WHICH OF THESE BELONGS HERE? (Interviewer then puts each of
the four choices out on the table one by one in the prescribed
order. He leaves them out so that the S can examine all the
possibilities simultaneously.) WHICH ONE GOES THE BEST WITH
THE OTHERS?
YOU CAN PUT THEM INTO THE EMPTY SPACE TO TRY THEM OUT IF
YOU WANT.

B. (After S has selected) HOW CAN YOU TELL IT GOES BEST WITH
THE OTHERS? _____

If S gives the correct response and explanation, the interviewer says, THAT'S RIGHT. THESE ROWS (he indicates the two
horizontal rows by pointing) HAVE RACING CARS THAT ARE THE
SAME SIZE, AND THESE TWO ROWS (he points to the two vertical
rows) HAVE RACING CARS THAT ARE THE SAME COLOR.

If S has not been able to choose the correct card, or if he
has chosen the correct card but is unable to articulate the
correct reason for doing so, the interviewer places the correct
card on the matrix saying: THIS IS THE CARD THAT GOES BEST
WITH THE OTHERS. THE RACING CARS IN THESE ROWS (indicating
two horizontal rows by pointing) ARE THE SAME SIZE, AND THE
RACING CARS IN THESE TWO ROWS (pointing to the vertical rows)
ARE THE SAME COLOR.

PRACTICE II

WHEN I SHOWED YOU THESE RACING CARS, THERE WERE 4 CHOICES AND THE
RIGHT ONE HAPPENED TO BE THE LAST ONE I PUT OUT. IN SOME OF THE
ONES I'M GOING TO SHOW YOU NOW, THERE ARE MORE CHOICES BUT THE
CORRECT CARD CAN BE THE ONE THAT IS SHOWN YOU 4th, 1st, 2nd OR
ANY PLACE AT ALL. FROM NOW ON I'M GOING TO SHOW YOU EACH OF THE
CARDS, ONE BY ONE, AND YOU JUST LOOK AT THEM CAREFULLY AND THINK
ABOUT WHICH ONE IS THE CORRECT ONE. THEN I'M GOING TO SHOW THEM

PRACTICE II, Continued

TO YOU AGAIN, AND THAT TIME, FOR EACH CARD, YOU TELL ME YES OR NO,
IS IT THE ONE THAT GOES BEST WITH THE OTHERS.

A. NOW LET'S TRY THIS ONE. REMEMBER FIRST I'LL SHOW YOU THEM
ONE BY ONE AND YOU LOOK CAREFULLY AND THINK ABOUT WHICH ONE
IS THE RIGHT ONE (interviewer shows each card in turn). NOW
LET'S GO THROUGH THEM AGAIN AND THIS TIME, AS I SHOW YOU EACH
CARD, YOU TELL ME YES OR NO. IS IT THE ONE THAT GOES BEST
WITH THE OTHERS? (Interviewer shows each card in turn)
____ IS IT THIS ONE? THIS ONE? THIS ONE? ....

B. HOW CAN YOU TELL THIS IS THE BEST ONE? _____

If the S gives the correct response and explanation, the interviewer says, THAT'S RIGHT. THESE TWO ROWS (pointing to the horizontal rows) GO BY SHAPE, AND THESE ROWS (pointing to the two
vertical rows) GO BY SIZE.

If S has not been able to choose the correct card, or if he is
unable to articulate the correct reason for doing so, the interviewer places the correct card on the matrix saying, THIS IS THE
CARD THAT GOES BEST WITH THE OTHERS. THESE ROWS (pointing to the
two horizontal rows) GO BY SHAPE. AND THESE ROWS (pointing to
the two vertical rows) GO BY SIZE.

Testing

NOW WE ARE GOING TO DO SOME MORE OF THESE.

A. Colored Geometric Shapes

1. LOOK AT EACH CARD CAREFULLY AS I SHOW IT TO YOU AND THINK
ABOUT WHICH ONE GOES BEST WITH THE OTHERS. (Interviewer
shows each card in turn.) NOW AS I SHOW YOU EACH CARD,
YOU TELL ME YES OR NO, IS IT THE ONE THAT GOES BEST WITH
____ THE OTHERS.

2. HOW CAN YOU TELL THIS IS THE BEST ONE?

(Interviewer checks dimension referred to by S)

	question	probe
Color		
Shape		

(Interviewer strictly adheres to same procedure for all remaining
items)

TESTING, Continued

  B. <u>Flowers and Fruit</u>

____   1. WHICH ONE GOES BEST WITH THE OTHERS?

      2. HOW CAN YOU TELL THIS IS THE BEST ONE?

	<u>question</u>	<u>probe</u>
Shape		
Shading		

  C. <u>Flowers and Fruit</u>

____   1. WHICH ONE GOES BEST WITH THE OTHERS?

      2. HOW CAN YOU TELL THIS IS THE BEST ONE?

	<u>question</u>	<u>probe</u>
Shape		
Shading		

  D. <u>Fish</u>

____   1. WHICH ONE GOES BEST WITH THE OTHERS?

      2. HOW CAN YOU TELL THIS IS THE BEST ONE?

	<u>question</u>	<u>probe</u>
Color		
Direction		

  E. <u>Fish and Birds</u>

____   1. WHICH ONE GOES BEST WITH THE OTHERS?

      2. HOW CAN YOU TELL THIS IS THE BEST ONE?

	<u>question</u>	<u>probe</u>
Shape		
Shading		
Direction		

  F. <u>Cats, Fish and Birds</u>

____   1. WHICH ONE GOES BEST WITH THE OTHERS?

      2. HOW CAN YOU TELL THIS IS THE BEST ONE?

TESTING, F, Continued

	question	probe
Shape		
Shading		
Direction		

G. Birds and Dogs

_____   1. WHICH ONE GOES BEST WITH THE OTHERS?

2. HOW CAN YOU TELL THIS IS THE BEST ONE?

	question	probe
Shape		
Shading		
Direction		

H. Daisies and Tulips

_____   1. WHICH ONES GOES BEST WITH THE OTHERS?

2. HOW CAN YOU TELL THIS IS THE BEST ONE?

	question	probe
Shape		
Color		
Size		

CONSERVATION OF WEIGHT

Materials: 4 balls of red play dough in varying sizes. The smallest (1) has 6 weights, next (2) has 4 wts., next (3) has 2 wts., and the largest (4) has no wts. One ball of blue play dough matching the largest red ball in size and weight.

ORIENTATION

(Interviewer places blue ball in front of S and the four red balls in front of himself, putting 3, 2, 4, 1 going from left to right.)

I'LL PUT THIS BALL IN FRONT OF YOU AND THESE BALLS IN FRONT OF ME. ONE OF THESE BALLS IS JUST AS HEAVY AS YOURS. CAN YOU FIND OUT WHICH RED BALL WEIGHS THE SAME AMOUNT AS YOUR BLUE BALL? TAKE YOUR BALL IN ONE HAND AND TRY EACH OF THE OTHERS IN TURN TO SEE WHICH ONE WEIGHS THE SAME.

(Circle one)   Correct   Incorrect

_____   Prompting: (If incorrect the interviewer corrects, saying:)

190

CONSERVATION OF WEIGHT, Continued
THAT'S A PRETTY GOOD CHOICE, BUT SEE THIS ONE IS HEAVIER (OR
LIGHTER) THAN THIS ONE IS. THIS IS THE ONE THAT WEIGHS THE
SAME AS YOUR BALL, ISN'T IT? (Interviewer must make sure that
the child agrees on this equality of the two largest balls
before he goes on to the next section.) (He then sets aside
the three remaining balls.)

TEST SECTION

A. (In full view of S, the interviewer elongates the red ball,
saying:)

I'M GOING TO DO THIS TO MY CLAY. DOES MINE WEIGH AS MUCH AS
YOURS OR DOES ONE OF THEM WEIGH MORE?

1. (Circle one)   Blue more   Red more   Same

Prompting: (If necessary, the interviewer asks:)

IS THE BLUE PLAY DOUGH HEAVIER, THE RED PLAY DOUGH HEAVIER,
OR DO THEY WEIGH THE SAME?

2. HOW CAN YOU TELL? _____

_____

B. (In full view of S, elongate the hot-dog (red) even further,
saying:)

I'M NOW GOING TO DO THIS TO MY CLAY AGAIN. DOES MINE WEIGH
AS MUCH AS YOURS OR DOES ONE OF THEM WEIGH MORE?

1. (Circle one)   Blue more   Red more   Same

Prompting: (If necessary, the interviewer asks:)

IS THE BLUE CLAY HEAVIER, THE RED CLAY HEAVIER, OR DO THEY
WEIGH THE SAME?

2. HOW CAN YOU TELL? _____

_____

C. (Break the blue ball into three pieces and ask about
equivalence of these pieces with the hot dog.)

DO THESE PIECES (gesture broadly to indicate the three blue
pieces) ALTOGETHER WEIGH MORE, LESS OR THE SAME AS THAT PIECE?
(point to hot dog.)

1. (Circle one)   Blue more   Red more   Same

Prompting: (If necessary, the interviewer asks:)

ARE THEY HEAVIER, LIGHTER, OR DO THEY WEIGH THE SAME?

2. HOW CAN YOU TELL? _____

_____

Appendix B

Coding System for Analyzing SCIS Lessons

DESCRIPTION OF CODING SYSTEM

The coding system described in the following pages involves break-ing up the stream of dialogue into units which are then further analyzed. The data to be coded are in the form of transcripts (typed) of tape recordings of teaching sessions. Analysis is made by listening to the tapes while reading the transcripts, and supplementing these activities with typed observations of non-verbal behavior of the teacher and students.

The unit of analysis chosen to divide up the data is the pedagogi-cal move described by Bellack (1966). As developed by Bellack there are four kinds of moves that teachers and students may make. Two of them (Soliciting and Structuring) are initiatory and two (Responding and Reacting) are reflexive.

A soliciting move is intended to elicit a response from the person(s) addressed. "Soliciting moves are clearly directive in intent and function. . . Although these moves may take all grammatical forms . . . the interrogative occurs most frequently" (Bellack, 1966, p. 18).

"Structuring moves serve the function of setting the context for subsequent behavior." They do not directly elicit a response nor are they themselves responses "and are not called out by anything in the immedi-ate classroom situation except the speaker's concept of what should be said or taught" (Bellack, 1966, p. 17-16).

Responding moves occur only in relation to soliciting moves, and may be an active verbal response, a cognitive response (e.g., focusing attention), or a physical response. Since responding moves occur only in relation to soliciting moves, they are coded only when so elicited.

Reacting moves "are occasioned by a structuring, soliciting, re-sponding, or prior reacting move, but are not directly elicited by them" (Bellack, 1966, p. 18). These moves modify and/or rate the moves that occasioned them.

The coder should read pages 4 and 16 through 19 of the Language of the Classroom, as well as examine sections 1 and 2 of the General Coding Instructions (included in this booklet) before trying to use the system.

After having identified a move, the coder then performs the analyses summarized in lines 3 through 9 of the format. The General Coding Instructions which have been adapted from Bellack's system pro-vide detailed instructions for carrying out the analysis and for using the category systems mentioned in lines 3, 4, 5, 6, 7. In addition, there is an introduction and explanation of each separate category system included in the booklet.

Format of Coding Unit

1. Person speaking: Teacher, Pupil

2. Pedagogical Move: Solicitation, Response, Structuring, Reaction.

3. SCIS content: Objects, Properties, Materials, Change, Variation in Properties, Science Procedures, and No substantive content.

4. Cognitive actions: Class Relations, Conservation, Seriation, Ordination, and Transitivity.

5. Medium of Expected Response: Manipulative.

6. Explanation.

7. Number of half-lines in parts three and four.

8. Number of half-lines remaining in move.

```
   1        2      3        4          5           6            7 & 8
Speaker / Move / SCIS / Cognitive / Medium / Explanation / Number of
                                                             lines
Example:                                                    Coding
   T:  Order your sticks by how long they are.     1  2  3  4  5  7
                                                   T/SOL/VL/S/Man/2
```

SCIS CONCEPTS

The concepts and information which the teacher and students discuss in the classroom are coded in the group of categories entitled SCIS content. These categories comprise a content analysis of the SCIS manual Material Objects which the teachers used as a lesson guide. The categories summarize only the information aspects of the manual. They have been organized into five major concept classes, each ranging from specific to general. A sixth category includes references to scientific procedures and instruments mentioned in the manual.

The task of the coder is to decide, for each move, the concept class which provides the context, and then for the variation concept the particular way in which the concept is mentioned in the move (which of the categories within each major concept classes is relevant). More detailed instructions for coding can be found in section 3 of the General Coding Instructions.

I. CONCEPT OF OBJECT (O)
   In this grouping are listed moves that have to do with the notion of object as it is used in the teacher's manual. "Object" is the scientific term used to refer to a piece of matter. Thus,

I. CONCEPT OF OBJECT, Continued

abstractions are not considered objects, and neither are states of mind or emotions. The word "thing" is often used to refer to both objects and non-objects.

II. CONCEPT OF PROPERTY (P)

The moves to be grouped here focus on contexts referring to properties. A property is considered to be an objective character- istic of an object. It is different "from the influence or effect the objects have on one another, from the patterns in which they may be arranged, and from the emotions they arouse" (SCIS Manual, p. 3). Such object characteristics as shape, texture, weight, flota- bility, and whether it bounces, are examples of properties of objects.

III. CONCEPT OF MATERIAL (M)

The moves grouped here focus on contexts involving the material com- position of an object. "The material of an object is what it is made of . . . the concept of material involves a degree of abstrac- tion from the observations of the actual specimens: it incorporates certain properties (such as density and hardness), while other properties (such as size and shape) are irrelevant" (SCIS Manual, p. 19).

IV. CONCEPT OF CHANGE (C)

In this grouping are categories that involve transformations of objects, changes in the form and appearance of objects, as well as the notion of change as a series of events over times with a speci- fied relationship between the initial phase observed and the final phase observed. All moves whose context is change in the state of an object or matter belong here.

V. CONCEPT OF VARIATION IN PROPERTIES (V)

These categories deal with the notion that properties exhibit quan- titative variation. The concept is presented in the manual by the device of comparing objects with respect to quantifiable properties.

A. Ordered Variation V

Code here moves that focus on the idea of variation along a continuum, or on the notion of ordered arrangement of such variation. A discussion about what is meant by serial ordering would provide context that would be coded here. Similarly references to what is meant by measurement would be coded here.

	Example:	Coding
T:	We made some steps and what do you call them?	T/SOL/V/C/2
P:	But it's not by size so it can't be a serial ordering.	P/REA/V/C/2
T:	A serial ordering is when you put things from smallest to greatest.	T/STR/V/S/3

V. B. <u>Serial Orderings of Objects</u> VV
Code here moves that focus on particular serial orderings, what
was done by the person making the ordering, and on the particular properties serialized. Add to the V consonant identifying
the property used to make the serial ordering or being discussed
as governing an ordering when possible. Select from the follow-
ing the appropriate underlined consonant: <u>L</u>ength, <u>H</u>eight (<u>Ht</u>),
<u>W</u>idth, <u>Sh</u>ape, <u>C</u>olor Brightness, Si<u>z</u>e (<u>Z</u>), <u>F</u>orm, Weight (<u>G</u>),
<u>T</u>exture, <u>B</u>ounciness, <u>N</u>on-property, Hardness (<u>Hr</u>), and <u>O</u>ther.

Example:		Coding
T:	What property did you use to order your sticks?	T/SOL/VV/C/2
P:	Color.	P/RES/VC/C/1
T:	Order your corks from big to little.	T/SOL/VZ/S/Man/2
P:	First I put the fattest and then the next fattest and then the next all the way down to the skinniest.	P/RES/VF/S/Xpl/4

C. <u>Quantifying a Property in Two or More Objects</u> VVV
Code here moves that focus on the variation of a single property
in two or more objects, with the properties being described or
compared as more, less, or equal in value, or otherwise quantified. When possible, select from the list in B the consonant
indicating the property being quantified and substitute it for
the final V in the symbol pattern.

Example:		Coding
T:	See which bounces more.	T/SOL/VVB/Man/1
P:	This is heavier than that.	P/RES/VVG/S/1
P:	These are the same height.	P/RES/VVHT/S/1

D. <u>Failure to Quantify</u> VVVV
Code here when there is a non-quantitative comparison of
properties in objects. The property is merely recognized as
present or absent in one or both objects when there has been
clearly established a context of making quantified comparisons.

Example:		Coding
T:	Which is more bouncy?	T/SOL/VVB/S/1
P:	This bounces and that doesn't.	P/RES/VVVB/S/1

VI. SCIENCE PROCEDURES (SP)
Code in this category when the focus of the move is use of a scientific instrument, the interpretation of such an instrument, it's
purposes. Using magnifiers, inequality signs, equality signs, metal

VI., Continued
files, air pumps, aerosol cans, medicine droppers, sand papers, and mortar and pestle. (Do not code cognitive acts for this category.)

Example:	Coding
T: What does this mean this way?	T/SOL/SP/--/1
P: More than.	P/RES/SP/--/1

COGNITIVE ACTS INVOLVED IN OPERATIONAL STRUCTURE

The following categories are to be used to code cognitive acts related to the acquisition of operational structure in conservation, seriation, class relations, ordination, and transitivity problems and situations. The category headings have been devised from Piaget's writings and are assumed to name classes of cognitive actions, be they overt behaviors or covert actions.

For each move, the task of the coder is to determine the context of the cognitive act (conservation, seriation, class relations, ordination or transitivity problem).

More detailed instructions for using the following group of categories are to be found in Section 4 of the General Coding Instructions.

I.   CLASS RELATIONS (C)
Situations dealing with class relations involve the membership of an element (e.g., an object or idea) in a class or a collection or the relation of one class to another as represented by the inclusions of one class within another. Membership in a class involves properties common to members of the class and to those of other classes to which the element belongs as well as the specific properties that differentiate class members from members of other classes. Achievement of operational structure for class inclusion relations involves the quantification of the relation between a sub-class and a sub-suming class; that is, the understanding that all of a sub-class is necessarily only some of a larger class.

Categorize a move as involving class relations if its focus is on the membership of an element in a class, the forming of elements into classes or groups by their properties, or on the relation between classes of elements.

Example:	Coding
T: How are these two alike?	T/SOL/P/C/1
P: I put all the red together.	P/RES/P/C/1
T: What properties does this object have?	T/SOL/P/C/1

196

II. CONSERVATION (Q)

Conservation deals with the notion that the identity of a substance or the quantity of a set or volume remains unchanged irrespective of certain modifications in the relationship among the elements or irrespective of certain changes in the appearance of the substance. Psychologically it is "the cognition that certain properties (quantity, number, length, etc.) remain invariant (are conserved) in the face of certain transformations (displacing objects or object parts in space, sectioning an object into pieces, changing its shape, etc.)" (Flavell, 1963, p. 245). For example, a set of ten blocks contains ten blocks whether the blocks are arranged in a line or formed into a circle. Certain properties are not relevant (in this example shape) in evaluating the numerical value of a set of objects.

Categorize a move in this group of categories when the context of the discussion is focused on changing or transforming elements or on the relationship between earlier forms or states and later modified forms or states.

Example: Coding

P: This dust was rubbed off from
this piece of wood but it's
still the same wood.   P/RES/C/Q/Xpl/5

III. SERIATION (S)

The operational construction of a series involves the coordination of relations such that each element is both greater than all those preceding it and less than those following it. Perceptual relations between big and small elements or the relationships bigger and smaller are relevant to achieving seriation, but these do not involve the simultaneous coordination of bigger than and smaller than relations among three or more elements.

Moves which focus on the ordering of elements by properties that vary on comparative relationships between the properties of objects, and on discriminating relationships within a serial ordering should be coded here.

Example: Coding

T: Which is the biggest in
your ordering?   T/SOL/VZ/S/2

P: I made steps out of my
sticks.   P/RES/VHt/S/1

IV. ORDINATION (O)

Ordination tasks involve finding the position of an element in a series and understanding that the position is correlated with a cardinal value, and not merely the situation of the element in a qualitative scale. Achieving ordination requires the counting of

IV. ORDINATION, Continued
elements as equivalent units, and considering the element whose
position is to be determined as a unit comparable to other units.

Categorize as dealing with ordination those moves whose
context is a coordination of cardinal and ordinal values.

Example:	Coding

P: This is the first one,
   this is the second, and
   the third, and all the
   way down to the sixth.   P/REA/VL/O/4

V. TRANSITIVITY (T)
Transitivity refers to the coordination of two relations
between three elements in such a way that a conclusion can be reached
about the relation between two of the elements although they are
not directly compared. In other words, given a relation between
x and y, and y and z, a conclusion can be reached about the relation
between x and z.

Categorize as involving transitivity moves which focus on reach-
ing a conclusion about the relation between two elements from information about the relation of each element to a third.

Example:	Coding

P: I put my finger here, and
   this one came up to here on it,
   and the other up to here,
   so this is longer.   P/RES/VVL/T/Xp1/4

REFERENCE MEDIUM

This category presents one way in which the teacher may structure
the student's interactions with the environment and the lesson material.
The categories refer to the mode of interaction in which the teacher,
either explicitly or implicitly, specifies responses to solicitations
are to be made.

The task of the coder is to determine for each move with either an
SCIS or cognitive act analyzed (SOL's only) the medium specified for
the expected response. Of course there may very well be SOL's which do
not specify a medium, in which case the categorization cannot be made.

Manipulation of Materials Man

Code here SOL's which are intended to elicit actual physical manipulation of materials and objects, such as actually grouping objects,
placing signs, circling objects, pasting things, rubbing or otherwise
acting on objects, and demonstrating use of materials and tools.

Manipulation of Materials, Continued

                    Example:
                    T: Sand your wood down until you get
                        some fine dust.

Explanation (Xpl)

This part of the coding is designed to collect all moves which
either are explanations, or in the case of solicitations, request
explanatory responses.

Mark with the symbol Xpl all moves which are explanations or
request them. Requests for reasons, statements giving reasons, sub-
stantation of answers and requests about procedures are typical of
moves that would be categorized as involving explanations. Explanations will generally involve a child's constructing a response and
not merely affirming a teacher's remark or choosing between alternative
possibilities.

                    Examples:

                    How did you know?
                    It's larger because there's more.
                    What is your evidence?
                    How did you order your objects?
                    Why did you put it there?
                    How does it look like brass?
                    I put them in order from smallest to biggest.

GENERAL CODING INSTRUCTIONS

1. CODING

1.1 Coding is from the viewpoint of the coder with pedagogical
meaning inferred from the speaker's verbal behavior as supplemented by
the commentary of non-verbal behavior made by the observer present
during the taping sessions. The coder should listen to the tapes as
the analysis is made, using the playback of the observer's commentary
to synchronize the dialogue and observer transcripts. The playback of
the teacher-student dialogue is essential for identifying the moves,
voice expressions often being the clue to the kind of pedagogical move
being made.

1.2 Grammatical form may give a clue, but is not decisive in coding.
For example, SOL may be found in declarative, interrogative, or imperative form. Likewise, RES may be in the form of a question--frequently
indicating tentativeness on the part of the speaker.

1.3 One move ends and a new move begins with the end of the utterance, indicated by either a change in speaker or a pause in the tape,
or a change in the function and direction of the discourse.

GENERAL CODING INSTRUCTIONS, Continued

1.4 Partially missed statements are coded only if there is enough information to code the pedagogical move and either the SCIS or cognitive aspects. Those moves immediately following a move coded T/NOC or P/NOC are coded as usual, if the context is clear and unambiguous. If alternative codings are clearly possible, code NOC for these moves also.

1.5 A four and a half inch segment of transcript in elite type comprises two half-lines of discourse.

1.6 All complete utterances of less than four and one-half inches are counted one half-line while an utterance of a whole four and one-half inch line is counted as two half-lines. The numerals used to give the line count in the coding are understood to refer to half-lines.

1.7 In utterances longer than one line, if the partial line segment comprises half a half-line, it should be counted as one half-line; otherwise it should be dropped.

1.8 In utterances that comprise more than one pedagogical move, partial line segments are combined in determining the line count.

Example:	Coding
T: Yes that's right.	T/REA-A/P/-/1
Can you name another property?	T/SOL/P/C/1

1.9 In utterances that contain more than one pedagogical move, each pedagogical move is counted as at least one half-line.

1.10 Utterances which do not contain either an SCIS content or relevant cognitive act will not be coded except for identifying the pedagogical move involved and adding the symbol NCC. When such contents are only mentioned as part of some housekeeping routine or task, but there is no substantive reference to them, the utterance will not be coded either except for identifying the move and adding NCC.

1.11 The line count should be given for all identified moves, including those mentioned in 1.10. The number indicating the line count for moves with no SCIS or cognitive aspects should be circled. Also, if a move contains discourse which is not SCIS or cognitive, the line count for this should be made and the circled numeral placed adjacent to the line count for the rest of the move.

Example: Coding

T: Go ahead. Circle the pieces of   T/SOL/M/C/Man/1/⑦
   wood. Don't worry about what
   someone else does. You worry about
   what you're doing. This is your
   paper. This is your work. Whatever
   you think is right.
T: When you win one just put yours   T/SOL/NCC/③
   in one pile and hers in another.

GENERAL CODING INSTRUCTIONS, Continued

    1.12 Underline the letter indicating speaker when a group is speaking in unison. This is indicated on the transcript also by underlining the initial indicating speaker.

2. PEDAGOGICAL MOVES

    2.1 The postscript -INT is added to the coding of a pedagogical move when the speaker resumes the same move after it has been interrupted or mediated by one or more intervening pedagogical moves. If the interlarded move is ambiguous (e.g., mm, er, ah), code it T/NOC or P/NOC. An interrupted move is coded on the final segment of the move and counted as a single move.

Example:	Coding
T: Put them in order.	T/SOL-INT
P: Mrs. Johnson	P/SOL/NCC/①
T: Just a minute. From the	T/SOL/NCC/①
shortest to the longest.	T/SOL/VL/S/Man/1

    2.2 When coding do not be misled by the linguistic habits of the speaker which have no function within the frame of reference of the units coded here.

Example:	Coding
T: O.K., hand in your papers	T/SOL/NCC/①

This remark is coded solicitation even though the "O.K." occurring within it might be considered a reaction. In this case it happens to be a habit of the teacher who typically precedes a statement with "O.K."

    2.3 Do not code speech by persons who are not students or teachers.

    2.4 A SOL begins with the first manifestly eductive statement and ends with:
- a. The end of the utterance signalled by a change in speaker or a pause in the tape.
- b. The beginning of a STR, RES, or REA.
- c. With the occurrence of a physical response as indicated by the non-verbal commentary or the occurrence of an REA-P.
- d. The beginning of another SOL involving a different context, different requests, or an explicit change in medium.

Example:	Coding
T: Gail, go around the other way sweetie, and then come back again. Brian your	T/SOL/NCC/②
plastic bag is on the floor again today. Regis, all of the boys and	T/SOL/NCC/②
girls who sit in Mike's row and all of the boys and girls who sit in	
Tommy's row.	T/SOL/NCC/④

GENERAL CODING INSTRUCTIONS, Continued

Example	Coding
T: Would you do something else? Use your magnifier to look at the piece of balsa wood that you have been working with. How does it look where you have been rubbing it against the sandpaper?	T/SOL/SP/--/5 T/SOL/C/Q/3

2.5 Solicitations whose only function is to give someone permission to speak should be coded with the postscript -A and only the SCIS context (where there is one).

Example	Coding
T: Mike?	T/SOL-A/M/---/1

Acknowledging solicitations are not coded separately when they occur in connection with another solicitation. The only type of response (RES) that can follow this kind of SOL is a RES-M or RES-R (see 2.10, 2.12, and 2.14), but any other kind of pedagogical move may occur.

2.6 Tentative and optional assignments, as well as prescribed ones, are coded as SOL's.

2.7 When checking statements (e.g., "Follow me?" "Get it?") occur within a STR or a REA, SOL is not coded unless there is a pause or verbal cue indicating a RES is expected. Such statements when they occur within a larger move do not appear as part of the code for the larger move.

2.8 Implicit in any SOL is the concept of knowing or not knowing. Therefore, code RES for any one of the range of possible responses (including invalid ones), and also for any reply referring to knowing or not knowing (e.g., "I don't know").

2.9 Occasionally a teacher or student responds to a SOL with a question. Coding in these instances is in terms of context and intent. For example, students frequently respond with a question to indicate the tentativeness of their responses. These are coded RES. If, however, the responding question is a genuine solicitation (i.e., expects a RES), it is coded SOL.

2.10 Responses are normally coded as having been elicited by the immediately preceding pedagogical move. When the solicitation which elicits the response occurs earlier in the discourse, the postscript -M, along with a numeral indicating the position of the soliciting move, is added. The number is determined by counting back to the last explicit expression of the solicitation.

GENERAL CODING INSTRUCTIONS, Continued

Example:	Coding

T: What did we decide about this object?
    Does it contain one material or
    more than one material? Alice?   T/SOL/M/C/4
P: One material.   P/RES/M/C/1
T: One material. Mike?   T/REA-R/M/C/1; T/SOL-A/M/-/1
P: One material.   P/RES-M4/C/1

2.11 A speaker cannot respond to his own solicitation. (1) If the
speaker answers his own question immediately after asking it, the question is taken to be rhetorical and a stylistic device rather than a true
SOL. (2) If a speaker answers his own question after an intervening
incorrect answer, the correct answer to the solicitation is coded as a
reaction to the incorrect answer, since the purpose of the question was
not to elicit a response from the questioner. (3) If a speaker answers
his own question after a pause, the answer is coded as a reaction, indicating that the speaker is primarily reacting to the absence of an
expected response. An asterisk is indicated as part of the coding of
the REA (REA-*) when this occurs.

2.12 The postscript -R is added to the coding of responses (RES)
that are repetitions of an earlier response by the same speaker.

2.13 The postscript -P is added to the coding of reactions when the
reactions are occasioned by a physical action rather than a verbal one.

Example:	Coding

T: Does anybody else think that tin is   T/SOL/M/C/2
    one material? I see Mike does .   T/REA-P/M/C/1

2.14 The postscript -R is added to the coding of reactions when
the reaction repeats the occasioning move.

Example:	Coding

T: Mike?   T/SOL-A/M/-/1
P: One material   P/RES-M4/M/C/1
T: One material. Who else...   T/REA-R/M/C/1

2.15 One word reactions that reflect acknowledgment of a remark and
refer to substantive material but are not in themselves substantive
should be coded as REA-A parallel to acknowledging solicitations.

Example:	Coding

P: This is limestone.   P/RES/M/C/1
T: Right   T/REA-A/M/---/1

2.16 A reaction begins at the beginning of an utterance or following a nonverbal response or the absence of an expected move. A REA is
still in progress when the speaker:

GENERAL CODING INSTRUCTIONS, Continued

   a. Evaluates or otherwise discusses a previous move.
   b. Rephrases a previous move or makes reference to it.
   c. Expands a previous move by stating its implications,
       interpreting it, or drawing conclusions from the
       same point or sub-point.

A REA ends when any of the following occurs:

   a. The utterance ends.
   b. A SOL begins.
   c. The speaker indicates the end of the REA by some verbal
       convention, such as "All right, now let's turn to ...."
   d. A distinct (not parenthetic) shift occurs to another
       context not heretofore mentioned or not under immediate
       discussion.

Note that although such phrases as "all right" are typical of REA's,
sometimes they also serve to move on to another topic, rather than
serving as a comment on previous material.

          Example: Coding

   T: All right now, let's talk
       about these properties.   T/STR/P/---/2

   2.17 When a REA to a verbal move is followed by a summary reaction
(REA), both reactions are coded separately even when they occur within
the same utterance.

   2.18 A brief or passing reference to what has gone before does not
constitute a summary reaction (REA). REA is coded for a genuine summary
or review and/or reaction to more than one move.

   2.19 A reaction to a solicitation occurs only when the reaction is
about the solicitation and not a response to the solicitation.

   2.20 REA frequently occurs when a teacher concludes one part of a
discussion and moves to something else. In such instances it is necessary for the coder to determine when the summary (if any) or reacting
part of the utterance ends and the focusing on new material begins (STR)
and to code appropriately. In general the coding should be in terms of
the moves that carry the discourse ahead the furthest.   Often the clue
to a STR move is the introduction of new material even though it may be
related to what has gone on before. In the following example, the children had been trying to decide whether or not a rubber band they had cut
apart was composed of one or two materials when the teacher made the
following remarks:

          Example: Coding
   T: Do you think that maybe the rubber
       band has a different property inside
       than it does outside because Regis has
       been playing with it--there's been
       dirt on his fingers? I wonder if I

GENERAL CODING INSTRUCTIONS, Continued

<u>2.20</u>   took a brand new rubber band and   Coding
     this is around something we put on
     the tray. I wonder if we cut this
     one if we would see any difference
     in color. You cut.   T/STR/P/C/12
                                                      T/SOL/P/---/Man/1

The teacher here, although referring to previous discussion, is introducing a new idea and actually trying to move the discussion onward
since the children had become stalled on one point. Noticing the flow
and context of episodes between teacher and students will help the coder
distinguish true structuring moves from moves which merely assume the
form of a structuring move by being phrased indirectly.

          Example:

          P: How do you spell Aegean, A e or A g?
          T: Why?
          P: I just want to know.
          T: Well, let's take a look at the map. See.
              Well it's not here.

In this interchange the teacher's comment, "Well, let's ..." although of
the form of many structuring moves, in this case serves the function of
a solicitation. Since the context had been established by the child's
question and the teacher was merely continuing along with the child's
context and not re-directing the discussion or providing a new context,
his comment is not a structuring move. If the teacher had said, "Well
you could look in the dictionary, or at maps, or globes and then see,"
the comment would qualify as a structuring move.

     The tapes often clarify doubts about whether or not a move serves
a structuring function by the tempo and pace of the discourse.

     Structuring moves set the context so that later solicitations have
meaning with the actual response, perhaps even implied by the structuring move, being directly elicited by these later SOL's.

     Compare the following examples:

          T: I'll leave the buttons here so that way they won't get
              lost. When you win one just put yours in one pile and
              hers in another.

          T: I'll be calling some names. If I call yours please
              come up with your folder.

In the first case the first sentence is coded STR and the last sentence
as SOL because the last sentence suffices to elicit the response with no
further teacher soliciting. In the second case the teacher must call
the student's name in order for the response to occur, and so the whole
utterance is coded STR even though a response is implied by the utterance. Note that structuring moves are not necessarily extended verbal
statements. What is essential is that structuring moves serve as an

GENERAL CODING INSTRUCTIONS, Continued

introduction to the forthcoming activity and serve to move the discussion forward. (Note, however, that moves that serve to focus attention are specifically coded as SOL's.) The following is a short structuring move.

> T: The reason I had you sing the song today about the thermometer was because we're going to use something that is very cold.

2.21 Utterances that seem to be self-addressed and comprise a kind of reverie or verbal accompaniment to behavior should be coded as are other utterances, but the coding should be underlined.

Example: Coding

T: All right now, put your name at the
   bottom in crayon. I'll let you do
   it in crayon today.   T/SOL/NCC/③
P: Red and green and brown.   P/REA/P/C/1
T: All right, pass that down to
   Madeline please.   T/SOL/NCC/②

3. SCIS CONTENT

3.1 Code each move in terms of the context of the discussion even though the concept being discussed may not be explicitly mentioned in the move. Of course there may be shifts in the context from one concept class to another, but these shifts should be explicit.

3.2 If the primary focus of the move cannot be determined use the following list to resolve conflicts, the first listed having highest priority: Variation, Change, Material, Property, Objects, and Science Procedures.

3.3 Within the Material concept if discussion centers on the number of materials in an object, add a raised # symbol to the coding, and if a specific number of materials is mentioned, indicate by adding the appropriate raised symbol to the coding.

Example: Coding

T: Is it made of one material or
   more than one? $T/SOL/M^{\#}/C/2$
P: It's made of metal and wood. $P/RES/M^{2}/C/1$

3.4 When coding in the Variation in Properties concept, code by adding the appropriate letter to the coding pattern. (See description of this in the explanation of this category.)

3.5 When other school subjects comprise the primary context of the move code NCC as when procedural and housekeeping matters are the focus.

3.6 When SCIS concepts are applied to non-SCIS materials or to items not mentioned in the manual, code the appropriate SCIS category and circle the code.

GENERAL CODING INSTRUCTIONS, Continued

    <u>3.6</u>   Example: Coding

        P: Mrs. J., my bracelet is
            made of two materials.   P/REA/M/C/1

4. COGNITIVE ACTS INVOLVED IN OPERATIONAL STRUCTURE

    <u>4.1</u>   Coding of the cognitive acts is in terms of the main context of the discussion, even though this may not be explicit in every move. There may be shifts from acts of one area (i.e., conservation to class relations) to another, but such shifts should be explicit.

    <u>4.2</u> If the primary focus of a move cannot be determined, use the following list to resolve conflicts, the first listed having highest priority: Transitivity, Ordination, Seriation, Conservation, Class Relations. Not every move, however, can be categorized for cognitive content.

    <u>4.3</u> If a particular cognitive act falls into a particular class of acts, but the class misrepresents the actual context of the move, circle the coding.

        Example: Coding

        T: How many objects are on
            the tray?   T/SOL/O/C/1

5. REFERENCE MEDIUM

    <u>5.1</u> The medium is coded for the expected response elicited by a solicitation, when the response is to be manipulatory.

    <u>5.2</u> Code the central focus of the SCIS and cognitive content of a move.

        Example: Coding

        T: Now look at your paper. Make
            sure you put your name on the
            bottom. Take your green crayon
            and circle the pieces of wood. T/SOL/M/C/Man/2/3

6. EXPLANATIONS

    <u>6.1</u> Code every move that is an explanation and every solicitation that requests an explanatory response as Xpl.

Appendix C

Supplementary Tables

Table 50

Number of Second Grade Children in Six Instructional Programs
Clearly Operational in Post-Test Tasks,[a] Grouped According
to Program and Program Combined and by Sex, I.Q.,[b] S.E.S.,[c]
and Conservation Status[d] in Kindergarten and First Grade

Group	Conservation of No.	Class Wt.	Inclusion	Seriation	Ordination	Reordering	Transitivity	Total No. of Children[e]
				Number Operational				
	Conservation Class		Serial Ordering					
Programs Initiated in Kindergarten								
AAAS (GCMP)								
All Children	65	38	8	22	33	6	37	93
Sex								
Males	33	22	3	13	20	3	18	50
Females	32	17	5	9	13	3	19	44
Peabody Picture Vocabulary Test								
I.Q. 110+	34	21	7	14	15	3	17	42
90-109	26	15	1	8	16	2	16	35
89 & below	5	2	0	0	2	1	4	16
Socioeconomic Status								
80+	49	29	7	20	28	6	31	65
40-79	9	5	1	0	4	0	1	16
39 & below	3	2	0	1	0	0	2	3
Conservation Status in Kindergarten								
Pattern 1	16	11	0	3	5	0	10	32
2	28	15	5	8	14	3	18	34
3	8	3	2	4	6	1	4	10
4	7	6	1	4	3	2	4	7
Conservation Status in First Grade								
Pattern 1	1	0	0	0	1	0	0	4
2	11	7	2	3	4	0	7	21
3	10	5	1	2	5	0	4	15
4	38	23	5	15	22	6	23	44

Table 50, Continued

Group	Conservation of No.	Conservation Wt.	Class Inclu- sion	Seria- tion	Ordina- tion	Reorder- ing	Transi- tivity	Total No. of Children[e]
					Number Operational			
				Serial Ordering				
All Children	54	32	10	28	29	10	10	79

Programs Initiated in Kindergarten

SCIS (GCMP)

Group	Conservation of No.	Conservation Wt.	Class Inclu- sion	Seria- tion	Ordina- tion	Reorder- ing	Transi- tivity	Total No. of Children[e]
Sex								
Males	29	14	8	16	16	6	7	43
Females	25	18	2	12	13	4	3	36
Peabody Picture Vocabulary Test								
I.Q. 110+	23	16	6	14	9	7	6	29
90-109	22	12	4	12	16	3	4	33
89 & below	9	4	0	2	4	0	0	17
Socioeconomic Status								
80+	29	20	8	20	14	7	6	39
40-79	10	4	1	4	6	0	4	20
39 & below	5	2	0	0	3	0	0	9
Conservation Status in Kindergarten								
Pattern 1	17	7	0	5	10	2	3	33
2	14	8	5	8	9	2	5	20
3	10	8	2	4	6	3	0	10
4	4	4	1	4	0	1	1	6
Conservation Status in First Grade								
Pattern 1	3	0	1	5	0	0	0	9
2	7	2	0	1	5	0	1	14
3	7	5	1	3	4	1	0	10
4	29	20	7	16	13	9	8	34

209

Table 50, Continued

Number Operational

Group	Conservation of No.	Wt.	Class Inclusion	Seriation	Ordination	Reordering	Transitivity	Total No. of Children[e]

Programs Initiated in Kindergarten

GCMP Only

| All Children | 67 | 46 | 14 | 41 | 60 | 18 | 23 | 122 |

Sex

| Males | 32 | 21 | 7 | 17 | 32 | 7 | 13 | 67 |
| Females | 35 | 25 | 7 | 24 | 28 | 11 | 9 | 55 |

Peabody Picture Vocabulary Test

I.Q. 110+	30	25	10	16	28	8	12	47
90-109	34	21	4	24	30	9	11	67
89 & below	3	0	0	1	2	1	0	8

Socioeconomic Status

80+	55	37	13	35	45	16	17	85
40-79	7	7	0	5	10	1	4	23
39 & below	1	1	0	0	2	0	0	4

Conservation Status in Kindergarten

Pattern 1	23	12	3	9	15	4	7	48
2	26	18	6	19	29	7	12	48
3	5	5	2	3	6	3	1	10
4	7	5	2	7	6	1	1	8

Conservation Status in First Grade

Pattern 1	5	2	1	2	5	1	2	16
2	6	2	1	5	11	2	4	22
3	16	15	3	10	13	5	3	26
4	29	19	7	18	20	6	9	43

Table 50, Continued

Group	Conservation of No.	Wt.	Class Inclu-sion	Seria-tion	Ordina-tion	Reorder-ing	Transi-tivity	Total No. of Children[e]

Number Operational

Programs Initiated in Kindergarten

No Prescribed Lessons

| All Children | 91 | 53 | 6 | 51 | 66 | 8 | 50 | 136 |

Sex

| Males | 41 | 31 | 3 | 21 | 35 | 3 | 25 | 63 |
| Females | 50 | 22 | 3 | 30 | 31 | 5 | 25 | 73 |

Peabody Picture Vocabulary Test

I.Q. 110+	47	33	6	32	38	7	28	63
90–109	38	19	0	17	26	1	21	60
89 & below	6	1	0	2	2	0	1	13

Socioeconomic Status

80+	71	41	6	40	51	6	39	106
40–79	12	7	0	6	7	0	7	17
39 & below	-	-	-	-	-	-	-	-

Conservation Status in Kindergarten

Pattern 1	30	16	1	15	22	1	16	57
2	39	19	3	26	29	5	20	46
3	8	6	2	3	4	2	6	11
4	3	2	0	0	3	0	1	5

Conservation Status in First Grade

Pattern 1	4	4	0	1	2	0	2	19
2	12	4	0	8	4	0	4	19
3	14	8	0	5	12	0	5	18
4	52	30	5	28	37	5	29	61

Table 50, Continued

	Number Operational							
	Conservation		Class	Serial Ordering				Total No.
	of		Inclu-	Seria-	Ordina-	Reorder-	Transi-	of
Group	No.	Wt.	sion	tion	tion	ing	tivity	Children[e]

Programs Initiated in First Grade

SCIS (Math)

| All Children | 51 | 31 | 8 | 26 | 36 | 14 | 22 | 113 |

Sex

| Males | 26 | 18 | 3 | 16 | 18 | 7 | 11 | 59 |
| Females | 25 | 13 | 5 | 10 | 18 | 7 | 11 | 54 |

Peabody Picture Vocabulary Test

I.Q. 110+	23	17	4	14	18	7	8	45
90-109	25	13	4	12	17	6	13	58
89 & below	3	1	0	0	1	1	1	10

Socioeconomic Status

80+	26	15	5	15	13	7	9	38
40-79	12	11	1	4	11	2	6	40
39 & below	10	2	1	3	6	1	4	16

Conservation Status in First Grade

Pattern 1	6	3	0	2	3	1	3	19
2	9	3	0	4	9	1	3	30
3	8	6	0	4	6	3	6	21
4	20	10	6	11	9	6	7	25

Table 50, Continued

Group	Conservation of No.	Class Wt.	Inclu-sion	Seria-tion	Ordina-tion	Reorder-ing	Transi-tivity	Total No. of Children[e]
					Number Operational			
	Conservation of	Class		Serial Ordering				Total No. of
	No.	Wt.	Inclu-sion	Seria-tion	Ordina-tion	Reorder-ing	Transi-tivity	Children[e]
			Programs Initiated in First Grade					
				Math Only				
All Children	38	21	4	21	29	6	19	85
				Sex				
Males	17	11	1	10	12	3	9	43
Females	21	10	3	11	17	3	10	42
			Peabody Picture Vocabulary Test					
I.Q. 110+	24	16	3	14	15	3	11	34
90-109	12	5	1	5	12	3	6	36
89 & below	2	0	0	2	2	0	2	15
			Socioeconomic Status					
80+	20	13	3	13	14	3	10	30
40-79	14	7	1	6	10	1	4	33
39 & below	4	1	0	2	4	1	4	14
			Conservation Status in First Grade					
Pattern 1	5	1	0	1	2	0	2	16
2	3	2	0	2	5	0	3	22
3	9	4	0	5	8	1	3	15
4	14	9	3	9	8	4	9	20

Table 50, Continued

Group	Conservation No.	of Wt.	Class Inclu- sion	Seria- tion	Ordina- tion	Reorder- ing	Transi- tivity	Total No. of Children[e]
					Serial Ordering			

Number Operational

Combined Programs Initiated in Kindergarten

AAAS (GCMP) + SCIS (GCMP) + GCMP Only

| All Children | 186 | 116 | 32 | 91 | 122 | 34 | 70 | 294 |

Sex

| Males | 94 | 57 | 18 | 46 | 68 | 16 | 38 | 160 |
| Females | 92 | 60 | 14 | 45 | 54 | 18 | 31 | 135 |

Peabody Picture Vocabulary Test

I.Q. 110+	87	62	23	44	52	18	35	118
90-109	82	48	9	44	62	14	31	135
89 & below	17	6	0	3	8	2	4	41

Socioeconomic Status

80+	133	86	28	75	87	29	54	189
40-79	26	16	2	9	20	1	9	59
39 & below	9	5	0	1	5	0	2	16

Conservation Status in Kindergarten

Pattern 1	56	30	3	17	30	6	20	113
2	68	41	16	35	52	12	35	102
3	23	16	6	11	18	7	5	30
4	18	15	4	15	9	4	6	21

Conservation Status in First Grade

Pattern 1	9	2	2	7	6	1	2	29
2	24	11	3	9	20	2	12	57
3	33	25	5	15	22	6	7	51
4	96	62	19	49	55	21	40	121

Table 50, Continued

	Number Operational							
	Conservation of		Class Inclu-sion	Serial Ordering				Total No. of Children[e]
Group	No.	Wt.		Seria-tion	Ordina-tion	Reorder-ing	Transi-tivity	

Combined Programs Initiated in Kindergarten

AAAS (GCMP) + SCIS (GCMP)

Group	No.	Wt.	Class Inclu-sion	Seria-tion	Ordina-tion	Reorder-ing	Transi-tivity	Total
All Children	119	70	18	50	62	16	47	172
Sex								
Males	62	36	11	29	36	9	25	93
Females	57	35	7	21	26	7	22	80
Peabody Picture Vocabulary Test								
I.Q. 110+	57	37	13	28	24	10	23	71
90-109	48	27	5	20	32	5	20	68
89 & below	14	6	0	2	6	1	4	33
Socioeconomic Status								
80+	78	49	15	40	42	13	37	104
40-79	19	9	2	4	10	0	5	36
39 & below	8	4	0	1	3	0	2	12
Conservation Status in First Grade								
Pattern 1	4	0	1	5	1	0	0	13
2	18	9	2	4	9	0	8	35
3	17	10	2	5	9	1	4	25
4	67	43	12	31	35	15	31	78

[a]Based on 0-1 scoring procedures. Numbers presented indicate how many children scored 1 in each task.

[b]Based on Peabody Picture Vocabulary Test, Form A.

[c]Based on U.S. Bureau of the Census, Methodology and scores of socioeconomic status, Working Paper No. 15, Washington, D. C., 1963.

[d]Pattern 1:   Conservation in no task
   2:   Conservation in task B only
   3:   Conservation in only task B and task A
   4:   Conservation in tasks B, A, and C

[e]Total, including those not operational who attempted each of the seven kinds of tasks.

Appendix C, Continued

Table 51

Number of Second Grade Children Clearly Operational in
Post-Test Tasks Grouped According to Scores on the Matrix Tasks
(N = 629)

Matrix Score	Conservation of No.	Conservation Wt.	Class Inclusion	Serial Ordering Seriation	Serial Ordering Ordination	Reordering	Transitivity	Total No. of Children
				Number Receiving Designated Score				
5	6	3	0	2	2	1	3	11
6	4	4	0	2	5	2	2	14
7	17	8	0	8	13	1	4	49
8	20	13	2	3	15	2	7	45
9	30	14	1	12	17	0	8	61
10	17	12	2	7	11	1	9	41
11	24	12	2	7	17	3	12	54
12	20	14	3	6	10	3	8	38
13	29	20	6	18	26	6	12	44
14	39	23	5	24	30	4	21	60
15	32	16	5	18	28	4	14	47
16	40	28	7	26	27	10	16	52
17	31	15	7	21	24	13	18	45
18	29	18	3	12	14	4	12	33
19	20	16	4	14	11	4	9	24
20	7	5	3	8	3	4	4	10

22-101